D0073310

MONTGOMERY COUNTY COMMUNITY COLLEGE

3 0473 00038532 1

87079

HQ
769   Miller, Alice
M531613   For your own good
1983

DATE DUE			
SEP 14 1983			
MAR 2 1984			
MAY 10 1986			
SEP 26 1991			
FEB 3 1992			
NOV 9 1995			
DEC 18 1995			

LEARNING RESOURCES CENTER
MONTGOMERY COUNTY COMMUNITY COLLEGE
BLUE BELL, PENNSYLVANIA

For Your Own Good

Farrar • Straus • Giroux

NEW YORK

ALICE MILLER

For Your Own Good

Hidden Cruelty
in Child-Rearing
and the Roots
of Violence

TRANSLATED BY

Hildegarde and Hunter Hannum

Translation copyright © 1983 by Alice Miller
Originally published in German under the title
Am Anfang war Erziehung © Suhrkamp Verlag
Frankfurt am Main 1980
All rights reserved
Published simultaneously in Canada by
McGraw-Hill Ryerson Ltd., Toronto
Printed in the United States of America
DESIGNED BY HERBERT H. JOHNSON

FIRST PRINTING, 1983

Grateful acknowledgment is made to Desmond Elliott Publisher, Ltd. (New York) and Arlington Books (Publishers), Ltd. (London), for permission to reprint excerpts from *Christiane F.: Autobiography of a Girl of the Streets and Heroin Addict*, adapted from the translation by Susanne Flatauer, copyright © 1980 by Arlington Books; to Harcourt Brace Jovanovich, Inc., for permission to reprint excerpts from *Hitler* by Joachim C. Fest, adapted from the translation of Richard and Clara Winston, copyright © 1974 by Harcourt Brace Jovanovich, Inc.; to Olwyn Hughes, Literary Agent, for permission to reprint excerpts from *Letters Home: Correspondence 1950–1963*, by Sylvia Plath, selected and edited with commentary by Aurelia Schober Plath, published by Harper & Row, Inc., copyright © 1975 by Ted Hughes; to Paul Moor, for permission to include translated excerpts from his book *Das Selbstporträt des Jürgen Bartsch*, published by Fischer Taschenbuchverlag (Frankfurt), copyright © 1972 by Paul Moor; to Pantheon Books, a Division of Random House, Inc., for permission to reprint excerpts from *The Face of the Third Reich* by Joachim C. Fest, translated by Michael Bullock, copyright © 1970 by Weidenfeld & Nicolson; to Verlag Ullstein (Berlin), for permission to include translated excerpts from *Schwarze Pädagogik*, edited by Katharina Rutschky, Ullstein Series nr. 35087, copyright © 1978 by Verlag Ullstein GmbH.

Library of Congress Cataloging in Publication Data
Miller, Alice.
For your own good.
Translation of: Am Anfang war Erziehung.
Bibliography: p.
1. Child rearing—Psychological aspects.
2. Discipline of children—Psychological aspects.
3. Violence—Psychological aspects.   I. Title.
HQ769.M531613   1983   649'.1   82-24249

87079

Contents

Preface
to the American Edition

THIS BOOK is appearing in America some two and a half years after its first publication in Germany, and it is probably just as well that it wasn't available before now in this country. Had it appeared here earlier, American readers might well have asked: "Why should we still bother with Hitler today? That's all ancient history," and "Who is this Christiane F.?" But now, after so many young Americans have seen their own tragedies mirrored in the film and book about Christiane F., the teenage German drug addict, and after all the talk in the media the past few years about the danger of nuclear war, it should come as no surprise that I have chosen Adolf Hitler and Christiane F. as representatives, respectively, of extreme destructiveness on a world-historical scale and of extreme self-destructiveness on a personal one.

Since the end of World War II, I have been haunted by the question of what could make a person conceive the plan of gassing millions of human beings to death and of how it could then be possible for millions of others to acclaim him and assist in carrying out this plan. The solution to this enigma, which I found only a short while ago, is what I have tried to present in this book. Readers' reactions to my work convinced me how crucial others find this problem too and how the terrifying stockpiling of nuclear weapons worldwide raises the same question in an even more acute form: namely, what could motivate a person to misuse power in such a way as to cause, completely without scruples and with the use of beguiling ideologies, the destruction of humanity, an act that is altogether conceivable today? It can hardly be considered an idle academic exercise when somebody attempts to expose the roots of an unbounded and insatiable hatred like Hitler's; an investigation of this sort is a matter of life and death for all of us, since it is easier today than ever before for us to fall victim to such hatred.

A great deal has already been written about Hitler by historians, sociologists, psychologists, and psychoanalysts. As I attempt to show in the pages that follow, all his biographers have tried to exonerate his parents (particularly his father), thus refusing to explore what really happened to this man during his childhood, what experiences he stored up within, and what ways of treating other people were available as models for him.

Once I was able to move beyond the distorting perspectives associated with the idea of a "good upbringing" (what is described in this book as "poisonous pedagogy") and show how Hitler's childhood anticipated the later concentration camps, countless readers were amazed by the convincing evidence I presented for my view. At the same time, however, their letters expressed confusion: "Basically, my childhood differed little from Hitler's; I, too, had a very strict upbringing, was beaten and mistreated. Why then didn't I become a mass murderer instead of, say, a scientist, a lawyer, a politician, or a writer?"

Actually, my book provides clear answers here, although they often seem to be overlooked: e.g., Hitler never had a single other human being in whom he could confide his true feelings; he was not only mistreated but also prevented from experiencing and expressing his pain; he didn't have any children who could have served as objects for abreacting his hatred; and, finally, his lack of education did not allow him to ward off his hatred by intellectualizing it. Had a single one of these factors been different, perhaps he would never have become the arch-criminal he did.

On the other hand, Hitler was certainly not an isolated phenomenon. He would not have had millions of followers if they had not experienced the same sort of upbringing. I anticipated a great deal of resistance on the part of the public when I advanced this thesis—which I am convinced is a correct one —so I was surprised to discover how many readers, both young and old, agreed with me. They were familiar from their own backgrounds with what I depicted. I didn't have to adduce elaborate arguments; all I needed to do was describe Hitler's childhood in such a way that it served as a mirror, and suddenly Germans caught their own reflections in it.

It was the personal nature of their responses to the three examples I present in my book that enabled many people to understand in a more than purely intellectual sense that every act of cruelty, no matter how brutal and shocking, has traceable antecedents in its perpetrator's past. The diverse reactions to my book range from unmistakable "aha" experiences to angry rejection. In the latter cases, as I have already indicated, the following comment keeps recurring like a refrain: "I am living proof that beating [or spanking] children is not necessarily harmful, for in spite of it I became a decent person."

Although people tend to make a distinction between "spanking" and "beating" a child, considering the former a less severe measure than the latter, the line between the two is a tenuous one. I just heard a report on an American radio station about a man—a member of a Christian fundamentalist sect in West Virginia—who "spanked" his son for two hours. The little boy died as a result. But even when a spanking is a gentler form of physical violence, the psychic pain and humiliation and the need to repress these feelings are the same as in the case of more severe punishment. It is important to point this out so that readers who receive or give what they call "spankings" will not think they or their children are exempt from the consequences of child beating discussed in this book.

Probably the majority of us belong to the category of "decent people who were once beaten," since such treatment of children was a matter of course in past generations. Be that as it may, to some degree we can all be numbered among the survivors of "poisonous pedagogy." Yet it would be just as false to deduce from this fact of survival that our upbringing caused us no harm as it would be to maintain that a limited nuclear war would be harmless because a part of humanity would still be alive when it was over. Quite apart from the culpably frivolous attitude toward the victims this view betrays, it also fails to take into account the question of what aftereffects the survivors of a nuclear conflict would have to face. The situation is analogous to "poisonous pedagogy," for even if we, as survivors of severe childhood humiliations we all too readily make light of, don't kill ourselves or others, are not drug addicts or criminals, and are fortunate enough not to pass on the absurdities of our own childhood to our children so that they become psychotic, we can still function as dangerous carriers of infections. We will continue to infect the next generation with the virus of "poisonous pedagogy" as long as we claim that this kind of upbringing is harmless. It is here that we experience the harmful aftereffects of our survival, because we can protect ourselves from a poison only if it is clearly labeled as such, not if it is mixed, as it were, with ice cream advertised as being "For Your Own Good." Our children will find themselves helpless when confronted with such labeling. When people who have been beaten or spanked as children attempt to play down the consequences by setting themselves up as examples, even claiming it was good for them, they are inevitably contributing to the continuation of cruelty in the world by this refusal to take their childhood tragedies seriously. Taking over this attitude, their children, pupils, and students will in turn beat their own children, citing their parents, teachers, and professors as authorities. Don't the consequences of having been a battered child find their most tragic expression in this type of thinking?

Although the general public is beginning to understand that this suffering is transmitted to one's children in the form of an upbringing supposedly "for their own good," many people with whom I have spoken in the United States still believe that permissive methods of child-rearing allow children "too much" freedom and that it is this permissiveness, not "poisonous pedagogy," that is responsible for the marked increase in crime and drug addiction. Even cartoons and jokes make fun of parents who have a tolerant and supportive attitude toward their children, emphasizing the dangers if parents allow themselves to be tyrannized by their children. King Solomon's mistaken belief (if you spare the rod you will spoil the child) is still accepted today in all seriousness as great wisdom and is still being passed on to the next generation. These attitudes, although they now take a more subtle and less apparent form, are not far removed from those quoted in the following pages to illustrate the detrimental effects of child-rearing methods. Such views have not been borne out by my many years of experience. Theoretically, I can imagine that someday we will regard our children not as creatures to manipulate or to change but rather as messengers from a world we once deeply knew, but which we have long since forgotten, who can reveal to us more about the true secrets of life, and also our own lives, than our parents were ever able to. We do not need to be told whether to be strict or permissive with our children. What we do need is to have respect for their needs, their feelings, and their individuality, as well as for our own.

It is no mere accident that all three of the people I write about in this book had no children of their own. One of my readers wrote to me: "Who knows, perhaps the Jews would not have been sent to the gas ovens if Hitler had had five sons on whom he could have taken revenge for what his father did to him." We punish our children for the arbitrary actions of our parents that we were not able to defend ourselves against, thanks to the Fourth Commandment. I have discovered that we are less a prey to this form of the repetition compulsion if we are willing to acknowledge what happened to us, if we do not claim that we were mistreated "for our own good," and if we have not had to ward off completely our painful reactions to the past. The more we idealize the past, however, and refuse to acknowledge our childhood sufferings, the more we pass them on unconsciously to the next generation. For this reason, I attempt to point out in these pages some underlying connections, with the hope of breaking a vicious circle. For a decisive change could well come about in our culture if parents would only stop combating their own parents in their children, often

when the latter are still infants—something they do because
their parents were able to attain a position of guiltlessness and
inviolability by forcible means, i.e., thanks to the Fourth Commandment and to the methods of child-rearing they employed.

On a recent trip to America I encountered many people,
especially women, who have discovered the power of their
knowledge. They do not shrink from pointing out the poisonous
nature of false information, even though it has been well concealed for millennia behind sacrosanct and well-meaning
pedagogical labels. The conversations I had in the United
States gave support to my own experience that courage can
be just as infectious as fear. And if we are courageous enough
to face the truth, the world will change, for the power of that
"poisonous pedagogy" which has dominated us for so long has
been dependent upon our fear, our confusion, and our childish
credulity; once it is exposed to the light of truth, it will inevitably disappear.

A.M.
November 1982

Preface
to the Original Edition

THE most psychoanalysis is able to do—according to a typical reproach—is help a privileged minority, and only to a very limited extent at that. This is certainly a legitimate complaint as long as the benefits derived from analysis remain the exclusive property of a privileged few. But this need not be the case.

The reactions to my first book, *Prisoners of Childhood: The Drama of the Gifted Child and the Search for the True Self,** convinced me that resistance to what I have to say is no greater outside the psychoanalytic community than among members of the profession—in fact, the younger generation of the lay public shows perhaps even more openness to my ideas than do my professional colleagues. Reflecting on this, I realized how essential it is to make the insights gained from analysis of a few available to the public at large rather than hide these insights away on dusty library shelves. Thus, I decided to devote the next several years of my life to writing.

I am primarily interested in describing everyday situations occurring outside the psychoanalytic setting that can, however, be more fully understood if viewed from a psychoanalytic perspective. This does not mean applying a ready-made theory to society, for I believe I can truly understand a person only if I hear and feel what he or she is saying to me without hiding or barricading myself behind theories. Depth psychology practiced both on others and on ourselves provides us as analysts with insights into the human psyche that accompany us every-

---

* Published in hardcover in 1981 by Basic Books, New York, as *Prisoners of Childhood;* now available in paperback under the original title, translated from the German: *The Drama of the Gifted Child.* This is also the title of the British edition.

where in life, sharpening our sensitivity outside as well as inside the consulting room.

On the other hand, the general public is still far from realizing that our earliest experiences unfailingly affect society as a whole; that psychoses, drug addiction, and criminality are encoded expressions of these experiences. This fact is usually either disputed or accepted only on a strictly intellectual level. Since the intellect fails to influence the area of the emotions, the practical world (of politics, law, or psychiatry) continues to be dominated by medieval concepts characterized by the outward projection of evil. Can a book help to bring about knowledge of an emotional nature? I do not know the answer, but the hope that my writings will set an inner process in motion at least for some readers seems reason enough to make the attempt.

Although the numerous letters I received from readers of *Prisoners of Childhood* were of the utmost interest to me, I was unable to answer them all personally. Hence this book. My inability to reply directly to my readers was partly due to other demands on my time, but I also soon realized that when it comes to presenting my thoughts and experiences of recent years I must go into a great deal of detail, for there is no body of existing literature I can refer to. From the professional questions of my colleagues and the general human questions of those affected by the problems I described (which are not to be understood as mutually exclusive), two distinct issues emerged: the extent to which my interpretation of the nature of early childhood deviates from the psychoanalytic drive* theory, and the need to distinguish more clearly between feelings of guilt and of sorrow. Related to the latter issue is the urgent and frequently asked question raised by concerned parents: Is there still something we can do for our children once we have realized to what degree we are victims of the repetition compulsion?

Since I do not believe in the effectiveness of giving pre-

---

* The author prefers to have Freud's word *Trieb* translated as "drive" instead of "instinct" (the choice of Strachey, Freud's official English translator), which she considers misleading.—Trans.

scriptions and advice, at least when unconscious behavior is involved, I do not consider it my task to admonish parents to treat their child in ways that are impossible for them. Instead, I see it as my role to convey relevant information of a vivid and emotional nature to the child in the adult. As long as this child within is not allowed to become aware of what happened to him or her, a part of his or her emotional life will remain frozen, and sensitivity to the humiliations of childhood will therefore be dulled.

All appeals to love, solidarity, and compassion will be useless if this crucial prerequisite of sympathy and understanding is missing.

This fact has special implications for trained psychologists, because without empathy they cannot apply their professional knowledge in a beneficial way, regardless of how much time they devote to their patients. The same is true for parents; even if they are highly educated and have sufficient time at their disposal, they are helpless when it comes to understanding their child so long as they must keep the sufferings of their own childhood at an emotional distance. On the other hand, it is possible for a working mother, for example, to grasp her child's situation immediately, provided she has the necessary inner openness and freedom.

Thus, I see it as my task to sensitize the general public to the sufferings of early childhood. Addressing the child in my adult readers, I attempt to accomplish this in two different ways. In the first section of the present work I describe "poisonous pedagogy," the methods of child-rearing practiced when our parents and grandparents were growing up. It is possible that many readers will respond to my first chapter with feelings of anger and rage, which can turn out to have a very therapeutic effect. In the second part I recount the childhoods of a drug addict, a political leader, and a murderer of young boys, all of whom were subjected to severe humiliation and mistreatment as children. In two cases in particular, I draw upon their own accounts of their childhoods and later fate, trying to bring the reader to listen to their shattering testimony with my analytic ear. All three histories bear witness to the devastating role of child-rearing, its destruction of vitality, its danger for society. Even in psychoanalysis, especially in its theory of drives, we find traces of traditional pedagogy. I first planned to devote a chapter to this theme, but its scope forced me to make it the subject of another work, soon to appear.* There I stress the distinctions between my ideas and specific psychoanalytic theories and models more clearly than in my previous writings.

This book is a product of my inner dialogue with the readers of *Prisoners of Childhood: The Drama of the Gifted Child* and is to be understood as a continuation of that work. It is possible to read it without knowing the earlier book, but if the subjects discussed here evoke feelings of guilt in the reader rather than of sadness, then it would be advisable to read the earlier work as well. It is important and helpful always to keep in mind in reading my present work that when I speak of parents and children I do not mean specific persons but rather certain conditions, situations, or questions of relative status that concern us all, because all parents were once children and most of those who are children today will one day be parents themselves.

In conclusion, I should like to express my gratitude to several people without whose assistance this book could never have been written, at least not in its present form.

I first became fully aware of what pedagogy really is by experiencing its complete opposite in my second analysis. Therefore, my very special thanks go to my second analyst, Gertrud Boller-Schwing, the author of an extraordinary book about her experiences with institutionalized patients, *The Way to the Soul of the Mentally Ill. Being* was always more important to her than *behavior;* she never tried to "train" or instruct me, neither directly nor "between the lines." As a result of this experience, I was able to learn a great deal in

---

* *Du sollst nicht merken* appeared in Germany in 1981 and will be published in the United States under the title *Thou Shalt Not Be Aware.*

my own very personal way and to become sensitive to the pedagogical atmosphere surrounding us all.

Countless conversations with my son, Martin Miller, played an equally important role in this learning process. Again and again, he forced me to become aware of my unconscious compulsions, internalized during childhood and stemming from the upbringing common to my generation. His full, clear account of his experiences is partially responsible for my own liberation from these compulsions, a liberation that could be achieved only after I had developed an ear for the sophisticated and minute nuances of the pedagogical approach. Before writing down many of the ideas developed here, I discussed them thoroughly with my son.

Lisbeth Brunner's assistance in preparing the manuscript was invaluable. She not only typed it but reacted spontaneously to every chapter with interest and empathy, thereby becoming my first reader.

Finally, I had the good fortune of finding in Suhrkamp's Friedhelm Herborth an editor who showed a profound understanding of my concerns. He never saw fit to do violence to my text and suggested only those stylistic changes that left the original meaning fully intact. His circumspect treatment of my words as well as the respect and understanding he showed for another person's ideas had already impressed me in his labors on my first book. I consider myself extremely fortunate to have received this unusual treatment.

It is thanks to Siegfried Unseld's enthusiastic response to *The Drama of the Gifted Child* (*Prisoners of Childhood*) and to his energetic efforts on my behalf that my works did not disappear on the list of a technical publisher but were able to reach a wider circle of "patients," i.e., of the suffering people for whom they were actually written. Since the editors of the German professional journal *Psyche* rejected the first of the three studies making up *Prisoners of Childhood* and since other publishers were not particularly interested in my work at that time either, it was Suhrkamp's sympathetic reception that made publication in Germany possible.

A.M.

*The young child which lieth in the cradle is both wayward
and full of affections; and though his body be but small,
yet he hath a reat [wrong-doing] heart, and is altogether
inclined to evil. . . . If this sparkle be suffered to increase,
it will rage over and burn down the whole house. For we
are changed and become good not by birth but by education. . . . Therefore parents must be wary and circumspect
. . . they must correct and sharply reprove their children
for saying or doing ill.*
ROBERT CLEAVER AND JOHN DOD, A Godly
Form of Household Government</i> (1621)</p>

*The gentle rod of the mother is a very soft and gentle
thing; it will break neither bone nore skin; yet by the
blessing of God with it, and upon the wise application of it,
it would break the bond that bindeth up corruption in the
heart. . . . Withhold not correction from the child, for if
thou beatest him with the rod he shall not die, thou shalt
beat him with the rod and deliver his soul from hell.*
JOHN ELIOT, The Harmony of the Gospels (1678)

*It is quite natural for the child's soul to want to have a will
of its own, and things that are not done correctly in the first
two years will be difficult to rectify thereafter. One of the
advantages of these early years is that then force and
compulsion can be used. Over the years children forget
everything that happened to them in early childhood. If
their wills can be broken at this time, they will never*

remember afterwards that they had a will, and for this
very reason the severity that is required will not have any
serious consequences.

J. SULZER, "Versuch von der Erziehung
und Unterweisung der Kinder" [An Essay
on the Education and Instruction of
Children] (1748)

Such disobedience amounts to a declaration of war against
you. Your son is trying to usurp your authority, and you are
justified in answering force with force in order to insure
his respect, without which you will be unable to train him.
The blows you administer should not be merely playful
ones but should convince him that you are his master.

J. G. KRÜGER, "Gedanken von der Erziehung
der Kinder" [Some Thoughts on the
Education of Children] (1752)

It was constantly impressed upon me in forceful terms that
I must obey promptly the wishes and commands of my
parents, teachers, and priests, and indeed of all grown-up
people, including servants, and that nothing must distract
me from this duty. Whatever they said was always right.
These basic principles by which I was brought up became
second nature to me.

RUDOLF HÖSS, *Commandant at Auschwitz*

What good fortune for those in power that people do not
think. ADOLF HITLER

How Child-Rearing Crushes Spontaneous Feelings: Glimpses of a Revered Tradition

"Poisonous Pedagogy"

*Punishment followed on a grand scale. For ten days, an
unconscionable length of time, my father blessed the palms
of his child's outstretched, four-year-old hands with a sharp
switch. Seven strokes a day on each hand: that makes one
hundred forty strokes and then some. This put an end to
the child's innocence. Whatever it was that happened in
Paradise involving Adam, Eve, Lilith, the serpent, and the
apple, the well-deserved Biblical thunderbolt of prehistoric
times, the roar of the Almighty and His pointed finger
signifying expulsion—I know nothing about all that. It was
my father who drove me out of Paradise.*

CHRISTOPH MECKEL

*Whoever inquires about our childhood wants to know
something about our soul. If the question is not just a
rhetorical one and the questioner has the patience to listen,
he will come to realize that we love with horror and
hate with an inexplicable love whatever caused us our
greatest pain and difficulty.*

ERIKA BURKART

Introduction

ANYONE who has ever been a mother or father and is at all
honest knows from experience how difficult it can be for
parents to accept certain aspects of their children. It is especially painful to have to admit this if we really love our child
and want to respect his or her individuality yet are unable to
do so. Intellectual knowledge is no guarantee of understanding
and tolerance. If it was never possible for us to relive on a
conscious level the rejection we experienced in our own child-

3

hood and to work it through, then we in turn will pass this rejection on to our children. A merely intellectual knowledge of the laws of child development does not protect us from irritation or anger if our child's behavior does not correspond to our expectations or needs or if—even worse—it should pose a threat to our defense mechanisms.

It is very different for children: they have no previous history standing in their way, and their tolerance for their parents knows no bounds. The love a child has for his or her parents ensures that their conscious or unconscious acts of mental cruelty will go undetected. Descriptions of what can be done to children without fear of reprisal are readily available in recent works dealing with the history of childhood (cf., for example, Philippe Ariès, Lloyd de Mause, Morton Schatzman, and Ray E. Helfer and C. Henry Kempe [see Bibliography]).

The former practice of physically maiming, exploiting, and abusing children seems to have been gradually replaced in modern times by a form of mental cruelty that is masked by the honorific term *child-rearing*. Since training in many cultures begins in infancy during the initial symbiotic relationship between mother and child, this early conditioning makes it virtually impossible for the child to discover what is actually happening to him. The child's dependence on his or her parents' love also makes it impossible in later years to recognize these traumatizations, which often remain hidden behind the early idealization of the parents for the rest of the child's life.

In the mid-nineteenth century a man named Schreber, the father of a paranoid patient described by Freud, wrote a series of books on child-rearing. They were so popular in Germany that some of them went through forty printings and were translated into several languages. In these works it is stressed again and again that children should start being trained as soon as possible, even as early as their fifth month of life, if the soil is to be "kept free of harmful weeds." I have encountered similar views in parents' letters and diaries, which provide the outsider with a clear indication of the underlying causes of the serious illnesses that developed in their children, who were later to become my patients. But initially, these patients of mine were unable to derive much benefit from these diaries and had to undergo long and deep analysis before they could begin to see the truth in them. First they had to become detached from their parents and develop their own individuality.

The conviction that parents are always right and that every act of cruelty, whether conscious or unconscious, is an expression of their love is so deeply rooted in human beings because it is based on the process of internalization that takes place during the first months of life—in other words, during the period preceding separation from the primary care giver.

Two passages from Dr. Schreber's advice to parents, written in 1858, will illustrate the method of raising children prevalent at the time:

> The little ones' displays of temper as indicated by screaming or crying without cause should be regarded as the first test of your spiritual and pedagogical principles. . . . Once you have established that nothing is really wrong, that the child is not ill, distressed, or in pain, then you can rest assured that the screaming is nothing more than an outburst of temper, a whim, the first appearance of willfulness. Now you should no longer simply wait for it to pass as you did in the beginning but should proceed in a somewhat more positive way: by quickly diverting its attention, by stern words, threatening gestures, rapping on the bed . . . or if none of this helps, by appropriately mild corporal admonitions repeated persistently at brief intervals until the child quiets down or falls asleep. . . .
>
> This procedure will be necessary only once or at most twice, and then you will be *master* of the child *forever*. From now on, a glance, a word, a single threatening gesture will be sufficient to control the child. Remember that this will be of the greatest benefit to your child since it will spare him many hours of agitation inimicable to his successful growth, freeing him from all those inner torments that can, moreover, very easily lead to a proliferation of pernicious character traits that will become increasingly difficult to conquer. [Quoted in Morton Schatzman, *Soul Murder*]

Dr. Schreber doesn't realize that what he is in fact attempting to curb in children are his own impulses, and there is no doubt in his mind that he is recommending the exercise of power purely for the child's own good:

> If parents are consistent in this, they will soon be rewarded by the emergence of that desirable situation in which the child will be controlled almost entirely by a parental glance alone.

Children raised in this way frequently do not notice, even at an advanced age, when someone is taking advantage of them as long as the person uses a "friendly" tone of voice.

I have often been asked why I refer mostly to mothers and so seldom to fathers in *Prisoners of Childhood: The Drama of the Gifted Child.* I designate the most important care giver in the child's first year of life as the "mother." This does not necessarily have to be the biological mother or even a woman. In *Prisoners of Childhood* I took pains to point out that looks expressing disapproval and rejection that are directed at the infant can contribute to the development of severe disturbances, including perversions and compulsion neuroses, in the adult. In the Schreber family it was not the mother who "controlled" her two infant sons with "glances," it was the father. (Both sons later suffered from mental illness accompanied by delusions of persecution.) In the last decades, however, there has been an increasing number of fathers who have assumed positive maternal functions and have been able to give their child tenderness and warmth and to empathize with his or her needs. In contrast to the era of the patriarchal family, we now find ourselves in a phase of healthy experimentation with sex roles, and this being the case, I have difficulty speaking about the "social roles" of the father or mother without resorting to outdated normative categories. I can only state that every small child needs an empathic and not a "controlling" human being (whether it be father or mother) as care giver.

An enormous amount can be done to a child in the first two years: he or she can be molded, dominated, taught good habits, scolded, and punished—without any repercussions for the person raising the child and without the child taking revenge. The child will overcome the serious consequences of the injustice he has suffered only if he succeeds in defending himself, i.e., if he is allowed to express his pain and anger. If he is prevented from reacting in his own way because the parents cannot tolerate his reactions (crying, sadness, rage) and forbid them by means of looks or other pedagogical methods, then the child will learn to be silent. This silence is a sign of the effectiveness of the pedagogical principles applied, but at the same time it is a danger signal pointing to future pathological development. If there is absolutely no possibility of reacting appropriately to hurt, humiliation, and coercion, then these experiences cannot be integrated into the personality; the feelings they evoke are repressed, and the need to articulate them remains unsatisfied, without any hope of being fulfilled. It is this lack of hope of ever being able to express repressed traumata by means of relevant feelings that most often causes severe psychological problems. We already know that neuroses are a result of repression, not of events themselves. I shall try to demonstrate that neuroses are not the only tragic consequences of repression.

Because this process does not begin in adulthood but in the very first days of life as a result of the efforts of often well-meaning parents, in later life the individual cannot get to the roots of this repression without help. It is as though someone has had stamped on his back a mark that he will never be able to see without a mirror. One of the functions of psychotherapy is to provide the mirror.

It is true that psychoanalysis is still a privilege of the few, and its therapeutic achievements are often questioned. But having witnessed in case after case the forces that are set free when the results of child-rearing are counteracted; having seen how these forces would otherwise have to be mobilized on all fronts to destroy vital spontaneity in oneself and in others because this quality has been regarded as bad and threatening from an early age, I want to communicate to society something of what I have learned in the analytic process. Society has a right to know, to the extent that this is at all possible, what actually takes place in the analytic setting; for what comes to light there is not only the private affair of a few ill or disturbed people; it concerns us all.

Breeding Grounds of Hatred

GUIDES TO CHILD-REARING
FROM TWO CENTURIES

F OR a long time I asked myself how I could go about giving a vivid and not purely intellectual portrayal of what is done to many children in their earliest days and the consequences this has for society. How could I best tell others, I often wondered, what it is people have discovered concerning the beginning of their life after having gone through a lengthy and laborious process of reconstruction? In addition to the difficulty involved in presenting this material, there is the old dilemma: on the one hand, there is my pledge of professional secrecy; on the other, my conviction that principles are at work here that ought not to remain the special knowledge of a few insiders. Furthermore, I am aware of the resistance on the part of the reader who has not been in analysis, of the guilt feelings that arise when cruel treatment is discussed and the way to mourning still remains blocked. What, then, should be done with this sad fund of knowledge?

We are so used to perceiving everything we hear in terms of moralizing rules and regulations that sometimes even pure information may be interpreted as a reproach and thus cannot be absorbed at all. We justifiably resist new exhortations if moral demands were frequently imposed upon us at too young an age. Love of one's neighbor, altruism, willingness to sacrifice—how splendid these words sound and yet what cruelty can lie hidden in them simply because they are forced upon a child at a time when the prerequisites for altruism cannot possibly be present. Coercion often nips the development of these prerequisites in the bud and what then remains is a lifelong condition of strain. This is like soil too hard for anything to grow in, and the only hope at all of forcibly producing the love demanded of one as a child lies in the upbringing given one's own children, from whom one then demands love in the same merciless fashion.

For this reason, it is my intention to refrain from all moralizing. I definitely do not want to say someone ought or ought not to do this or that (for example, ought not to hate), for I consider maxims of this sort to be useless. Rather, I see it as my task to expose the roots of hatred, which only a few people seem to recognize, and to search for the explanation of why there are so few of these people.

I was giving serious thought to these questions when I came upon Katharina Rutschky's *Schwarze Pädagogik* (*Black Pedagogy*), a collection of excerpts from books on child-rearing, published in Germany in 1977. These texts describe all the techniques, which I refer to in this book as "poisonous pedagogy," that are used to condition a child at an early age not to become aware of what is really being done to him or her; they offer clear corroboration on a concrete level of the conjectural reconstructions I have arrived at in the long course of my analytic work. This gave me the idea of juxtaposing certain passages from this excellent but very lengthy book so that with their help readers can answer for themselves and on their own personal terms the following questions I shall be raising: How were our parents brought up? How were they permitted—even forced—to treat us? How could we, as young children, have become aware of this? How could we have treated our own children differently? Can this vicious circle ever be broken? And finally, is our guilt any less if we shut our eyes to the situation?

It may be that I am trying to attain something with these texts that either is not possible at all or is completely superfluous. For as long as you are not allowed to see something, you have no choice but to overlook it, to misunderstand it, to protect yourself against it in one way or another. But if you have already perceived it for yourself, then you don't need me to tell you about it. Although this observation is correct, I still do not want to give up the attempt, for it strikes me as worthwhile, even though at the moment only a few readers may profit from these excerpts.

I believe the quotations I have chosen will reveal methods that have been used to train children not to become aware of what was being done to them—not only "certain children" but more or less *all* of us (and our parents and forebears). I use the word *reveal* here although there was nothing secretive about these writings; they were widely distributed and went through numerous editions. We of the present generation can learn something from them that concerns us personally and was still hidden from our parents. Reading them, we may have the feeling of getting to the bottom of a mystery, of discovering something new but at the same time long familiar that until now has simultaneously clouded and determined our lives. This was my own experience when I read Rutschky's book about the phenomenon of "poisonous pedagogy." Suddenly I became more keenly aware of its many traces in psychoanalytic theories, in politics, and in the countless compulsions of everyday life.

Those concerned with raising children have always had great trouble dealing with "obstinacy," willfulness, defiance, and the exuberant character of children's emotions. They are repeatedly reminded that they cannot begin to teach obedience too soon. The following passage by J. Sulzer, written in 1748, will serve as an illustration of this:

> As far as willfulness is concerned, this expresses itself as a natural recourse in tenderest childhood as soon as children are able to make their desire for something known by means of gestures. They see something they want but cannot have; they become angry, cry, and flail about. Or they are given something that does not please them; they fling it aside and begin to cry. These are dangerous faults that hinder their entire education and encourage undesirable qualities in children. If willfulness and wickedness are not driven out, it is impossible to give a

child a good education. The moment these flaws appear in a child, it is high time to resist this evil so that it does not become ingrained through habit and the children do not become thoroughly depraved.

Therefore, I advise all those whose concern is the education of children to make it their main occupation to drive out willfulness and wickedness and to persist until they have reached their goal. As I have remarked above, it is impossible to reason with young children; thus, willfulness must be driven out in a methodical manner, and there is no other recourse for this purpose than to show children one is serious. If one gives in to their willfulness once, the second time it will be more pronounced and more difficult to drive out. Once children have learned that anger and tears will win them their own way, they will not fail to use the same methods again. They will finally become the masters of their parents and of their nursemaids and will have a bad, willful, and unbearable disposition with which they will trouble and torment their parents ever after as the well-earned reward for the "good" upbringing they were given. But if parents are fortunate enough to drive out willfulness from the very beginning by means of scolding and the rod, they will have obedient, docile, and good children whom they can later provide with a good education. If a good basis for education is to be established, then one must not cease toiling until one sees that all willfulness is gone, for there is absolutely no place for it. Let no one make the mistake of thinking he will be able to obtain any good results before he has eliminated these two major faults. He will toil in vain. This is where the foundation first must be laid.

These, then, are the two most important matters one must attend to in the child's first year. When he is over a year old, and is beginning to understand and speak somewhat, one must concentrate on other things as well, yet always with the understanding that willfulness must be the main target of all our toils until it is completely abolished. It is always our main purpose to make children into righteous, virtuous persons, and parents should be ever mindful of this when they regard their children so that they will miss no opportunity to labor over them. They must also keep very fresh in their minds the outline or image of a mind disposed to virtue, as described above, so that they know what is to be undertaken. The first and foremost matter to be attended to is implanting in children a love of order; this is the first step we require in the way of virtue. In the first three years, however, this—like all things one undertakes with children—can come about only in a quite mechanical way. Everything must follow the rules of orderliness. Food and drink, clothing, sleep, and indeed the child's entire little household must be orderly and must never be altered in the least to accommodate their willfulness or whims so that they may learn in earliest childhood to submit strictly to the rules of orderliness. The order one insists upon has an indisputable influence on their minds, and if children become accustomed to orderliness at a very early age, they will suppose thereafter that this is completely natural because they no longer realize that it has been artfully instilled in them. If, out of indulgence, one alters the order of the child's little household as often as his whim shall dictate, then he will come to think that orderliness is not of great importance but must always yield to our whim. Such a false assumption would cause widespread damage to the moral life, as may easily be deduced from what I have said above about order. When children are of an age to be reasoned with, one must take every opportunity to present order to them as something sacred and inviolable. If they want to have something that offends against order, then one should say to them: my dear child, this is impossible; this offends against order, which must never be breached, and so on. . . .

The second major matter to which one must dedicate oneself beginning with the second and third year is a strict obedience to parents and superiors and a trusting acceptance of all they do. These qualities are not only absolutely necessary for the success of the child's education, but they have a very strong influence on education in general. They are so essential because they impart to the mind orderliness per se and a spirit of submission to the laws. A child who is used to obeying his parents will also willingly submit to the laws and rules of reason once he is on his own and his own master, since he is already accustomed not to act in accordance with his own will. Obedience is so important that all education is actually nothing other than learning how to obey. It is a generally recognized principle that persons of high estate who are destined to rule whole nations must learn the art of governance by way of first learning obedience. *Qui nescit obedire, nescit imperare:* the reason for this is that obedience teaches a person to be zealous in observing the law, which is the first quality of a ruler. Thus, after one has driven out willfulness as a result of one's first labors with children, the chief goal of one's further labors must be obedience. It is not very easy, however, to implant obedience in children. It is quite natural for the child's soul to want to have a will of its own, and things that are not done correctly in the first two years will be difficult to rectify thereafter. One of the advantages of these early years is that then force and compulsion can be used. Over the years, children forget everything that happened to them in early childhood. If their wills can be broken at this time, they will never remember afterwards that they had a will, and for this very reason the severity that is required will not have any serious consequences.

Just as soon as children develop awareness, it is essential to demonstrate to them by word and deed that they must submit to the will of their parents. Obedience requires children to (1) willingly do as they are told, (2) willingly refrain from doing what is forbidden, and (3) accept the rules made for their sake. [J. Sulzer, *Versuch von der Erziehung und Unterweisung der Kinder (An Essay on the Education and Instruction of Children)*, 1748, quoted in Rutschky]

It is astonishing that this pedagogue had so much psychological insight over two hundred years ago. It is in fact true that over the years children forget everything that happened to them in early childhood; "they will never remember afterwards that they had a will"—to be sure. But, unfortunately, the rest of the sentence, "the severity that is required will not have any serious consequences," is *not* true.

The opposite is the case: throughout their professional lives, lawyers, politicians, psychiatrists, physicians, and prison guards must deal with these serious consequences, usually without knowing their cause. The psychoanalytical process takes years to work its cautious way back to the roots of the trouble, but when successful, it does in fact bring release from symptoms.

Lay persons repeatedly raise the objection that there are people who had a demonstrably difficult childhood without becoming neurotic, whereas others, who grew up in apparently favorable circumstances, become mentally ill. This is supposed to be proof of an innate predisposition and thus a refutation of the importance of parental influence.

The Sulzer passage helps us to understand how this error can (and is meant to?) arise on all levels of society. Neuroses and psychoses are not direct consequences of actual frustrations but the expression of repressed traumata. If primary emphasis is placed upon raising children so that they are not aware of what is being done to them or what is being taken from them, of what they are losing in the process, of who they otherwise would have been and who they actually are, and if this is begun early enough, then as adults, regardless of their intelligence, they will later look upon the will of another person as if it were their own. How can they know that their own will was broken since they were never allowed to express it? Yet something one is not aware of can still make one ill. If, on the other hand, children experience hunger, air raids, and the loss of their home, for instance, but in such a way that they feel they are being taken seriously and respected as individuals by their parents, then they will not become ill as a result of these actual traumata. There is even a chance for them to remember these experiences (because they have had the support of devoted attachment figures) and thus enrich their inner world.

The next passage, by J. G. Krüger, reveals why it was (and still is) so important to pedagogues to combat "obstinacy" vigorously:

> It is my view that one should never strike children for offenses they commit out of weakness. The only vice deserving of blows is obstinacy. It is therefore wrong to strike children at their lessons, it is wrong to strike them for falling down, it is wrong to strike them for wreaking harm unwittingly; it is wrong to strike them for crying; but it is right and proper to strike them for all of these transgressions and for even more trivial ones if they have committed them out of wickedness. If your son does not want to learn because it is your will, if he cries with the intent

of defying you, if he does harm in order to offend you, in short, if he insists on having his own way:

> *Then whip him well till he cries so:*
> *Oh no, Papa, oh no!*

Such disobedience amounts to a declaration of war against you. Your son is trying to usurp your authority, and you are justified in answering force with force in order to insure his respect, without which you will be unable to train him. The blows you administer should not be merely playful ones but should convince him that you are his master. Therefore, you must not desist until he does what he previously refused out of wickedness to do. If you do not pay heed to this, you will have engaged him in a battle that will cause his wicked heart to swell with triumph and him to make the firm resolve to continue disregarding your blows so that he need not submit to his parents' domination. If, however, he has seen that he is vanquished the first time and has been obliged to humble himself before you, this will rob him of his courage to rebel anew. But you must pay especial heed that in chastising him you not allow yourself to be overcome by anger. For the child will be sharp-witted enough to perceive your weakness and regard as a result of anger what he should deem a meting out of justice. If you are unable to practice moderation in this regard, then yield the execution of the chastisement to another, but be sure to impress upon the person not to desist until the child has fulfilled his father's will and comes to beg you for forgiveness. You should not withhold your forgiveness entirely, as Locke justly observes, but should make it somewhat difficult of attainment and not show your complete approbation again until he has made good his previous transgression by total obedience and has proven that he is determined to be a faithful subject of his parents. If children are educated with befitting prudence at a young age, then surely it will very rarely be necessary to resort to such forceful measures; this can hardly be avoided, however, if one takes children in to be reared after they have already developed a will of their own. But sometimes, especially when they are of a proud nature, one can, even in the case of serious transgressions, dispense with beatings if one makes them, for example, go barefoot and hungry and serve at table or otherwise inflicts pain upon them where it hurts. [*Gedanken von der Erziehung der Kinder (Some Thoughts on the Education of Children)*, 1752, quoted in Rutschky]

Here, everything is still stated openly; in modern books on child-rearing the authors carefully mask their emphasis on the importance of gaining control over the child. Over the years a sophisticated repertory of arguments was developed to prove the necessity of corporal punishment for the child's own good. In the eighteenth century, however, one still spoke freely of "usurping authority," of "faithful subjects," etc., and this language reveals the sad truth, which unfortunately still holds today. For parents' motives are the same today as they were then: in beating their children, they are struggling to regain the power they once lost to their own parents. For the first time, they see the vulnerability of their own earliest years, which they are unable to recall, reflected in their children (cf. Sulzer). Only now, when someone weaker than they is involved, do they finally fight back, often quite fiercely. There are countless rationalizations, still used today, to justify their behavior. Although parents *always* mistreat their children for psychological reasons, i.e., because of their own needs, there is a basic assumption in our society that this treatment is good for children. Last but not least, the pains that are taken to defend this line of reasoning betray its dubious nature. The arguments used contradict every psychological insight we have gained, yet they are passed on from generation to generation.

There must be an explanation for this that has deep emotional roots in all of us. It is unlikely that someone could proclaim "truths" that are counter to physical laws for very long (for example, that it is healthy for children to run around in bathing suits in winter and in fur coats in summer) without appearing ridiculous. But it is perfectly normal to speak of the necessity of striking and humiliating children and robbing them of their autonomy, at the same time using such high-sounding words as *chastising, upbringing,* and *guiding onto the right path.* The excerpts from *Schwarze Pädagogik* which follow indicate how much a parent's hidden, unrecognized needs stand to profit from such an ideology. This also explains the great resistance to accepting and integrating the indisputable body of knowledge about psychological principles that has been built up in recent decades.

There are many good books available describing the harmful and cruel aspects of traditional methods of child-rearing (by Ekkehard von Braunmühl, Lloyd de Mause, Katharina Rutschky, Morton Schatzman, and Katharina Zimmer, to mention a few). Why has all this information brought about so little change in the attitudes of the public at large? I used to try to address the numerous individual reasons for problems resulting from child-rearing, but I now believe that there is a universal psychological phenomenon involved here that must be brought to light: namely, the way the adult exercises power over the child, a use of power that can go undetected and unpunished like no other. Seen superficially, it is not in the best interest of any of us to expose this universal mechanism, for who is willing to relinquish either the opportunity to discharge pent-up affect or the rationalizations that enable us to keep a clear conscience? Nevertheless, making these undercurrents of our behavior known is crucial for the sake of future generations. The easier it becomes by means of technology to destroy human life with the touch of a button, the more important it is for the public to understand how it can be possible for someone to want to extinguish the lives of millions of human beings. Beatings, which are only one form of mistreatment, are *always* degrading, because the child not only is unable to defend him- or herself but is also supposed to show gratitude and respect to the parents in return. And along with corporal punishment there is a whole gamut of ingenious measures applied "for the child's own good" which are difficult for a child to comprehend and which for that very reason often have devastating effects in later life. What is our reaction, for example, when we, as adults, try to empathize with the child raised according to the methods recommended by Villaume:

If a child is caught in the act, then it isn't difficult to coax a confession from him. It would be very easy to say to him, so-and-so saw you do this or that. I prefer to take a detour, however, and there are a variety of them.

You have questioned the child about his peaked appearance. You have even gotten him to confess to certain aches and pains that you describe to him. I would then continue:

"You see, my child, that I am aware of your present ailments; I have even enumerated them. You see, then, that I know about your condition. I know even more: I know how you are going to suffer in the future, and I'll tell you about it. Listen. Your face will shrivel, your hair will turn brown; your hands will tremble, your face will be covered with pustules; your eyes will grow dim, your memory weak, your brain dull. You will lose all your good spirits, you won't be able to sleep, and you'll lose your appetite, etc."

It is hard to find a child who will not be dismayed by this. To continue:

"Now I am going to tell you something else. Pay attention! Do you know what the cause of all your suffering is? You may not know, but I do. You have brought it on yourself!—I am going to tell you what it is you do in secret. . . ."

A child would have to be extremely obdurate if he did not make a tearful confession.

Here is another path to the truth! I am taking this passage from the *Pedagogical Discourses:*

I called Heinrich to me. "Listen, Heinrich, I am quite concerned about the seizure you had" (H. had had several epileptic seizures). "I have been searching in my mind for a likely cause but can come up with nothing. Think about it: do you know of anything?"

H.: "No, I know of nothing." (He could hardly know of anything, for a child in this condition does not know what he is doing. In any case, the question was only meant to lead up to what follows.)

"It certainly is strange! Did you perhaps get overheated and then drink something too quickly?"

H.: "No. You know I haven't been out for a long time unless you have taken me with you."

"I can't understand it—I do know a very sad story about a lad of around twelve" (that was Heinrich's age); "he finally died."

(The author now gives a description of Heinrich himself, but with a different name, and frightens the lad.—V.)

"He also had spells without warning, the way you do, and he said it was as though someone were tickling him violently."

H.: "Oh, dear! I'm not going to die? That's the way I feel too."

"And sometimes the tickling seemed as if it would take his breath away."

H.: "Mine too. Didn't you notice that?" (From this, one can see that the poor child really didn't know what the cause of his misery was.)

"Then he began to laugh very hard."

H.: "No, I become so frightened I don't know what to do."

(The author has invented the laughter, perhaps to hide his intention. I think it would have been better to adhere to the truth.—V.)

"This all lasted for a while until he was finally overcome by such hearty, violent, and uncontrollable laughter that he smothered and died."

(I related all this with the greatest equanimity, paying no attention to his responses. I tried to make my facial expressions and my gestures lend what I was saying the appearance of friendly conversation.)

H.: "He died of laughter? Can someone die of laughter?"

"Yes, indeed; that's what I'm telling you. Haven't you ever laughed very hard? Your chest becomes constricted, and the tears come to your eyes."

H.: "Yes, I've had that happen."

"Well, then, just imagine if that had lasted for a very long time; would you have been able to stand it? You were able to stop because the cause of your laughter stopped having an effect on you or because it didn't seem so funny any more. But in the case of our poor lad there weren't any external circumstances that made him laugh; what caused it was the tickle of his nerves, which he couldn't stop by an act of will, and as long as that lasted, his laughter lasted too and in the end caused his death."

H.: "The poor lad!—What was his name?"

"His name was Heinrich."

H.: "Heinrich—!" (He looked at me aghast.)

(Nonchalantly) "Yes! He was a merchant's son in Leipzig."

H.: "Oh! But what made it happen?"

(I had been waiting for this question. Until now I had been walking about the room; now I stopped and looked him straight in the eye in order to observe him closely.)

"What do you think, Heinrich?"

H.: "I don't know."

"I'll tell you what caused it." (I said what follows in a slow and emphatic voice.) "The boy had seen someone doing harm to the most delicate nerves of his body, at the same time making strange motions. Our lad, without knowing that it would harm him, imitated what he had seen. He liked it so well that by this act he caused an unwonted agitation of the nerves of his body, thus weakening them and bringing about his death." (Heinrich blushed violently and was visibly embarrassed.) "What's wrong, Heinrich?"

H.: "Oh, nothing!"

"Do you think you are about to have a seizure again?"

H.: "Oh, no! Will you permit me to leave?"

"Why, Heinrich? Don't you like being here with me?"

H.: "Oh, yes! But—"

"Well?"

H.: "Oh, nothing!"

"Listen, Heinrich, I'm your friend, isn't that true? Be honest. Why did you blush and become so upset upon hearing the tale of the poor lad who came to such an unfortunate and untimely end?"

H.: "Blushed? Oh, I don't know—I felt sorry for him."

"Is that all?—No, Heinrich, there must be another reason; your face betrays it. You are becoming more upset. Be honest, Heinrich; by being honest, you make yourself pleasing in the sight of God, our Heavenly Father, and all men."

H.: "Oh, dear—" (He began to cry loudly and was so pitiable that tears came to my own eyes—he perceived this, grasped my hand, and kissed it passionately.)

"Well, Heinrich, why are you crying?"

H.: "Oh, dear."

"Shall I spare you your confession? Is it not true that you have done what that unfortunate lad did?"

H.: "Oh, dear! Yes."

This second method is perhaps preferable to the first if one is dealing with children of a gentle, sensitive character. There is something severe about the first one in the way it almost assaults the child. [1787, quoted in Rutschky]

Feelings of resentment and rage over this devious form of manipulation cannot surface in the child here because he does not see through the subterfuge. At the most, he will experience feelings of anxiety, shame, insecurity, and helplessness, which may soon be forgotten, especially when the child finds a victim of his own. Villaume, like other pedagogues, takes pains that his methods remain undetected:

One must observe the child closely but in such a way that he does not notice, otherwise he will be secretive and suspicious, and there will be no way of reaching him. Since a sense of shame will always impel the child to try to conceal this sin, we are not dealing with an easy matter here.

If we constantly spy upon a child, especially in secret places, it can happen that we catch him in the act.

Send the children to bed early. When they have just fallen asleep, gently pull aside the blanket to see where their hands are or whether you can detect any other signs. Again in the morning before they are fully awake.

Children, especially if they have a feeling or suspicion that their secret behavior is wicked, are timid and evasive with adults. For this reason I would assign the task of observing the child to one of his friends, and in the case of a girl to a girl friend or faithful maidservant. It goes without saying that these observers must already be familiar with the secret or must be of such age and character as to render its disclosure innocuous. These persons would now perform their observations under the guise of friendship (and it would indeed be a great act of friendship). I would advise, if you are quite sure of them and if it is necessary to their task, that these observers sleep in the same bed with the little ones. In bed, shame and suspicion are easily cast off. In any case, it will not be long before the little ones betray themselves by word or deed.

The conscious use of humiliation (whose function is to satisfy the *parents'* needs) destroys the child's self-confidence, making him or her insecure and inhibited; nevertheless, this approach is considered beneficial:

It goes without saying that pedagogues themselves not infrequently awaken and help to swell a child's conceit by foolishly emphasizing his merits, since they are often merely large children themselves and are filled with the same conceit. . . . It is then important to eliminate this conceit. Undisputedly, it is a fault that, if not combatted in time, becomes ingrained and, combining with other egocentric traits, can be extremely dangerous for the moral life, quite apart from the fact that conceit which rises to the level of excessive pride is offensive or ridiculous to others. Moreover, conceit frequently hinders a pedagogue's effectiveness; the conceited pupil believes he already possesses the good qualities the pedagogue teaches and expects of him or at least considers them easily attainable. Warnings he deems signs of exaggerated apprehensiveness; words of censure, signs of a peevish severity. Only humiliation can be of help here. But how should this be applied? Above all, not with many words. Words are surely not the way to establish and develop moral behavior or to eradicate and remove immoral behavior. They are effective only when part of a more thoroughgoing procedure. Detailed and direct instructions and long homilies, acerbic satire, and biting mockery are the least efficient paths to our goal; the former produce boredom and indifference, the latter bitterness and low spirits. Life itself is always the most convincing teacher. The conceited pupil should be led into situations where he is made aware of his imperfections without the pedagogue having to say a word. Someone who is unduly proud of his accomplishments should be assigned tasks far beyond his abilities and should not be dissuaded if he attempts to take on more than he can handle; halfhearted measures and superficiality should not be tolerated in these attempts. If someone who boasts of his diligence slackens in class, this should be sternly but briefly pointed out to him, and his attention should even be called to a missing or incorrect word in his written assignment; just be sure that the pupil does not suspect any special intent here. It will be no less effective if the pedagogue often brings his charge into the presence of what is great and noble. Hold up to a talented lad the examples of living or historical figures who possess far more splendid talent than his and who have used their talent to accomplish admirable deeds; or hold up as examples those lacking in any especially brilliant mental powers who have nevertheless achieved far more by means of a sustained iron discipline than has a frivolous talent—here too, of course, without explicit reference to your charge, who will of his own accord make the comparison privately. Finally, it will be useful to call to mind the dubious and transitory nature of merely material things by occasionally pointing out appropriate illustrations of this: the sight of a youthful corpse or the report of the collapse of a commercial house has a more humbling effect than often repeated warnings and censure. [K. G. Hergang, ed., *Pädagogische Realenzyklopädie (Encyclopedia of Pedagogy)*, 1851, quoted in Rutschky]

Feigning friendliness helps even more to conceal this type of cruel treatment:

When I once asked a schoolmaster how he had been able to bring it about that the children obeyed him without being whipped, he replied: I attempt to persuade my pupils by my entire demeanor that I mean well by them, and I demonstrate to them through example and illustration that it is to their disadvantage if they do not obey me. Further, I reward the one who is the most amenable, the most obedient, the most diligent in his lessons by preferring him over the others; I call on him the most, I permit him to read his composition before the class, I let him do the necessary writing on the blackboard. This way I awaken the children's zeal so that each wishes to excel, to be preferred. When one of them then upon occasion does something that deserves punishment, I reduce his status in the class, I don't call on him, I don't let him read aloud, I act as though he were not there. This distresses the children so much that those who are punished weep copious tears. If there is upon occasion someone who cannot be educated by such gentle means, then, to be sure, I must whip him; however, for the execution thereof I first make such lengthy preparations that he is more affected by them than by the lashes themselves. I do not whip him at that moment when he earns the punishment but postpone it until the following day or the day thereafter. This provides me with two advantages: first, my blood cools down in the meantime, and I have leisure to consider how best to go about the matter; later, the little delinquent will feel the punishment tenfold more sharply because he has had to devote constant thought to it.

When the day of reckoning arrives, directly after the morning prayer I make a pathetic address to all the children and tell them this is a very sad day for me since the disobedience of one of my dear pupils has imposed on me the necessity of whipping him. The tears begin to flow, not only his who is to be chastised but also those of his fellow pupils. After this lecture is over, I bid the children be seated and I begin the lesson. Not until school is over do I have the little sinner step forward; I then pronounce my verdict and ask him if he knows what he has done to deserve it. After he has given a proper answer, I administer the lashes in the presence of all the children, turn then to the spectators and tell them it is my heartfelt desire that this may be the last time I am constrained to whip a child. [C. G. Salzman (1796), quoted in Rutschky]

For purposes of self-protection, it is only the adult's friendly manner that remains in the child's memory, accompanied by a predictable submissiveness on the part of "the little transgressor" and the loss of his capacity for spontaneous feeling.

Fortunate are those parents and teachers who have educated their children so wisely that their counsel is as forceful as a command, that they seldom have cause to mete out an actual punishment, and that even in these few cases such methods as withdrawing certain pleasant but dispensable things, banishing the children from one's presence, recounting their disobedience to persons whose approbation they desire, etc., are feared as the harshest punishment. Yet few parents are so fortunate. Most of them must occasionally resort to more severe measures. But if they want to instill genuine obedience in their children by so doing, both their miens and words during the chastisement must be serious but not cruel or hostile.

One should be composed and serious, announce the punishment, carry it out, and say nothing more until the act is completed and the little transgressor is once again ready to accept counsel and commands. . . .

If after the chastisement the pain lasts for a time, it is unnatural to forbid weeping and groaning at once. But if the chastised use these annoying sounds as a means of revenge, then the first step is to distract them by assigning little tasks or activities.

If this does not help, it is permissible to forbid the weeping and to punish them if it persists, until it finally ceases after the new chastisement. [J. B. Basedow, *Methodenbuch für Väter und Mütter der Familien und Völker (Handbook for Fathers and Mothers of Families and Nations)*, 1773, quoted in Rutschky]

Crying as a natural reaction to pain is suppressed here by means of renewed beating. To suppress feelings, various techniques may be used:

Now let us see how exercises can aid in the complete suppression of affect. Those who know the strength of a deep-seated habit also know that self-control and perseverance are required in order to break it. Affects can be regarded in the same category as deep-rooted habits. The more persevering and patient one's disposition in general, the more efficient it is in specific cases in overcoming an inclination or bad habit. Thus, all exercises that teach children self-control, that make them patient and persevering, aid in the suppression of inclinations. For this reason, all exercises of this sort deserve special attention in the education of children and are to be regarded as one of its most important elements even though they are almost universally ignored.

There are many such exercises and they can be presented in such a way that children gladly submit to them; you need only know the correct manner of approaching the children and choose a time when they are in a good humor. An example of such an exercise is keeping silent. Ask a child: Do you think you could remain silent for a few hours sometime, without saying a word? Make it pleasurable for him to make the attempt, until he eventually passes the test. Afterwards spare nothing in persuading him that it is an accomplishment to practice such self-control. Repeat the exercise, making it more difficult each time, partly by lengthening the period of silence, partly by giving him cause to speak or by depriving him of something. Continue these exercises until you see that the child has attained a degree of skill therein. Then entrust him with secrets and see if he can be silent even then. If he reaches the point of being able to restrain his tongue, then he is also capable of other things, and the honor attained thereby will encourage him to undertake other tests. One such test is to go without certain things one loves. Children especially love the pleasures of the senses. One must occasionally test whether they can control themselves in this regard. Give them fine fruits and when they reach for them, put them to the test. Could you bring yourself to save this fruit until tomorrow? Could you make someone a present of it? Proceed as I have just instructed in connection with keeping silent. Children love movement. They do not like to keep still. Train them here as well to learn self-control. Also put their bodies to the test insofar as their health permits: let them go hungry and thirsty, bear heat and cold, perform difficult labors, but see that this occurs with their acquiescence; force must not be applied or these exercises will lose their efficacy. I promise you that they will give children brave, persevering, and patient dispositions that will later be all the more efficient in suppressing evil inclinations. Let us take the case of a child who prattles, very often talking for no reason at all. This habit can be broken by the following exercise. After you have thoroughly explained his misbehavior to the child, say: "Now let us test whether you can stop prattling. I shall see how many times you speak today without thinking first." Then one pays careful heed to everything he says, and when he prattles, one makes clear that he is in error and makes note of how many times this has happened in one day. The following day, say to him: "Yesterday you prattled so and so many times. Now let us see how many times you will be in error today." And one continues in this manner. If the child still has any sense of honor and good instincts, he will be sure to forsake his error little by little in this way.

Along with these general exercises, one must also undertake special ones that are directly aimed at restraining affect, but these must not be tried until the above mentioned methods have first been used. A single example can stand for all the rest, because I must pull in my sails a little in order not to go on at too great length. Let us assume a child is vindictive and your methods have brought him to the point of being inclined to suppress this passion. After he has promised to do so, put him to the test in the following manner: tell him you intend to put his perserverance in controlling this passion to the test; admonish him to be on his guard and to be watchful for the first attacks of the enemy. Then secretly order someone to give the child an undeserved reproof when he is not expecting it so that you can see how he will behave. If he succeeds in self-control then you must praise his accomplishment and cause him to perceive as much as possible the satisfaction proceeding from self-control. Later, one must repeat the same test. If he cannot pass it, one must punish him lovingly and admonish him to behave better another time. One need not be severe with him. Where there are many children, one must hold up as examples to the others those who have done well in the test.

One must help the children as much as possible with these tests. One must teach them how to be on their guard. One must make them take as much pleasure as possible in the process so that they are not intimidated by the difficulties. For it should be mentioned that if the children do not take pleasure in these tests, all will be in vain. So much for the exercises. [Sulzer, quoted in Rutschky]

The results of this struggle against strong emotions are so disastrous because the suppression begins in infancy, i.e., before the child's self has had a chance to develop.

Another rule with very important consequences: Even the child's permissible desires should always be satisfied *only* if the child is in an amiable or at least calm mood but *never* while he is crying or behaving in an unruly fashion. First he must have regained his composure even if his previous behavior has been caused, for example, by his legitimate and periodic need to be fed—only then, after a brief pause, should one grant the child's wish. This interval is necessary because the child must not be given even the slightest impression that anything can be won by crying or by unruly behavior. On the contrary, the child perceives very quickly that he will reach his goal only by means of the opposite sort of behavior, by self-control (albeit still unconscious). A good, sound habit can be formed with incredible swiftness (as, on the other hand, can its contrary). Much will have been gained by this, for a good foundation has an infinite number of far-reaching consequences for the future. Here again, however, it is clear how infeasible are these and all similar principles—which must be regarded as of the utmost importance —if, as is usually the case, children of this age are entrusted almost exclusively to domestics, who rarely have the requisite understanding, at least in these matters.

The training just described will give the child a substantial head start in the art of waiting and will prepare him for another, more important one: the art of self-denial. After what has been said, it can be taken almost for granted that every impermissible desire, be it to the child's own disadvantage or not, must be met with an unfailingly consistent and absolute refusal. Refusal alone, however, is not enough. One must at the same time see to it that the child accepts the refusal calmly; one must take care that this calm acceptance becomes a sound habit, if need be by making use of a harsh word, a threatening gesture, and the like. Be sure not to make any exceptions!—then this too will take place much more easily and quickly than one thinks possible. Every exception of course invalidates the rule, both prolonging the training and making it more difficult.—On the other hand, accede to the child's every permissible desire lovingly and gladly.

Only in this way can one aid the child in the salutary and indispensable process of learning to subordinate and control his will, to distinguish for himself the difference between what is permissible and what is not. This cannot be done by anxiously removing everything that arouses impermissible desires. The foundation for the requisite spiritual strength must be laid at an early age, and it—like every other kind of strength—can be increased only through practice. If one waits until later to begin, then success will be much more difficult to attain, and the child, who has had no preparation for this, will become bitter in his disposition.

A very good exercise in the art of self-denial, appropriate for this age, is to give the child frequent opportunity to learn to watch other people in his immediate vicinity eating and drinking without desiring the same for himself. [D. G. M. Schreber (1858), quoted in Rutschky]

Thus, the child is supposed to learn "self-renunciation" from the very beginning, to destroy as early as possible everything in himself that is not "pleasing to God":

True love flows from the heart of God, the source and image of all fatherhood (Ephesians 3:15), is revealed and prefigured in the love of the Redeemer, and is engendered, nourished, and preserved in man by the Spirit of Christ. This love emanating from above purifies, sanctifies, transfigures, and strengthens natural parental love. This hallowed love has as its primary goal the growth of the child's interior self, his spiritual life, his liberation from the power of the flesh, his elevation above the demands of the merely natural life of the senses, his inner independence from the world threatening to engulf him. Therefore, this love is concerned that the child learn at an early age to renounce, control, and master himself, that he not blindly follow the promptings of the flesh and the senses but rather the higher will and the promptings of the spirit. This hallowed love can thus be severe even as it can be mild, can deny even as it can bestow, each according to its time; it also knows how to bring good by causing hurt, it can impose harsh renunciation like a physician who prescribes bitter medicine, like a surgeon who knows very well that the cut of his knife will cause pain and yet cuts in order to save a life. "Thou shalt beat him [the child] with the rod, and shalt deliver his soul from hell" (Proverbs 23:14). With these words, Solomon reveals to us that true love can also be severe. This is not the kind of stoic or narrowly legalistic severity that is full of self-satisfaction and would rather sacrifice its charge than ever deviate from its principles; no, however severe, it always lets its tender concern shine through, like the sun through the clouds, in a spirit of friendliness, compassion, and patient hope. For all its steadfastness, it is yet yielding and always knows what it does and why. [K. A. Schmid, ed., *Enzyklopädie des gesamten Erziehungs- und Unterrichtswesens (A Comprehensive Encyclopedia of Education and Instruction)*, 1887, quoted in Rutschky]

It is a foregone conclusion exactly which feelings are good and valuable for the child (or the adult) and which are not; exuberance, actually a sign of strength, is assigned to the latter category and consequently attacked:

One of the traits in children that border on abnormality is exuberance, which can take many forms but usually begins with exceptionally agitated activity of the voluntary muscles, followed to a greater or lesser degree by other manifestations, should an aroused desire not be immediately satisfied. Children who are just beginning to learn to talk and whose dexterity is still limited to reaching for nearby objects need only be unable to grasp an object or not be allowed to keep it; if they have a tendency toward an excitable disposition, they will then start to scream and make unrestrained movements. Malice develops quite naturally in this child, for whom feelings are no longer subject to the general laws of pleasure and pain but have degenerated from their natural state to such an extent that the child not only loses all capacity for sympathy but evinces pleasure in the discomfort and pain of others. A child's ever-growing discomfort at the loss of the pleasure he would have had if his wishes had been granted eventually finds satisfaction only in revenge, i.e., in the comforting knowledge that his peers have been subjected to the same feeling of discomfort or pain. The more often the child experiences the comforting feeling of revenge, the more this becomes a need, which seeks satisfaction at every idle moment. In this stage, the child uses unruly behavior to inflict every possible unpleasantness, every conceivable annoyance, on others, only for the sake of alleviating the pain he feels because his wishes are not being fulfilled. This fault leads with logical consistency to the next; his fear of punishment awakens the need to tell lies, to be devious and deceitful, to use these stratagems that require only some practice in order to be successful. The irresistible desire to be malicious gradually develops in the same way, as does the penchant for stealing, kleptomania. Willfulness also appears as a secondary but no less serious consequence of the original fault.

. . . Mothers, who are ordinarily entrusted with their children's education, very rarely know how to deal with unruly behavior successfully.

. . . As in the case of all illnesses that are difficult to cure, so too, in the case of the psychic fault of exuberance, the greatest care must be devoted to prophylaxis, to prevention of the disorder. The best way for an education to reach this goal is by adhering unswervingly to the principle of shielding the child as much as possible from all influences that might stimulate feelings, be they pleasant or painful. [S. Landmann, *Über den Kinderfehler der Heftigkeit (On the Character Fault of Exuberance in Children)*, 1896, quoted in Rutschky]

Significantly, cause and effect are confused here and what is attacked as a cause is something that the pedagogues have themselves brought about. This is the case not only in pedagogy but in psychiatry and criminology as well. Once "wickedness" has been produced in a child by suppressing vitality, any measure taken to stamp it out is justified:

> . . . In school, discipline precedes the actual teaching. There is no sounder pedagogical axiom than the one that children must first be trained before they can be taught. There can be discipline without instruction, as we have seen above, but no instruction without discipline.
>
> We insist therefore that learning in and of itself is not discipline, is not a moral endeavor, but discipline is an essential part of learning.
>
> This must be kept in mind when administering discipline. Discipline is, as stated above, not primarily words but deeds; if presented in words, it is not instruction but commands.
>
> . . . It proceeds from this that discipline, as the Old Testament word indicates, is basically chastisement (*musar*). The perverse will, which to its own and others' detriment is not in command of itself, must be broken. Discipline is, as Schleiermacher puts it, life-inhibiting, is at the very least curtailment of vital activity insofar as the latter cannot develop as it wishes but is confined within specific limits and subjected to specific rules. Depending on the circumstances, however, it can also mean restraint; in other words, partial suppression of enjoyment, of the joy of living. This can be true even on a spiritual level: for example, the member of a church congregation can be deprived temporarily of the highest possible enjoyment, the enjoyment of Holy Communion, until he has regained his religious resolve. A consideration of the idea of punishment reveals that, in the task of education, healthy discipline must always include corporal punishment. Its early and firm but sparing application is the very basis of all genuine discipline because it is the power of the flesh that needs most to be broken. . . .
>
> Where human authorities are no longer capable of maintaining discipline, divine authority steps in forcibly and bows down both individuals and nations under the insufferable yoke of their own wickedness. [*Enzyklopädie* . . . quoted in Rutschky]

Schleiermacher's "inhibition of life" is openly avowed here and extolled as a virtue. But, like many moralists, the author overlooks the fact that warm and genuine feelings are unable to grow without the vital soil of "exuberance." Theologians and pedagogues who take a moral viewpoint must be especially inventive if they are not to resort to the rod, for charitable feelings do not grow easily in soil that has been dried out by early disciplining. Still, the possibility remains of "charitable feelings" based on duty and obedience, in other words: another case of hypocrisy.

In her book *Der Mann auf der Kanzel* (*The Man in the Pulpit*) (1979), Ruth Rehmann, herself a minister's daughter, describes the atmosphere in which ministers' children have sometimes had to grow up:

> They are told that their values, by virtue of their nonmaterial nature, are superior to all tangible values. The possession of hidden values encourages conceit and self-righteousness, which quickly and imperceptibly blend in with the required humility. No one can undo this, not even they themselves. No matter what they do, they have to deal not only with their physical parents but with the omnipresent super-Father, whom they cannot offend without paying for it with a guilty conscience. It is less painful to give in, to "be a dear." One does not say "love" in these families, but rather "like" and "be a dear." By avoiding use of the verb "love," they take the sting away from Eros' arrow, bending it into a wedding ring and family ties. Warmth is prevented from becoming dangerous by being relegated to the home fire. Those who have warmed themselves by it will be cold ever after wherever they may be.

After telling her father's story from a daughter's perspective, Rehmann sums up her feelings with these words:

> This is what makes me uneasy about the story: this particular kind of loneliness, which doesn't look like loneliness at all because it is surrounded by well-meaning people; it's only that the one who is lonely has no way of approaching them except from above by bending down as St. Martin bent down from his lofty steed to the poor beggar. This can be given a variety of names: to do good, to help, to give, to counsel, to comfort, to instruct, even to serve; this does not change the fact that above remains above and below below and that the one who is above cannot

have others do good to him, counsel, comfort, or instruct him no matter how much he may be in need of this, for in this fixed constellation no reciprocity is possible—no matter how much love there is, there is not a spark of what we call solidarity. No misery is miserable enough to make such a person come down from the lofty steed of his humble conceit.

This may well be the particular kind of loneliness of a person who, in spite of his meticulous daily observance of God's word and commandments, could incur guilt without being aware of any guilt because the recognition of certain sins presupposes a knowledge based on seeing, hearing, and understanding, not on dialogues with one's own soul. Camillo Torres had to study sociology in addition to theology in order to understand the sufferings of his people and to act accordingly. The Church did not look with favor on this. The sins associated with wanting to know have always seemed more sinful to it than those of not wanting to know, and it has always considered those people more pleasing to God who have sought what is essential in the invisible and have ignored the visible as non-essential.

The pedagogue must also put a very early stop to the desire to know, so that the child does not become aware too early of what is being done to him.

Boy: Where do children come from, dear tutor?

Tutor: They grow in their mother's body. When they have gotten so large that there is no more room for them, the mother must push them out, something like what we do when we have eaten a lot and then go to the privy. But it hurts the mother very much.

Boy: And then the baby is born?

Tutor: Yes.

Boy: But how does the baby get into the mother's body?

Tutor: That we don't know; we only know that it grows there.

Boy: That's very strange.

Tutor: No, not at all.—Look at that whole forest that has grown over there. No one is surprised by this because everyone knows that trees grow out of the earth. In the same way, no reasonable person is surprised that a baby grows in its mother's body. For this has been so as long as people have been on earth.

Boy: And do midwives have to be there when a baby is born?

Tutor: Yes, because the mothers are in such pain that they can't take care of themselves all alone. Since not all women are so hardhearted and fearless that they can be around people who must undergo so much pain, there are women in every town who are paid to stay with the mothers until the pain has passed. They are like the women who prepare dead bodies for burial; washing the dead or undressing and dressing them are also tasks not to everyone's liking, which people therefore perform for money.

Boy: I would like to be there sometime when a baby is born.

Tutor: If you want an idea of the pain and distress mothers experience, you don't need to go and see a baby being born; one doesn't have that chance because mothers do not know themselves at what moment the pains will begin. Instead, I will take you to Dr. R. when he is about to amputate a patient's leg or remove a stone from someone's body. Those people wail and scream just like mothers giving birth. . . .

Boy: My mother told me not long ago that the midwife can tell right away whether the baby is a boy or a girl. How does the midwife know?

Tutor: I will tell you. Boys are much more broad-shouldered and large-boned than girls; but primarily, boys' hands and feet are always broader and coarser than girls' hands and feet. For example, you need only look at the hand of your sister, who is nearly a year and a half older than you; your hand is much broader than hers, and your fingers are thicker and fleshier. That makes them look shorter too, although they are not. [J. Heusinger (1801), quoted in Rutschky]

Once the child's intelligence has been stultified by answers such as these, then he can easily be manipulated:

It is rarely useful and often harmful for you to give them [children] reasons why you are not granting their wishes. Even when you are willing to do what they desire, accustom them now and again to postponement, to being satisfied with just part of what they want, and to accepting gratefully a boon other than the one they requested. Divert a desire you must oppose, either through some activity or by satisfying a different one. In the midst of eating, drinking, or playing, tell them from time to time with friendly gravity to interrupt their enjoyment for a few minutes and undertake something different. Fulfill no request you have once denied. Seek to satisfy children with a frequent "perhaps." You should grant this "perhaps," however, only occasionally and not always, but when they repeat a request, having been forbidden to, you should never grant it.—If they have a distaste for certain foods, determine whether these foods are of common or rare variety. If the latter is the case, you need not take great pains to combat their aversion; in the former case, see if they would rather go hungry and thirsty for a time than eat that to which they have an aversion. When, after abstaining for a time, they do partake of nourishment again, mix the despised food with others without their knowledge; if it tastes good and agrees with them, use this fact to persuade them they have been in error. If vomiting or other harmful bodily symptoms result, say nothing, but see if secretly adding the food in question will help their bodies gradually become accustomed to it. If this is not possible, then your attempts to coerce them will be in vain. If you have discovered, however, that the reason for their aversion is a figment of their imagination, attempt to remedy this by making them go hungry for a considerable period or by other methods of coercion. This will be more difficult to accomplish if children see that their parents or those who take care of them show aversion to this and that food. . . .

If parents or caretakers are unable to take medicine without grimacing or making woeful complaints, they must never let the children see this but rather must frequently pretend they are making use of these vile-tasting medicines that the children may have to take someday. These and other difficulties will usually be overcome if children become accustomed to perfect obedience. The greatest problems are presented by surgical operations. If only one is necessary, say not a word about it to young children ahead of time, but conceal all preparations, perform the operation in silence, and then say, My child, now you are cured; the pain will soon be gone. If more than one operation is required, then I have no general counsel to give as to whether an explanation should be given in advance or not, because the former may be advisable for some, the latter for others.—If children are afraid of the dark, then we have only ourselves to blame. In their first weeks of life, especially when they are being fed during the night, we must occasionally extinguish the light.

Once they have been spoiled, this condition must be cured little by little. The light is snuffed out; after a time it is reintroduced, then again after a longer time, finally after more than an hour. Meanwhile, there is cheerful conversation and the children are given something they like to eat. Now there is no light at all any more; now they are led by the hand through pitch-dark rooms; now they are sent into these same rooms to fetch something agreeable to them. But if parents and caretakers are frightened of the dark themselves, then I have no counsel for them except to use deception. [Basedow (1773), quoted in Rutschky]

Deception seems to be a universal method of control, even in pedagogy. Here too, as in the political sphere, ultimate victory is presented as "the successful resolution" of the conflict.

Similarly, self-control must be demanded from one's charge, and in order to learn it he must be made to practice it. Along with this, as Stoy explains very nicely in his encyclopedia, goes teaching him to observe himself, but without spending time before the looking glass, so he will recognize those faults he must devote his energy to subduing. Then, too, certain accomplishments are expected of him. The boy must learn to go without, must learn to deny himself things, and must learn to be silent when he is rebuked, to be patient when something disagreeable happens; he must learn to keep a secret, to break off in the midst of something pleasant. . . .

Moreover, in the case of practicing self-control, fortitude is required only in the beginning. "Success breeds success" is a favorite adage of educators. With each victory, the power of the will increases and weakness of will wanes until it is vanquished entirely. We have known boys to become so angry that they were beside themselves with rage, as the saying goes, and just a few years later have seen them become the amazed spectators of outbursts of rage in others, and we have heard them express their gratitude to those who trained them. [*Enzyklopädie* . . . quoted in Rutschky]

If this feeling of gratitude is to emerge, conditioning must begin at a very early age:

It is hard to go wrong if one bends a sapling in the direction in which it should grow, something that cannot be done in the case of an old oak. . . .

The infant is fond of something he is playing with that amuses him. Look at him kindly, then smilingly and very calmly take it from him, with a light air; replace it immediately, without making him wait long, with another toy and pastime. He will then forget the first object and eagerly accept the second. Frequent and early repetition of this procedure . . . will prove that the child is not so intractable as he is accused of being and as he would have been had he not been sensibly trained. He is not so likely to turn out to be headstrong with a familiar person who has won his confidence by means of love, play, and tender supervision. Initially, a child does not become agitated and refractory because something has been taken away from him or because his will has been thwarted but because he does not want to give up his amusement and endure boredom. The new diversion he is offered induces him to relinquish the one he had so strongly desired before. If he should show displeasure when an object he covets is withdrawn, should also cry and scream, then pay no heed nor seek to pacify the child by caressing him or by returning the object. Rather, continue your efforts to divert his attention to a new pastime. [F. S. Bock, *Lehrbuch der Erziehungskunst zum Gebrauch für christliche Eltern und künftige Junglehrer (A Manual of the Art of Pedagogy for the Use of Christian Parents and Future Teachers of the Young)*, 1789, quoted in Rutschky]

This advice reminds me of one of my patients, who was successfully conditioned at a very early age not to heed his hunger pangs; his attention was diverted from his hunger "solely by demonstrations of affection." A complicated set of compulsive symptoms concealing his deep feelings of insecurity later resulted from this early training. Naturally, this attempt to divert his attention was only one of many ways used to stifle his vitality; facial expressions and tone of voice are very popular and often unconsciously used methods too:

A very fine and worthy position is assumed by silent punishment or silent reproof, which expresses itself by a look or an appropriate gesture. Silence often has more force than many words and the eye more force than the mouth. It has been correctly pointed out that man uses his gaze to tame wild beasts; should it not therefore be easy for him to restrain all the bad and perverse instincts and impulses of a young mind? If we have nurtured and properly trained our children's sensitivity from the beginning, then a single glance will have more effect than a cane or switch on those children whose senses have not been dulled to gentler influences. "The eye discerns, the heart burns," should be our preferred motto in punishing. Let us assume that one of our children has told a lie but we are unable to prove it. When the family is together at the table or elsewhere, we happen to bring up the subject of people who tell lies, and with a sharp glance at the wrongdoer refer to the shameful, cowardly, and pernicious nature of lying. If he is still otherwise uncorrupted, he will sit there as if on hot coals and will lose his taste for untruthfulness. The silent, pedagogical rapport between us and him will grow stronger. —The right gestures are also among the silent servants of child-rearing. A slight movement of the hand, shaking of the head, or shrugging of the shoulders can have a greater influence than many words. —In addition to silent reproof, we can also use verbal reproof. Here, too, there is not always a need for many high-flown words. *C'est le ton qui fait la musique,* and this applies to pedagogy as well. Anyone fortunate enough to possess a voice whose tone can convey the most diverse moods and emotions has received from Mother Nature a fortuitous means of meting out punishment. This can be observed even in very small children. Their faces light up when Mother or Father speaks to them in a kindly tone, their wailing mouths close when Father's grave and resonant voice enjoins them to be quiet. And when a certain tone of reproof is used to order an infant to drink, it will often obediently take the bottle it had pushed away but a short time ago. . . . The child does not yet understand enough, cannot yet read our feelings clearly enough to perceive that we are compelled to administer the pain of punishment only because we want what is best for him, only because of our good will. Our protestations of love would only strike him as hypocritical or contradictory. Even we adults do not always understand the biblical words, "For whom the Lord loveth, he correcteth." Only long years of experience and observation along with the belief that the salvation of the immortal soul takes precedence over all earthly values can give us a glimpse of the profound truth and wisdom of this verse. —Losing control of ourselves should not be a part of moral censure, which can still be emphatic and forceful without it; losing control only lessens respect and never shows us from our best side. However, one should not shy away from anger, from noble anger that arises from the depths of injured and outraged moral feelings. The less accustomed a child is to see lack of control in the adult and the less the adult's anger is accompanied by lack of control, the stronger will be the impact if there is finally thunder and lightning to clear the air. [A. Matthias, *Wie erziehen wir unseren Sohn Benjamin? (How Shall We Rear our Son Benjamin?)*, 1902, quoted in Rutschky]

Can it ever occur to a small child that the need for thunder and lightning arises from the unconscious depths of the adult psyche and has nothing to do with his or her own psyche? The biblical quotation, "For whom the Lord loveth, he correcteth," implies that the adult shares in the divine omnipotence, and just as the truly devout person is not to question God's motives (see the Book of Genesis), so too the child is supposed to defer to the adult without asking for explanations:

One of the vile products of a misguided philanthropy is the idea that, in order to obey gladly, the child has to understand the reasons why an order is given and that blind obedience offends human dignity. Whoever presumes to spread these views in home or school forgets that our faith requires us adults to bow to the higher wisdom of Divine Providence and that human reason must never lose sight of this faith. He forgets that all of us here on earth live by faith alone, not by cogitation. Just as we must act with humble faith in the higher wisdom and unfathomable love of God, so the child should let his actions be guided by faith in the wisdom of his parents and teachers and should regard this as schooling in obedience toward the Heavenly Father. Anyone who alters these circumstances is flagrantly replacing faith with presumptuous doubt and at the same time overlooking the nature of the child and his need for faith. —I do not know how we can continue to speak of obedience once reasons are given. These are meant to convince the child, and, once convinced, he is not obeying us but merely the reasons we have given him. Respect for a higher intelligence is then replaced by a self-satisfied allegiance to his own cleverness. The adult who gives reasons for his orders opens up the field to argument and thus alters the relationship to his charge. The latter starts to negotiate, thereby placing himself on the same level as the adult; this equality is incompatible with the respect required for successful education. Anyone who believes he can win love only if he is obeyed as a result of explanations is sorely mistaken, for he fails to recognize the nature of the child and his need to submit to someone stronger than himself. If there is obedience in our hearts, a poet tells us, then love will not be far away. In the family it is usually weak mothers who follow the philanthropic principle, whereas the father demands unconditional obedience without wasting words. In return, it is the mother who is most often tyrannized by her offspring and the father who enjoys their respect; for this reason, he is the head of the whole household and determines its atmosphere. [L. Kellner (1852), quoted in Rutschky]

Obedience appears to be the undisputed supreme principle of religious education as well. The word appears again and again in the Psalms and always in connection with the danger of loss of love if the sin of disobedience should be committed. Whoever finds this surprising "fails to recognize the nature of the child and his need to submit to someone stronger than himself."

The Bible is also cited to discourage the expression of natural maternal feelings, which are described as doting:

Is it not doting when the baby is coddled and pampered in every way from infancy? Instead of accustoming the baby from the very first day of his life on earth to discipline and regularity in his intake of nourishment and thereby laying the groundwork for moderation, patience, and human happiness, doting lets itself be guided by the infant's crying. . . .

A doting love cannot be severe, cannot refuse anything, cannot say no for the child's own good; it can only say yes, to the child's detriment. It allows itself to be dominated by a blind desire to be kind, as if this were a natural instinct; it permits when it should forbid, is lenient when it should punish, is indulgent when it should be strict. A doting love lacks any clear idea of the goal of education; it is shortsighted. It wants to do right by the child but chooses the wrong methods. It is led astray by the emotions of the moment instead of being guided by composure and reflection. It allows itself to be misled by the child instead of leading him. It does not have any calm and genuine power of resistance and allows itself to be tyrannized by the child's contradictions, by his willfulness and defiance, or even by the pleas, flattery, and tears of the young tyrant. It is the opposite of true love, which does not shrink from punishment. The Bible says, "He who loves his son chastises him often with the rod, that he may be his joy when he grows up" (Sirach 30:1), and, "Pamper your child and he will be a terror for you, indulge him and he will bring you grief" (Sirach 30:9). . . . Sometimes children raised dotingly are guilty of gross misbehavior toward their parents. [Matthias, quoted in Rutschky]

Parents fear this "misbehavior" so much that on occasion they feel thoroughly justified in using any means to prevent it. And for this purpose they have a rich palette of possibilities to choose from; prominent among them is the method of withdrawing love, which can take many forms. This is something no child can risk.

The infant must perceive order and discipline before he becomes conscious of them, so that he will proceed to the stage of awakening consciousness with good habits already formed and his imperious physical egoism under control. . . .

Thus, the adult must instill obedience by the exercise of his power; this is done with a severe glance, a firm word, possibly by means of physical force (which curbs bad behavior although it is unable to produce good behavior) and by means of punishment. Punishment, however, need not primarily cause physical pain but can utilize withdrawal of kindness and of expressions of love, depending on the type or frequency of the disobedience. For example, for a more sensitive child who is being quarrelsome, this can mean removing him from his mother's lap, refusal of his father's hand or of the bedtime kiss, etc. Since the child's affection can be gained by expressions of love, this same affection can be made use of to make him more amenable to discipline.

. . . We have defined obedience as submission of the will to the legitimate will of another person. . . .

The will of the adult must be a fortress, inaccessible to duplicity or defiance and granting admittance only when obedience knocks at the gates. [*Enzyklopädie* . . . quoted in Rutschky]

When still in diapers, the child learns to knock at the gates of love with "obedience," and unfortunately often does not unlearn this ever after:

. . . Turning now to the second major point, how to instill obedience, we begin by showing how this can be done at a very early age. Pedagogy correctly points out that even a baby in diapers has a will of his own and is to be treated accordingly. [*Enzyklopädie* . . .]

If treatment of this sort is carried through consistently enough and early enough, then all the requirements will have been met to enable a citizen to live in a dictatorship without minding it; he or she will even be able to feel a euphoric identification with it, as happened in the Hitler period:

. . . for the health and vitality of a political commonwealth owe just as much to the flourishing of obedience to law and authority as to the prudent use of energy of its leaders. Likewise in the family, in all matters of child-rearing, the will that gives orders and the one that carries them out must not be regarded as antagonistic; they are both the organic expression of what is actually a single will. [*Enzyklopädie* . . .]

Just as in the symbiosis of the "diaper stage," there is no separation here of subject and object. If the child learns to view corporal punishment as "a necessary measure" against "wrongdoers," then as an adult he will attempt to protect himself from punishment by being obedient and will not hesitate to cooperate with the penal system. In a totalitarian state, which is a mirror of his upbringing, this citizen can also carry out any form of torture or persecution without having a guilty conscience. His "will" is completely identical with that of the government.

Now that we have seen how easy it is for intellectuals in a dictatorship to be corrupted, it would be a vestige of artisto-cratic snobbery to think that only "the uneducated masses" are susceptible to propaganda. Both Hitler and Stalin had a sur-prisingly large number of enthusiastic followers among intel-lectuals. Our capacity to resist has nothing to do with our intelligence but with the degree of access to our true self. Indeed, intelligence is capable of innumerable rationaliza-tions when it comes to the matter of adaptation. Educators have always known this and have exploited it for their own purposes, as the following proverb suggests: "The clever per-son gives in, the stupid one balks." For example, we read in a work on child raising by Grünewald (1899): "I have never yet found willfulness in an intellectually advanced or excep-tionally gifted child" (quoted in Rutschky). Such a child can, in later life, exhibit extraordinary acuity in criticizing the ideologies of his opponents—and in puberty even the views by his own parents—because in these cases his intellectual powers can function without impairment. Only within a group —such as one consisting of adherents of an ideology or a theoretical school—that represents the early family situation will this person on occasion still display a naïve submissiveness and uncritical attitude that completely belie his brilliance in other situations. Here, tragically, his early dependence upon tyrannical parents is preserved, a dependence that—in keeping with the program of "poisonous pedagogy"—goes undetected. This explains why Martin Heidegger, for example, who had no trouble in breaking with traditional philosophy and leaving behind the teachers of his adolescence, was not able to see the contradictions in Hitler's ideology that should have been ob-vious to someone of his intelligence. He responded to this ide-ology with an infantile fascination and devotion that brooked no criticism.

In the tradition we are dealing with, it was considered obstinacy and was therefore frowned upon to have a will and mind of one's own. It is easy to understand that an intelligent child would want to escape the punishments devised for those possessing these traits and that he or she could do so without any difficulty. What the child didn't realize was that escape came at a high price.

The father receives his powers from God (and from his own father). The teacher finds the soil already prepared for obedience, and the political leader has only to harvest what has been sown:

> With the most forceful form of punishment, corporal chastise-ment, we come to the ultimate in punishment. Just as the rod serves as the symbol of paternal discipline in the home, the stick is the primary emblem of school discipline. There was a time when the stick was the cure-all for any mischief in school as the rod was in the home. It is an age-old "indirect way of speak-ing from the soul," common to all nations. What can be more ob-vious than the rule, "He who won't hear must be made to feel"? Pedagogical blows provide a forceful accompaniment to words and intensify their effect. The most direct and natural way of administering them is by that box on the ears, preceded by a strong pulling on the ear, which we still remember from our own youth. This is an unmistakable reminder of the existence of an organ of hearing and of its intended use. It obviously has symbolic significance, as does a slap on the mouth, which is a reminder that there is an organ of speech and a warning to put it to better use. . . . The tried and true blow to the head and hair-pulling still convey a certain symbolism, too. . . .
> Even truly Christian pedagogy, which takes a person as he is, not as he should be, cannot in principle renounce every form of corporal chastisement, for it is exactly the proper punishment for certain kinds of delinquency: it humiliates and upsets the child, affirms the necessity of bowing to a higher order and at the same time reveals paternal love in all its vigor. . . . We would be in complete sympathy if a conscientious teacher de-clared: I would rather not be a teacher at all than have to relinquish my prerogative of reaching for the ultima ratio of the stick when necessary.
> . . . "The father strikes his child and himself feels the smart,/ Severity is a merit if you have a gentle heart," writes the poet Rückert. If the teacher is a true representative of the father, then he also knows how to display—with the stick when neces-

sary—a love that is often purer and deeper than that of many a natural father. And although we call the child's heart a sinful one, we believe we may still say: The childish heart as a rule understands this love, even if not always at the moment. [*Enzyklopädie* . . . quoted in Rutschky]

As an adult, this child will often allow himself to be manipulated by various forms of propaganda since he is already used to having his "inclinations" manipulated and has never known anything else:

First and foremost, the educator must take care that those inclinations hostile and adverse to the higher will, instead of being awakened and nourished by early education (as so commonly occurs), be prevented by every possible means from developing or at least be eradicated as soon as possible. . . .

Whereas the child should be as little acquainted as possible with those inclinations unfavorable to his higher development, he should, on the other hand, be zealously and frequently introduced to all the rest or at least to their first buddings.

Therefore, let the educator instill in the child at an early age abundant and enduring inclinations of the better sort. Let him rouse him often and in divers ways to merriment, joyfulness, delight, hope, etc., but occasionally, although less frequently and more briefly, let him also encourage fear, sadness, and the like. He will have opportunity enough for this by virtue of the fact that, in the normal course of events, some of the child's manifold needs, not only of the body but also and primarily of the soul, are satisfied; that others are not; and that there are various combinations of both conditions. He must arrange everything so that it be nature's doing and not his own, or at least so that this appear to be the case. The unpleasant occurrences in particular must not betray their origin if he is the one responsible for them. [K. Weiller, *Versuch eines Lehrgebäudes der Erziehungskunde (Toward a Theory of the Art of Education)*, 1805, quoted in Rutschky]

The person actually benefiting from this manipulation must not be detected. The child can be manipulated in another way: by frightening him in a manner that destroys or perverts his natural curiosity:

It is also well known how curious children are in this regard, especially when they are somewhat older, and what strange paths and means they often elect to acquaint themselves with the physical differences between the sexes. One can be sure that every discovery they make will feed their already heated imagination and thus endanger their innocence. For this reason alone, it would be advisable to anticipate this, and the instruction referred to earlier makes it necessary in any case. It would of course offend all modesty if one sex were permitted to disrobe freely in front of the other. And yet a boy should know how the female body is fashioned, and a girl should know how the male body is fashioned; otherwise, they will not receive correct impressions and their curiosity will know no bounds. Both sexes should learn about this in a solemn manner. Illustrations might give satisfaction in this matter, but do they present the matter clearly? Do they not inflame the imagination? Do they not awaken a wish for a comparison with nature? All these worries disappear if one makes use of a lifeless human body for this purpose. The sight of a corpse evokes solemnity and reflection, and this is the most appropriate mood for a child under such circumstances. By a natural association of ideas, his memory of the scene will also produce a solemn frame of mind in the future. The image imprinted in his soul will not have the seductive attractiveness of images freely engendered by the imagination or of those elicited by less solemn objects. If all young people could receive their instruction about human reproduction from an anatomical lecture, matters would be much simpler. But since there is so little opportunity for this, every teacher can also impart the necessary instruction in the manner described above. There is often opportunity to see a corpse. [J. Oest (1787), quoted in Rutschky]

Viewing corpses is here considered a legitimate means of combating the sex drive, of preserving "innocence"; at the same time, however, the groundwork is thus being laid for the development of future perversions. Systematically induced disgust with one's own body also fulfills this function:

Instilling modesty is not nearly so effective as teaching children to regard disrobing and all that goes with it as improper and as offensive to others, just as offensive as it would be, for example, to expect someone to carry out a chamber pot who is not paid to perform the task. For this reason I would suggest that children be cleansed from head to foot every two to four weeks by an old, dirty, and ugly woman, without anyone else being present; still, parents or those in charge should make sure that even this old woman doesn't linger unnecessarily over any part of the body. This task should be depicted to the children as disgusting, and they should be told that the old woman must be paid to undertake a task that, although necessary for purposes of health and cleanliness, is yet so disgusting that no other person can bring himself to do it. This would serve to prevent a shock to their sense of modesty. [Oest, quoted in Rutschky]

Causing a child to feel shame can also be a stratagem in the struggle against willfulness:

As already outlined above, willfulness must be broken "at an early age by making the child feel the adult's unquestionable superiority." Later on, shaming the child has a more lasting effect, especially on vigorous natures, for whom willfulness is often allied with boldness and energy. Toward the end of his education, either a veiled or an open reference to the ugly and immoral character of this fault must succeed in enlisting the child's thoughts and all his willpower against the last vestiges of willfulness. It has been our experience that a private conversation proves efficacious in this last stage. In view of the prevalence of willfulness in children, it is very surprising that the appearance, nature, and cure of this antisocial psychic phenomenon has received so little attention and elucidation in child psychology and pathology. [Grünewald, *Über den Kinderfehler des Eigensinns (On the Character Fault of Willfulness in Children)*, quoted in Rutschky]

It is always important to employ all these methods as early as possible:

If we frequently do not achieve our purpose, even in this manner, let this be a reminder for wise parents to make their child docile, malleable, and obedient at a very early age and to accustom him to conquer his own will. This is a major aspect of moral education and to neglect it is the worst mistake we can make. The correct observance of this duty without jeopardizing the other duty that obligates us to see that the child is kept in a happy frame of mind is the most important skill required in early training. [Bock (1780), quoted in Rutschky]

In the three scenes that follow, we see vivid examples of how the principles described above can be put into practice. I quote these passages at such length in order to give the reader an idea of the atmosphere these children (i.e., if not we ourselves, then at least our parents) breathed in daily. This material helps us to understand how neuroses develop. They are not caused by an external event but by repression of the innumerable psychological factors making up the child's daily life that the child is never capable of describing because he or she doesn't know that things can be any other way:

Until the time he was four, I taught little Konrad four essentials: to pay attention, to obey, to behave himself, and to be moderate in his desires.

The first I accomplished by continually showing him all kinds of animals, flowers, and other wonders of nature and by explaining pictures to him; the second by constantly making him, whenever he was in my presence, do things at my bidding; the third by inviting children to come play with him from time to time when I was present, and whenever a quarrel arose, I carefully determined who had started it and removed the culprit from the game for a time; the fourth I taught him by often denying him something he asked for with great agitation. Once, for example, I cut up a honeycomb and brought a large dishful into the room. "Honey! Honey!" he cried joyfully, "Father, give me some honey," pulled his chair to the table, sat down, and waited for me to spread a few rolls with honey for him. I didn't do it but set the honey before him and said: "I'm not going to give you any honey yet; first we will plant some peas in the garden; then, when that is done, we will enjoy a roll with honey together." He looked first at me, then at the honey, whereupon he went to the garden with me. Also, when serving food, I always arranged it so that he was the last one served. For example, my parents and little Christel were eating with us once, and we had rice pudding, which he especially liked. "Pudding!" he cried joyfully, embracing his mother. "Yes," I said, "it's rice pudding. Little Konrad shall have some, too. First the big people shall have some, and afterwards the little people. Here, Grandmother, is some pudding for you. Here, Grandfather, is some for you, too! Here, Mother, is some for you. This is for Father, this for Christel, and this? Whom do you think this is for?" " 'Onrad," he responded joyfully. He did not find this arrangement unjust, and I saved myself all the vexation parents have who give their children the first portion of whatever is brought to the table. [Salzmann (1796), quoted in Rutschky]

The "little people" sit quietly at the table and wait. This need not be demeaning. It all depends on the adult's intention —and here the adult in question shows unabashedly how much he enjoys his power and his bigness at the expense of the little ones.

Something similar occurs in the next story, in which telling a lie is the only possible way for the child to read in privacy:

A lie is something dishonorable. It is recognized as such even by those who tell one, and there probably isn't a single liar who has any self-respect. But someone who doesn't respect himself doesn't respect others either, and the liar thus finds himself excluded from human society to a certain extent.

It follows from this that a young liar needs to be treated very discreetly so that, in the process of being cured of his fault, his self-respect, which has already suffered as it is from knowing he has lied, will not be even more seriously damaged, and this is no doubt a rule that admits of no exception: a child who lies must never be publicly censured or punished for this fault or, except under the most extreme circumstances, even publicly reminded of it. —The adult will do well to appear to be more surprised and even astonished that the child has been untruthful than to appear outraged that he has told a lie, and the adult should pretend as long as possible that he takes a (deliberate) lie for an (unintentional) untruth. This is the key to the behavior assumed by Mr. Willich when he discovered traces of this vice even in his own little family group.

Katie was guilty of being untruthful on occasion. . . . She once had the opportunity to benefit from this, and she succumbed to the temptation. One evening she had done her knitting with such diligence that the portion she completed could pass for the work of two evenings. In addition, her mother happened to forget to have the girls show her what they had accomplished that evening.

On the following evening Katie secretly stole away from the rest of the family, took up a book that had come into her hands that day, and spent the whole evening reading it. She was cunning enough to conceal from her sisters, who were sent from time to time to see where she was and what she was doing, the fact that she was reading; they found her either with her knitting in her hand or at some other task.

This time her mother inspected the girls' work. Katie held up her stocking. It had indeed grown considerably in size, but her observant mother thought she noticed a certain evasiveness in the girl. She looked at the knitting, said nothing, but decided to make some inquiries. The next day, by asking some questions, she determined that Katie couldn't have done her knitting the previous evening. But, instead of indiscreetly accusing her of being untruthful, at a fitting moment she engaged the girl in conversation with the intention of setting a trap for her.

They spoke of woman's work. The mother remarked that at the present time it was usually very badly paid and added that she didn't believe a girl of Katie's age and skill could earn what she needed to live when food, clothing, and shelter were taken into account. Katie, however, believed the opposite and said she, for example, could accomplish twice as much with her knitting in a few hours as the mother had reckoned. The mother disagreed heartily. This in turn caused the girl to become very agitated; she forgot herself and exclaimed that two days ago she had knit twice as big a portion as usual.

"What am I to think of that?" the mother responded. "You told me yesterday that the evening before you had knit half the amount of what has been added to your stocking." —Katie turned red. She didn't know where to look and cast her eyes about uncontrollably. "Katie," her mother said to her in a grave but sympathetic tone of voice, "has the white ribbon in your hair been of no help?—I must sadly take my leave of you." She quickly rose from her chair and left the room, with a grave manner and without looking at the dismayed Katie, who wanted to run after her but instead remained behind, upset and in tears.

One will note that this was not the first time since Katie had been living with her foster parents that she had been guilty of this fault. Her mother had remonstrated with her about it and had finally told her that in the future she must wear a white ribbon in her hair. "White," she added, "is often considered the color of innocence and purity. You will do well, whenever you look in the mirror, to be reminded by your headband of purity and truthfulness, which should reign in your thoughts and words. Untruthfulness, on the other hand, is filth that stains your soul." —These measures had helped for a considerable time. But now, with this new lapse, all hope was gone that Katie's fault could remain a secret between her and her mother. For the latter had assured her at the time that if Katie proved guilty of this fault one more time, she, the mother, would feel obligated to call upon the father for assistance and thus reveal the matter to him.

Now things had reached this point, and it happened as the mother had promised. For she was not one to threaten to do something without carrying out her threat immediately if the need arose.

Mr. Willich appeared very displeased, ill-humored, and pensive all day long. All the children noticed it, but only for Katie were his stern looks like arrows in her heart. Her fear of what was coming tormented the girl all afternoon.

In the evening Katie's father called her to his room. She found him still with the same mien.

"Katie," he said to her, "I have been confronted with something exceedingly unpleasant today: I have found a liar among my children."

Katie started to cry and could not say a word.

Mr. Willich: "I was shocked when your mother told me you have demeaned yourself with this vice several times before. Tell me, for heaven's sake, child, how does it come about that you can go so far astray?" (After a pause) "Now dry your tears. Crying will not make it better. Tell me instead about yesterday's incident so that we can determine how to help prevent this wickedness in the future. Explain what happened yesterday evening. Where were you? What did you do or not do?"

Hereupon Katie related the episode as it had happened and as we already know it. She concealed nothing, not even the cunning she had employed to deceive her sisters about what she was doing. "Katie," responded Mr. Willich in a tone that inspired confidence, "you have told me things about yourself that you yourself cannot possibly welcome. When your mother examined your knitting yesterday evening, you told her you had been working hard on it. Knitting is undeniably something good; you told Mother something good about yourself. Now tell me, when did you feel lighter of heart—just now when you were telling something bad that is the truth, or yesterday when you were telling something good that was not the truth?"

Katie admitted she was relieved that she had confessed and that it was an ugly vice to tell lies. . . .

Katie: "It's true, I was very foolish. But forgive me, dear Father."

Willich: "It's not a question of forgiveness. You have offended me very little. Yourself, however, and your mother as well you have offended very severely. I shall proceed accordingly, and if you were to lie ten times more, you would not deceive me. If what you say is not obviously true, then in the future I shall treat your words like money one thinks is counterfeit. I shall test and question and examine. For me, you will be like a walking stick one cannot rely on; I shall always look at you with a measure of distrust."

Katie: "Ah, dear Father, as bad as all that . . ."

Willich: "Do not think, poor child, that I am exaggerating or joking. If I cannot rely on your truthfulness, then who will guarantee me that I shall not come to harm if I believe what you say? —I see, dear child, that you have *two* enemies to conquer if you wish to eradicate your inclination to tell lies. Do you want to know what they are, Katie?"

Katie (ingratiatingly, appearing a little too amiable and light-hearted): "Oh yes, dear Father."

Willich: "But are you sufficiently composed and prepared in your mind? I don't want to say it if it doesn't stay with you and is forgotten again by tomorrow."

Katie (more earnestly): "No, I will be sure to remember it."

Willich: "Poor girl, if you should take this lightly!" (After a pause) "Your first enemy is frivolity and thoughtlessness. —When you put the book in your pocket and stole away to read it in secret, you should have given some thought to what you were doing. How could you find it in your heart to do even the slightest thing you wanted to keep from us? Whatever put the idea into your head? If you regarded reading the book as permissible—good, then you needed only to say, 'I should like to read

this book today, and I ask that my diligence in knitting yesterday be counted toward today'—do you really think it would have
been denied you? Didn't you regard it as permissible? —Would
you have wanted to do something impermissible without our
knowledge? Certainly not. You are not that wicked. . . . Your
second enemy, dear daughter, is false modesty. You are ashamed
to confess it if you have done something wrong. Do away with
this fear. This enemy can be vanquished straightaway. Don't
permit yourself any more excuses or reticence, not even in the
case of the smallest mistake you make. Let us, let your sisters
know your heart even as you know it yourself. You are not yet
so depraved that you must be ashamed to confess what you
have done. Only hide nothing from yourself, and no longer tell
anything differently from the way you know it to be. Even in
the most trivial matters, even when joking, do not permit yourself to report anything other than the way it really is.

"Your mother has, as I see, taken the white ribbon from your
hair. You have forfeited it, that is true. You have besmirched your
soul with a lie. But you have also made amends. You have confessed your faults to me so faithfully that I cannot believe you
have concealed or misrepresented anything. This in turn proves
to me your sincerity and truthfulness. Here is another ribbon
for your hair. It is not as nice as the other one, but it is not a
question of how fine the ribbon is but of the worth of the one
who wears it. If she increases in worth, then I will not be averse
someday to showing my appreciation with an expensive hair
ribbon worked with silver." With this, he dismissed the girl, not
without concern that recurrences of this fault would occur because of her lively temperament, but also not without hope that
her keen intelligence and a skillful handling of the situation
would soon help the girl to become more steadfast in her ways
and thereby block off the wellspring of this ugly vice.

After a time, there was indeed a recurrence. . . . It was evening, and the children had just been asked what their tasks had
been and how they had performed them. Their accounts were
exceptionally good; even Katie could cite some things she had
done beyond the usual course of her duties. But she suddenly
remembered one thing she had neglected to do; she not only
kept it from her mother but, upon being questioned, professed
that she had done it. There were some holes in her stockings
that she was supposed to have darned and had forgotten about.

When she thought of it just as she was giving her accounting, she also remembered that for the past few days she had been rising earlier in the morning than the others. She hoped that this would be the case again the next morning and she would then quickly take care of it.

Things did not turn out at all as Katie had expected, however. Out of carelessness she had left her stockings where she wasn't supposed to, and her mother had already taken them away, whereas the girl believed they were still where she had put them. It was on the tip of the mother's tongue to ask Katie about the stockings again, while giving her a searching look. But she remembered just in time that her husband had forbidden her ever to accuse the girl of her fault in front of others, and she restrained herself. But it hurt her to the quick that the girl could utter a flagrant untruth with such ease.

The mother was also up early the next morning, for she had an idea of what Katie had in mind. She found her daughter already dressed, searching for something and more than a little worried. The girl was about to offer her mother her hand to bid her good morning and was attempting to assume her usual amiable manner. The mother took this to be the right moment. "Don't force yourself," she said, "to lie with your *mien* as well; your *mouth* already did so yesterday. Your stockings have been there in the closet since yesterday noon, and you didn't remember to darn them. How could you tell me yesterday evening that they were darned?"

Katie: "Oh, Mother, I could die."

"Here are your stockings," the mother said in a very cold and distant voice. "I want nothing more to do with you today. Come to your lessons or not, it's all the same to me. You are a wretched girl."

With this, the mother left the room, and Katie sat down, crying and sobbing, to do hurriedly what she had omitted to do the day before. Hardly had she begun, however, when Mr. Willich entered the room with a grave and mournful expression and silently paced up and down.

Willich: "You are crying, Katie. What has happened to you?"

Katie: "Oh, dear Father, you already know what it is."

Willich: "I want to know *from you*, Katie, what has happened."

Katie (hiding her face in her handkerchief): "I told another lie."

Willich: "Unhappy child. Is it really impossible for you to master your frivolous ways?"

Katie's tears and heavy heart prevented her from answering.

Willich: "I shall not besiege you with much talk, dear daughter. You already know well enough that a lie is a disgraceful thing, and I have also noted that at times, when you do not collect your thoughts, a lie pops out. What is to be done? You must take action, and I will lend you support as a friend.

"Let the present day be set to mourn over the mistake you made yesterday. The ribbons you put on today must be black. Go and do it before your sisters get up." When Katie returned, having done as she had been ordered, Mr. Willich continued: "Be comforted, you shall have in me a faithful source of support in your sorrow. So that you become more mindful of yourself, you are to come to my room every evening before you go to bed and enter into a notebook that I am going to prepare for this purpose either 'Today I told a lie' or 'Today I did not tell a lie.'

You need not fear a reprimand from me, even if you have to enter something unpleasant. I hope that just the reminder of a lie you have told will protect you from this vice for many days at a time. So that I, too, may do something to help you throughout the day to have something good in the evening to enter in the book rather than something bad, I forbid you from this evening on, when you take the black ribbon out of your hair, to wear any ribbons in your hair. I forbid this for an indefinite period until the record you keep convinces me that your earnest behavior and your truthfulness have become so ingrained that in my judgment a recurrence is no longer to be feared. If you reach that point, as I hope you will—then you will be able to choose for yourself which color hair ribbon you will wear." [Heusinger, *Die Familie Wertheim (The Wertheim Family)*, 1800, quoted in Rutschky]

Katie is without a doubt convinced that only she, the wicked creature, could harbor such a vice. In order to realize that her wonderful and kind father himself has difficulties with the truth and for this reason torments her so, the child would have to have some experience with psychoanalysis. As it is, she considers herself very bad compared to her exemplary parents.

And little Konrad's father? Can we perhaps see in him the problem of numerous fathers of our day?

I had made a firm resolve to raise him without ever striking him, but it didn't turn out as I had hoped. An occasion soon arose when I was compelled to use the rod.

It happened like this. Christel came to visit and brought a doll along. No sooner had Konrad seen it than he wanted to have it. I asked Christel to give it to him, and she did. After Konrad had held it for a while, Christel wanted it back, and Konrad didn't want to give it to her. What was I to do now? If I had brought him his picture book and then had said he should give the doll to Christel, perhaps he would have done it without objecting. But I didn't think of it, and even if I had, I don't know whether I would have done it. I thought it was high time for the child to accustom himself to obeying his father unquestioningly. I therefore said, "Konrad, don't you want to give Christel's doll back to her?"

"No!" he said with considerable vehemence.

"But poor Christel has no doll!"

"No!" he answered again, started to cry, clutched the doll, and turned his back to me.

Then I said to him in a severe tone of voice, "Konrad, you must return the doll to Christel at once; I insist."

And what did Konrad do? He threw the doll at Christel's feet.

Heavens, how upset I was by this. If my best cow had died, I don't think I would have been as shocked. Christel was about to pick up the doll, but I stopped her. "Konrad," I said, "pick the doll up at once and hand it to Christel."

"No! No!" cried Konrad.

Then I fetched a switch, showed it to him, and said, "Pick up the doll or I will have to give you a whipping." But the child remained obstinate and cried, "No! No!"

Then I raised the switch and was about to strike him when a new element was added to the scene. His mother cried, "Dear husband, I beg you, for heaven's sake—"

Now I was faced with a dilemma. I made a quick resolve, however, took the doll and the switch, picked up Konrad, ran out of the room and into another, locked the door behind me so his mother could not follow, threw the doll on the ground and said, "Pick up the doll or I will give you a whipping!" My Konrad persisted in saying no.

Then I lashed him, one! two! three! "Don't you want to pick up the doll now?" I asked.

"No!" was his reply.

Then I whipped him much harder and said: "Pick up the doll at once!"

Then he finally picked it up; I took him by the hand, led him back into the other room, and said: "Give the doll to Christel!"

He gave it to her.

Then he ran crying to his mother and wanted to put his head in her lap. But she had enough sense to push him away and said, "Go away, you're not my good Konrad."

To be sure, the tears were rolling down her cheeks as she said it. When I noticed this, I asked her please to leave the room. After she had gone, Konrad cried for perhaps another quarter hour; then he stopped.

I can certainly say that my heart was sore throughout this scene, partly because I felt pity for the child, partly because I was distressed by his stubbornness.

At mealtime I couldn't eat; I got up from the table and went to see our pastor and poured my heart out to him. I was comforted by what he said. "You did the right thing, dear Mr. Kiefer," he said. "When the nettles are still young, they can be pulled out easily; but if they are left for a long time, the roots will grow, and then if one attempts to pull them out, the roots will be deeply imbedded. It is the same way with misbehavior in children. The longer one overlooks it, the more difficult it is to eliminate. It was also a good thing for you to give the stubborn little fellow a thorough whipping. He won't forget it for a long time to come.

"If you had used the rod sparingly, not only would it have done no good on this occasion, but you would always have to whip him in the future, and the boy would become so accustomed to it that in the end he would think nothing of it. That is why children usually don't take it seriously when their mothers spank them, because mothers don't have the courage to strike them hard. This is also the reason why there are children who are so intractable that nothing can be accomplished any more by even the most severe thrashing. . . .

"Now while the lashes are still fresh in your Konrad's mind, I advise you to take advantage of it. When you come home, see that you order him about a good deal. Have him fetch you your boots, your shoes, your pipe, and take them away again; have him carry the stones in the yard from one place to another. He will do it all and will become accustomed to obeying." [Salzmann (1796), quoted in Rutschky]

Do the pastor's comforting words sound that outdated? Wasn't it reported in 1979 that two-thirds of the German population are in favor of corporal punishment? In England, flogging has not yet been prohibited in the schools and is accepted as routine in the boarding schools there. Who will bear the brunt of this humiliating treatment later when the colonies are no longer there to perform this function? Not every former pupil can become a teacher and attain revenge in this way . . .

SUMMARY

I have selected the foregoing passages in order to characterize an attitude that reveals itself more or less openly, not only in Fascism but in other ideologies as well. The scorn and abuse directed at the helpless child as well as the suppression of vitality, creativity, and feeling in the child and in oneself permeate so many areas of our life that we hardly notice it anymore. Almost everywhere we find the effort, marked by varying degrees of intensity and by the use of various coercive measures, to rid ourselves as quickly as possible of the child within us—i.e., the weak, helpless, dependent creature—in order to become an independent, competent adult deserving of respect. When we reencounter this creature in our children, we persecute it with the same measures once used on ourselves. And this is what we are accustomed to call "child-rearing."

In the following pages I shall apply the term *"poisonous pedagogy"* to this very complex endeavor. It will be clear from

the context in question which of its many facets I am emphasizing at the moment. The specific facets can be derived
directly from the preceding quotations from child-rearing
manuals. These passages teach us that:

1. Adults are the masters (not the servants!) of the dependent child.

2. They determine in godlike fashion what is right and
what is wrong.

3. The child is held responsible for their anger.

4. The parents must always be shielded.

5. The child's life-affirming feelings pose a threat to the
autocratic adult.

6. The child's will must be "broken" as soon as possible.

7. All this must happen at a very early age, so the child
"won't notice" and will therefore not be able to expose the
adults.

The methods that can be used to suppress vital spontaneity in the child are: laying traps, lying, duplicity, subterfuge, manipulation, "scare" tactics, withdrawal of love,
isolation, distrust, humiliating and disgracing the child, scorn,
ridicule, and coercion even to the point of torture.

It is also a part of "poisonous pedagogy" to impart to the
child from the beginning false information and beliefs that
have been passed on from generation to generation and duti-
fully accepted by the young even though they are not only
unproven but are demonstrably false. Examples of such beliefs
are:

1. A feeling of duty produces love.

2. Hatred can be done away with by forbidding it.

3. Parents deserve respect simply because they are
parents.

4. Children are undeserving of respect simply because
they are children.

5. Obedience makes a child strong.

6. A high degree of self-esteem is harmful.

7. A low degree of self-esteem makes a person altruistic.

8. Tenderness (doting) is harmful.

9. Responding to a child's needs is wrong.

10. Severity and coldness are a good preparation for life.

11. A pretense of gratitude is better than honest ingratitude.

12. The way you behave is more important than the way you really are.

13. Neither parents nor God would survive being offended.

14. The body is something dirty and disgusting.

15. Strong feelings are harmful.

16. Parents are creatures free of drives and guilt.

17. Parents are always right.

When we consider the major role intimidation plays in this ideology, which was still at the peak of its popularity at the turn of the century, it is not surprising that Sigmund Freud had to conceal his surprising discovery of adults' sexual abuse of their children, a discovery he was led to by the testimony of his patients. He disguised his insight with the aid of a theory that nullified this inadmissible knowledge. Children of his day were not allowed, under the severest of threats, to be aware of what adults were doing to them, and if Freud had persisted in his seduction theory, he not only would have had his introjected parents to fear but would no doubt have been discredited, and probably ostracized, by middle-class society. In order to protect himself, he had to devise a theory that would preserve appearances by attributing all "evil," guilt, and wrongdoing to the child's fantasies, in which the parents served only as the objects of projection. We can understand why this theory omitted the fact that it is the parents who not only project their sexual and aggressive fantasies onto the child but also are able to act out these fantasies because they wield the power. It is probably thanks to this omission that many professionals in the psychiatric field, themselves the products of "poisonous pedagogy," have been able to accept the Freudian theory of drives, because it did not force them to question their idealized image of their parents. With the aid of Freud's drive and structural theories, they have been able to continue obeying the commandment they internalized in early childhood: "Thou shalt not be aware of what your parents are doing to you."*

I consider the impact of "poisonous pedagogy" on the theory and practice of psychoanalysis so crucial that I intend to treat this theme much more extensively in another book (cf. page xvi). For now I must limit myself to stressing how important it is that we all be aware of the effect of the commandment to refrain from placing blame on our parents. This commandment, deeply imprinted in us by our upbringing, skillfully performs the function of hiding essential truths from us, or even making them appear as their exact opposites. The price many of us must pay for this is severe neurosis.

What becomes of all those people who are the successful products of a strict upbringing?

It is inconceivable that they were able to express and develop their true feelings as children, for anger and helpless rage, which they were forbidden to display, would have been among these feelings—particularly if these children were beaten, humiliated, lied to, and deceived. What becomes of this forbidden and therefore unexpressed anger? Unfortunately, it does not disappear, but is transformed with time into a more or less conscious hatred directed against either the self or substitute persons, a hatred that will seek to discharge itself in various ways permissible and suitable for an adult.

The little Katies and Konrads of all time have always been in agreement as adults that their childhood was the happiest

---

* I did not arrive at this insight until quite recently and solely on the basis of my psychoanalytic experiences. I was surprised to find striking corroboration in Marianne Krüll's fascinating book, *Freud und sein Vater (Freud and His Father)* (1979). Krüll is a sociologist who is not satisfied with theories; she tries to combine knowledge and experience. She visited Freud's birthplace, stood in the room where he spent his first years of life with his parents, and, after reading many books on the subject, attempted to *imagine* and *feel* what the child Sigmund Freud must have stored up in his mind in this room.

Since the appearance of my book in Germany, other books have appeared in the United States that also point to Freud's drive theory as a denial of what he had discovered to be true; for example, Florence Rush, *The Best Kept Secret: Sexual Abuse in Children* (McGraw-Hill, 1980); and Leon Sheleff, *Generations Apart: Adult Hostility to Youth* (McGraw-Hill, 1981).

period of their life. Only with today's younger generation are we seeing a change taking place in this regard. Lloyd de Mause is probably the first scholar who has made a thorough study of the history of childhood without glossing over the facts and without invalidating the results of his research with an idealizing commentary. Because this psychohistorian has the ability to empathize, he has no need to repress the truth. The truth laid bare in his book, *The History of Childhood,* is sad and depressing, but it holds hope for the future: those who read this book and realize that the children described here later turned into adults will no longer find the atrocities in human history hard to understand. They will locate the places where the seeds of cruelty have been sown and by virtue of their discovery will conclude that the human race need not remain the victim of such cruelty forever. For, by uncovering the unconscious rules of the power game and the methods by which it attains legitimacy, we are certainly in a position to bring about basic changes. The rules of the game cannot be fully comprehended, however, unless we develop an understanding of the hazards of early childhood, that time when the ideology of child-rearing is passed on to the next generation.

Without a doubt, the conscious ideals of young parents of the present generation have changed. Obedience, coercion, severity, and lack of feeling are no longer recognized as absolute values. But the road to the realization of the new ideals is frequently blocked by the need to repress the sufferings of one's childhood, and this leads to a lack of empathy. It is precisely the little Katies and Konrads who as adults close their ears to the subject of child abuse (or else minimize its harmfulness), because they themselves claim to have had a "happy childhood." Yet their very lack of empathy reveals the opposite: they had to keep a stiff upper lip at a very early age. Those who actually had the privilege of growing up in an empathic environment (which is extremely rare, for until recently it was not generally known how much a child can suffer), or who later create an inner empathic object, are more likely to be open to the suffering of others, or at least will not deny its existence. This is a necessary precondition if old wounds are to heal instead of merely being covered up with the help of the next generation.

The "Sacred" Values of Child-Rearing

It also gives us a very special, secret pleasure to see how unaware the people around us are of what is really happening to them. ADOLF HITLER

P EOPLE who have grown up within the value system of "poisonous pedagogy" and have remained untouched by psychoanalytic insights will probably respond to my antipedagogic position with either conscious anxiety or intellectual rejection. They will reproach me for being indifferent to "sacred" values or will say that I am displaying a naïve optimism and have no idea just how bad children can be. Such reproaches would come as no surprise, for the reasons behind them are all too familiar to me. Nevertheless, I would like to comment on the question of indifference to values.

Every pedagogue accepts as a foregone conclusion that it is wrong to tell a lie, to hurt or offend another human being, and to respond in kind to parental cruelty instead of showing understanding for the good intentions involved, etc. On the other hand, it is considered admirable and right for a child to tell the truth, to be grateful for the parents' intentions and overlook the cruelty of their actions, to accept the parents' ideas but still be able to express his or her own ideas independently, and above all not to be difficult when it comes to what is expected of him or her. In order to teach the child these almost universal values, which are rooted in the Judeo-Christian tradition, among others, adults believe they must sometimes resort to lying, deception, cruelty, mistreatment, and to subjecting the child to humiliation. In the case of adults, however, it is not a matter of "negative values," because they already have their upbringing behind them and use these means solely to achieve a sacred end: to save the child from telling lies in the future, from being deceitful, malicious, cruel, and egotistic.

It is clear from the foregoing that a relativity of traditional moral values is an intrinsic part of this system: in the last analysis, our status and degree of power determine whether our actions are judged to be good or bad. This same principle prevails throughout the whole world. The strong person dictates the verdict, and the victor in a war will sooner or later be applauded, regardless of the crimes that have been committed on the road to victory.

To these well-known examples of the relativity of values based upon one's position of power, I should like to add another, stemming from a psychoanalytic perspective. In our zeal to dictate to our children the rules of behavior referred to above, we forget that it is not always possible to tell the truth without hurting someone at the same time, to show gratitude one does not feel without lying, or to overlook parents' cruelty and still become an autonomous human being who can exercise independent critical judgment. These considerations arise of necessity as soon as we turn from the abstract ethical systems of religion or philosophy to concrete psychic reality. People unfamiliar with this concrete manner of thinking may find the way I relativize traditional pedagogical values and question the value of pedagogy per se to be shocking, nihilistic, threatening, or even naïve. This will depend on their own personal history. For my part, I can only say that there certainly are values I do not have to relativize. Our chances of survival probably depend, in the long run, on the practice of these values, among which are respect for those weaker than ourselves—including, of course, the child—and respect for life and its laws, without which all creativity would be stifled. Every brand of Fascism lacks this respect, causing psychic death and castrating the soul with the aid of its ideology. Among all the leading figures of the Third Reich, I have not been able to find a single one who did not have a strict and rigid upbringing. Shouldn't that give us a great deal of food for thought?

Those who were permitted to react appropriately throughout their childhood—i.e., with anger—to the pain, wrongs, and denial inflicted upon them either consciously or unconsciously will retain this ability to react appropriately in later life too. When someone wounds them as adults, they will be able to recognize and express this verbally. But they will not feel the need to lash out in response. This need arises only for people who must always be on their guard to keep the dam that restrains their feelings from breaking. For if this dam breaks, everything becomes unpredictable. Thus, it is understandable that some of these people, fearing unpredictable consequences, will shrink from any spontaneous reaction; the others will experience occasional outbursts of inexplicable rage directed against substitute objects or will resort repeatedly to violent behavior such as murder or acts of terrorism. A person who can understand and integrate his anger as part of himself will not become violent. He has the need to strike out at others only if he is thoroughly unable to understand his rage, if he was not permitted to become familiar with this feeling as a small child, was never able to experience it as a part of himself because such a thing was totally unthinkable in his surroundings.

With these dynamics in mind, we will not be surprised to learn from the statistics that 60 percent of German terrorists in recent years have been the children of Protestant ministers. The tragedy of this situation lies in the fact that the parents undoubtedly had the best of intentions; from the very beginning, they wanted their children to be good, responsive, well-behaved, agreeable, undemanding, considerate, unselfish, self-controlled, grateful, neither willful nor headstrong nor defiant, and above all meek. They wanted to inculcate these values in their children by whatever means, and if there was no other way, they were even ready to use force to obtain these admirable pedagogical ends. If the children then showed signs of violent behavior in adolescence, they were expressing both the unlived side of their own childhood as well as the unlived, suppressed, and hidden side of their parents' psyche, perceived only by the children themselves.

When terrorists take innocent women and children hostage in the service of a grand and idealistic cause, are they really doing anything different from what was once done to them? When they were little children full of vitality, their parents had offered them up as sacrifices to a grand pedagogic purpose, to lofty religious values, with the feeling of performing a great and good deed. Since these young people never were allowed to trust their own feelings, they continue to suppress them for ideological reasons. These intelligent and often very sensitive people, who had once been sacrificed to a "higher" morality, sacrifice themselves as adults to another—often opposite—ideology, in whose service they allow their inmost selves to be completely dominated, as had been the case in their childhood.

This is an example of the unrelenting, tragic nature of the unconscious compulsion to repeat. Its positive function must not be overlooked, however. Would it not be much worse if the parents' pedagogical aims were fully realized and it were possible successfully and irreversibly to murder the child's soul without this ever coming to public attention? When a terrorist commits violent actions against helpless people in the name of his ideals, thus putting himself at the mercy of the leaders who are manipulating him as well as of the police forces of the system he is fighting, he is unconsciously telling the story, in the form of his repetition compulsion, of what once happened to him in the name of the high ideals of his upbringing. The story he tells can be understood by the public as a warning signal or it can be completely misunderstood; if taken as a warning, it calls attention to a life that can still be saved.

But what happens when not a trace of vital spontaneity remains because the child's upbringing was a total and perfect success, as was the case with people such as Adolf Eichmann and Rudolf Höss? They were trained to be obedient so successfully and at such an early age that the training never lost its effectiveness; the structure never displayed any fissures, water never penetrated it at any point, nor did feelings of any kind ever jar it. To the end of their lives, these people carried out the orders they were given without ever questioning the content. They carried them out, just as "poisonous pedagogy" recommends (cf. page 39)—not out of any sense of their inherent rightness, but simply because they were orders.

This explains why Eichmann was able to listen to the most moving testimony of the witnesses at his trial without the slightest display of emotion, yet when he forgot to stand up at the reading of the verdict, he blushed with embarrassment when this was called to his attention.

The strong emphasis on obedience in Rudolf Höss's early upbringing left its indelible mark on him, too. Certainly his father did not intend to raise him to be a commandant at Auschwitz: on the contrary, as a strict Catholic, he had a missionary career in mind for his son. But he had instilled in him at an early age the principle that the authorities must always be obeyed, no matter what their demands. Höss writes:

Our guests were mostly priests of every sort. As the years passed, my father's religious fervor increased. Whenever time permitted, he would take me on pilgrimages to all the holy places in our own country, as well as to Einsiedeln in Switzerland and to Lourdes in France. He prayed passionately that the grace of God might be bestowed on me, so that I might one day become a priest blessed by God. I, too, was as deeply religious as was possible for a boy of my age, and I took my religious duties very seriously. I prayed with true, childlike gravity and performed my duties as acolyte with great earnestness. I had been brought up by my parents to be respectful and obedient toward all adults, and especially the elderly, regardless of their social status. I was taught that my highest duty was to help those in need. It was constantly impressed upon me in forceful terms that I must obey promptly the wishes and commands of my parents, teachers, and priests, and indeed of all adults, including servants, and that nothing must distract me from this duty. Whatever they said was always right.

These basic principles by which I was brought up became second nature to me.

When the authorities later required Höss to run the machinery of death in Auschwitz, how could he have refused? And later, after his arrest, when he was given the assignment of writing an account of his life, he not only performed this task faithfully and conscientiously but politely expressed gratitude for the fact that the time in prison passed more quickly because of "this interesting occupation." His account has provided the world with deep insight into the background of a multitude of otherwise incomprehensible crimes.

Rudolf Höss's first memories of his childhood are of washing compulsively, which was probably an attempt to free himself of everything his parents found impure or dirty in him. Since his parents showed him no affection, he sought this in animals, all the more since they were not beaten by his father, as he was, and thus enjoyed a higher status than children.

Similar attitudes were shared by Heinrich Himmler, who said, for example:

How can you find pleasure, Herr Kersten, in shooting from behind cover at poor creatures grazing on the edge of a wood, innocent, defenseless, and unsuspecting? It's really pure murder. Nature is so marvelously beautiful and every animal has a right to live. [Quoted by Joaquim Fest, *The Face of the Third Reich*]

Yet, it was also Himmler who said:

One principle must be absolute for the SS man: we must be honest, decent, loyal, and comradely to those of our own blood and to no one else. What happens to the Russians, what happens to the Czechs, is a matter of utter indifference to me. Good blood like ours that we find among other nationalities we shall acquire for ourselves, if necessary by taking away the children and bringing them up among us. Whether the other nationalities live in comfort or perish of hunger interests me only insofar as we need them as slaves for our society; apart from that, it does not interest me. Whether or not 10,000 Russian women collapse from exhaustion while digging a tank ditch interests me only insofar as it affects the completion of the tank ditch for Germany. We shall never be cruel or heartless when it is not necessary; that is clear. We Germans, who are the only people in the world who have a decent attitude toward animals, will also adopt a decent attitude toward these human animals, but it is a crime against our own blood to worry about them or to fill them with ideals. [Quoted by Fest]

Himmler, like Höss, was a nearly perfect product of the training given him by his father, who was first a tutor at the Bavarian court and then a headmaster by profession. Heinrich Himmler also dreamed of educating people and nations. Fest writes:

The doctor Felix Kersten, who treated him continuously from 1939 onwards and enjoyed his confidence, has asserted that Himmler himself would rather have educated foreign peoples than exterminate them. During the war he spoke enthusiastically —looking ahead to peace—of establishing military units who were "educated and trained, once education and training can be practiced again."

In contrast to Höss, who had been trained with total success to be blindly obedient, Himmler apparently was not entirely able to live up to the requirement of being hardhearted. Fest, who convincingly interprets Himmler's atrocities as the constant attempt to prove his harshness to himself and the world, says:

In the hopeless confusion of all criteria under the influence of a totalitarian ethic, harshness toward the victims was held justified by the harshness practiced toward oneself. "To be harsh toward ourselves and others, to give death and to take it," was one of the mottoes of the SS repeatedly emphasized by Himmler. Because murder was difficult, it was good, and justified. By the same reasoning, he was always able to point proudly, as though to a Roll of Honor, to the fact that the Order had suffered "no inner damage" from its murderous activity and had remained "decent."

Do we not see reflected in these words the principles of "poisonous pedagogy," with its violation of the impulses of the child's psyche?

These are only three examples of the endless number of people whose life took a similar course and who no doubt had received what is considered a good, strict upbringing. The results of the child's total subordination to the adults' will were not seen solely in his future political submissiveness (for example, to the totalitarian system of the Third Reich) but were already visible in his inner readiness for a new form of subordination as soon as he left home. For how could someone whose inner development had been limited to learning to obey the commands of others be expected to live on his own without experiencing a sudden sense of inner emptiness? Military service provided the best opportunity for him to continue the established pattern of taking orders. When someone like Adolf Hitler came along and claimed, just like Father, to know exactly what was good, right, and necessary for everyone it is not surprising that so many people who were longing for someone to tell them what to do welcomed him with open arms and helped him in his rise to power. Young people had finally found a father substitute, without which they were incapable of functioning. In *The Face of the Third Reich*, Fest documents the servile, uncritical, and almost infantile naïveté with which the men who were to enter the annals of infamy spoke of Hitler's omniscience, infallibility, and divinity. That is the way a little child sees his father. And these men never advanced beyond that stage. I shall quote several passages here because, without them, it might be hard for today's generation to believe that these men who later went down in history could have been so lacking in inner substance. Fest here quotes Hermann Goering:

If the Catholic Christian is convinced that the Pope is infallible in all religious and ethical matters, so we National Socialists declare with the same ardent conviction that for us, too, the Führer is absolutely infallible in all political and other matters having to do with the national and social interests of the people. . . . It is a blessing for Germany that in Hitler the rare union has taken place between the most acute logical thinker and truly profound philosopher and the iron man of action, tenacious to the limit.

And again:

Anyone who has any idea of how things stand with us . . . knows that we each possess just so much power as the Führer wishes to give. And only with the Führer and standing behind him is one really powerful, only then does one hold the strong powers of the state in one's hands; but against his will, or even just without his wish, one would instantly become totally powerless. A word from the Führer and anyone whom he wishes to be rid of falls. His prestige, his authority are boundless.

What is actually being described here is the way a little child feels toward his authoritarian father. Goering openly admitted:

It is not I who live, but the Führer who lives in me. . . . Every time I am in his presence, my heart stands still. . . . Often I couldn't eat anything again until midnight, because before then I should have vomited in my agitation. When I returned to Karinhall at about nine o'clock, I actually had to sit in a chair for some hours in order to calm down. This relationship turned into downright mental prostitution for me.

In his speech of June 30, 1934, Rudolf Hess, another top Nazi official, also admits openly to this attitude, without being hampered by any feelings of shame or discomfort—a situation we can hardly imagine today, half a century later. He says in this speech:

We note with pride that one man remains beyond all criticism, and that is the Führer. This is because everyone senses and knows: he is always right, and he will always be right. The

National Socialism of all of us is anchored in uncritical loyalty, in a surrender to the Führer that does not ask about the why in individual cases, in the silent execution of his orders. We believe that the Führer is obeying a higher call to shape German history. There can be no criticism of this belief.

Fest comments:

In his unbalanced approach to authority Hess resembles surprisingly many leading National Socialists who, like him, had "strict" parents. There is a good deal of evidence that Hitler profited considerably from the damage wrought by an educational system that took its models from the barracks and brought up its sons to be as tough as army cadets. The fixation on the military world, the determining feature of their early development, shows not only in the peculiar mixture of aggressiveness and doglike cringing so typical of the "Old Fighter" but also in the lack of inner independence and the need to receive orders. Whatever hidden rebellious feelings the young Rudolf Hess may have had against his father, who emphatically demonstrated his power one last time when he refused to let his son go to a university but forced him, against his wishes and the pleas of his teachers, to go into business with a view to taking over his own firm in Alexandria—the son, whose will had been broken over and over again, henceforth sought father and father substitute wherever he could find them. One must want leaders!

When non-Germans watched Adolf Hitler's appearances in newsreels, they were never able to understand the adulation he was given or the number of votes he received in 1933. It was easy for them to see through his human weaknesses, his artificial pose of self-assurance, his specious arguments; for them, it was not as though he were their father. For the Germans, however, it was much more difficult. A child cannot acknowledge the negative sides of his or her father, and yet these are stored up somewhere in the child's psyche, for the adult will then be attracted by precisely these negative, disavowed sides in the father substitutes he or she encounters. An outsider has trouble understanding this.

We often ask how a marriage can last, how, for example, a woman can go on living with a certain man, or vice versa.

It may be that the woman endures extreme torment in this relationship, continuing it only at the cost of her vitality. But she is mortally afraid at the thought of her husband leaving her. Actually, such a separation would probably be the great opportunity of her life, yet she is totally unable to see this as long as she is forced to repeat in her marriage the early torment, now relegated to her unconscious, inflicted on her by her father. For when she thinks about being abandoned by her husband, she is not reacting to her present situation but is reexperiencing her childhood fears of abandonment and the time when she was in fact dependent on her father. I am thinking here specifically of a woman whose father, a musician, took the mother's place when she died but who often disappeared suddenly when he went on tour. My patient was much too little at the time to bear these sudden separations without a feeling of panic. In her analysis we had been aware of this for a long time, but her fear of being abandoned by her husband did not subside until her dreams revealed to her what had hitherto been unconscious: the other—brutal and cruel—side of her father, whom she had until then remembered only as loving and tender. As a result of confronting this knowledge, she experienced an inner liberation and was now able to begin the process of becoming autonomous.

I mention this example because it demonstrates mechanisms that may have played a role in the election of 1933. The adulation accorded Hitler is understandable not only because of the promises he made (who doesn't make promises before an election?) but because of the way in which they were presented. It was precisely his theatrical gestures, ridiculous to a foreigner's eyes, that were so familiar to the masses and therefore held such a great power of suggestion for them. Small children are subject to this same sort of suggestion when their big father, whom they admire and love, talks to them. What he says is not important, it is *the way* he speaks that counts. The more he builds himself up, the more he will be admired, especially by a child raised according to the principles of "poisonous pedagogy." When a strict, inaccessible, and distant father condescends to speak with his child, this is certainly a festive occasion, and to earn this honor no sacrifice of self is too great. A properly raised child will never be able to detect it if this father—this big and mighty man—should happen to be power-hungry, dishonorable, or basically insecure. And so it goes; such a child can never gain any insight into this kind of situation because his or her ability to perceive has been blocked by the early enforcement of obedience and the suppression of feelings.

A father's nimbus is often composed of attributes (such as wisdom, kindness, courage) he lacks, along with those every father undoubtedly possesses, at least in the eyes of his children: uniqueness, bigness, importance, and power. If a father misuses his power by suppressing his children's critical faculties, then his weaknesses will stay hidden behind these fixed attributes. He could say to his children, just as Adolf Hitler cried out in all seriousness to the German people: "How fortunate you are to have me!"

If we keep this in mind, Hitler's legendary influence on the men who surrounded him loses its mystery. Two passages from Hermann Rauschning's book, *The Voice of Destruction,* illustrate this:

> [Gerhart] Hauptmann was introduced. The Führer shook hands with him and looked into his eyes. It was the famous gaze that makes everyone tremble, the glance which once made a distinguished old lawyer declare that after meeting it he had but one desire, to be back at home in order to master the experience in solitude.
>
> Hitler shook hands again with Hauptmann.
>
> Now, thought the witnesses of the meeting, now the great phrase will be uttered and go down in history.
>
> Now! thought Hauptmann.
>
> And the Führer of the German Reich shook hands a third time, warmly, with the great writer, and passed on to his neighbor.
>
> Later Gerhart Hauptmann said to his friends: "It was the greatest moment of my life."

Rauschning continues:

> I have frequently heard people confess that they are afraid of
> him, that they, grown though they are, cannot visit him without
> a pounding heart. They have the feeling that the man will sud-
> denly spring at them and strangle them, or throw the inkpot at
> them, or do some other senseless thing. There is a great deal of
> insincere enthusiasm, with eyes hypocritically cast up, and a
> great deal of self-deception behind this talk of an unforgettable
> experience. Most visitors *want* their interviews to be of this
> kind. . . . But these visitors who were fain to hide their dis-
> appointment gradually came out with it when they were pressed.
> Yes, it is true he did not say anything special. No, he does not
> look impressive, it is impossible to claim that he does. Why,
> then, make up things about him? Yes, they said, if you look
> critically at him he is, after all, rather ordinary. The nimbus—
> it is all the nimbus.

And so, when a man comes along and talks like one's
own father and acts like him, even adults will forget their
democratic rights or will not make use of them. They will
submit to this man, will acclaim him, allow themselves to be
manipulated by him, and put their trust in him, finally sur-
rendering totally to him without even being aware of their
enslavement. One is not normally aware of something that
is a continuation of one's own childhood. For those who become as dependent on someone as they once were as small
children on their parents, there is no escape. A child cannot
run away, and the citizen of a totalitarian regime cannot free
himself or herself. The only outlet one has is in raising one's
own children. Thus, the citizens who were captives of the
Third Reich had to rear their children to be captives as well,
if they were to feel any trace of their own power.

But these children, who now are parents themselves, did
have other possibilities. Many of them have recognized the
dangers of pedagogical ideology, and with a great deal of
courage and effort they are searching for new paths for themselves and their children.

Some of them, especially the creative writers, have found the path to experiencing the truth of their childhood, a path that was blocked for earlier generations. In *Lange Abwesenheit* (*Long Absence*), Brigitte Schwaiger, for example, writes:

> I hear Father's voice; he is calling my name. He wants something from me. He is far off in another room. And wants something from me, that's why I exist. He goes past me without saying a word. I am superfluous. I shouldn't even exist.

> If you had worn your wartime captain's uniform at home from the beginning, perhaps then many things would have been clearer. —A father, a real father, is someone who mustn't be hugged, who must be answered even if he asks the same question five times and it looks as though he is asking it for the fifth time just to be sure that his daughters are submissive enough to give an answer every time, a father who is free to interrupt one in midsentence.

Once a child's eyes are opened to the power game of child-rearing, there is hope that he or she will be freed from the chains of "poisonous pedagogy," for this child will be able to *remember* what happened to him or her.

When feelings are admitted into consciousness, the wall of silence disintegrates, and the truth can no longer be held back. Even intellectualizing about whether "there is a truth per se," whether or not "everything is relative," etc., is recognized as a defense mechanism once the truth, no matter how painful, has been uncovered. I found a good example of this in Christoph Meckel's portrayal of his father in *Suchbild: Über meinen Vater* (*Wanted: My Father's Portrait*):

> In the grown-up there is a child who wants to play.
> There is in him a dictator who wants to punish.
> In my grown-up father there was a child who played heaven on earth with his children. Part of him was an officer type who wanted to punish us in the name of discipline.
> Our happy father's pointless pampering. On the heels of the lavish dispenser of sweet treats came an officer with a whip. He had punishment ready for his children. He was the master of

what amounted to a spectrum of punishments, a whole cata-
logue. First there were scoldings and fits of rage—that was
bearable and passed over like a thunderstorm. Then came the
pulling, twisting, and pinching of the ear, the blow to the ear,
and the little, mean punches to the head. Next came being sent
from the room and after that being locked away in the cellar.
And further: the child was ignored, was humiliated and shamed
by reproachful silence. He was taken advantage of to run
errands, was banished to bed or ordered to carry coal. Finally, as
reminder and as climax came the punishment, the exemplary
punishment pure and simple. This punishment was a measure
reserved for Father, and it was administered with an iron hand.
Corporal punishment was used for the sake of order, obedience,
and humaneness so that justice might be done and this justice
might be imprinted in the child's memory. The officer type
reached for the switch and led the way down into the cellar,
followed by the child, who had no sense of guilt to speak of. He
had to stretch out his hands (palms up) or bend over his
father's knee. The thrashing was merciless and precise, accompanied by loud or soft counting, and took place without any
possibility of reprieve. The officer type expressed his regret at
being forced to take this step, claiming it hurt him too, and it
did hurt him. The shock of this "step" was followed by a pro-
longed period of dismay: the officer demanded cheerfulness. He
led the way up the stairs with exaggerated cheerfulness, set a
good example in a charged atmosphere, and was offended if the
child wasn't interested in being cheerful. For several days, always before breakfast, the punishment in the cellar was repeated. It became a ritual, and the obligatory cheerfulness became a form of harassment.

For the rest of the day, the punishment had to be forgotten.
Nothing was said about guilt or atonement, and justice and
injustice were kept out of sight. The children's cheerfulness did
not materialize. White as chalk, mute or crying furtively, brave,
dejected, resentful, and bitterly uncomprehending—even in the
night they were still in the clutches of justice. It rained down
on them and made its final impact, it had the last word out of
their father's mouth. The officer type also punished them when
he was home on leave and was downcast when his child asked
him if he didn't want to go back to war.

It is obvious that painful experiences are being described here; the subjective truth, at least, comes through in every sentence. Anyone who doubts the objective content because the story seems too monstrous to be true need only read the manuals of "poisonous pedagogy" to be convinced. There are even sophisticated analytical theories which suggest in all seriousness that the perceptions of the child as presented here by Christoph Meckel are the projections of his "aggressive or homosexual desires" and which interpret the actual events he describes as an expression of the child's fantasies. A child whom "poisonous pedagogy" has made unsure of the validity of his or her perceptions can easily be made even more unsure of these theories later as an adult and can be tyrannized by them even if the theories are belied by experience.

For this reason, it is always a miracle when a portrayal such as Meckel's is possible in spite of his "good upbringing." Perhaps the explanation in his case is that his upbringing, at least one side of it, was interrupted for several years while his father was away at war and then a prisoner of war. It is highly unlikely that someone who was consistently subjected to such treatment throughout childhood and adolescence would be able to write so honestly about his father. During his decisive years he would have had to learn day in and day out how to repress the misery he endured; if acknowledged, his misery would show him the truth about his childhood. He will not accept this truth, however, but will instead subscribe to theories that make the child the sole projecting subject instead of the victim of the parents' projections.

When someone suddenly gives vent to his or her rage, it is usually an expression of deep despair, but the ideology of child beating and the belief that beating is not harmful serve the function of covering up the consequences of the act and making them unrecognizable. The result of a child becoming dulled to pain is that access to the truth about himself will be denied him all his life. Only consciously experienced feelings would be powerful enough to subdue the guard at the gates, but these are exactly what he is not allowed to have.

The Central Mechanism of
"Poisonous Pedagogy"

SPLITTING OFF AND PROJECTION

IN 1943, Himmler gave his famous Posen Address, in which he, in the name of the German people, expressed his appreciation to the SS group leaders for their role in the extermination of the Jews. I shall quote here the part of his speech that finally enabled me, in 1979, to comprehend something for which I had been vainly seeking a psychological explanation for thirty years:

> I shall speak to you here with all frankness about a very serious subject. We shall now discuss it absolutely openly among ourselves, nevertheless we shall never speak of it in public. I mean the evacuation of the Jews, the extermination of the Jewish people. It is one of those things which is easy to say: "The Jewish people are to be exterminated," says every party member. "That's clear, it's part of our program, elimination of the Jews, extermination, right, we'll do it." And then they all come along, the eighty million upstanding Germans, and each one has his decent Jew. Of course the others are swine, but this one is a first-class Jew. Of all those who talk like this, not one has watched [the actual extermination], not one has had the stomach for it. Most of you know what it means to see a hundred corpses lying together, five hundred, or a thousand. To have gone through this and yet—apart from a few exceptions, examples of human weakness—to have remained decent, this has made us hard. This is a glorious page in our history that has never been written and never shall be written.

> The wealth which they [the Jews] had, we have taken from them. I have issued a strict command . . . that this wealth is as a matter of course to be delivered in its entirety to the Reich. We have taken none of it for ourselves. Individuals who have violated this principle will be punished according to an order which I issued at the beginning and which warns: Anyone who

takes so much as a mark shall die. A certain number of SS men —not very many—disobeyed this order and they will die, without mercy. We had the moral right, we had the duty to our own people, to kill this people that wanted to kill us. But we have no right to enrich ourselves by so much as a fur, a watch, a mark, or a cigarette, or anything else. In the last analysis, because we exterminated a bacillus we don't want to be infected by it and die. I shall never stand by and watch even the slightest spot of rot develop or establish itself here. Wherever it appears, we shall burn it out together. By and large, however, we can say that we have performed this most difficult task out of love for our people. And we have suffered no harm from it in our inner self, in our soul, in our character. [Quoted by Fest]

This speech contains all the elements of the complicated psychodynamic mechanism that can be described as splitting off and projection of parts of the self, which we encounter so often in the manuals of "poisonous pedagogy." Schooling oneself to be senselessly hard requires that all signs of weakness in oneself (including emotionalism, tears, pity, sympathy for oneself and others, and feelings of helplessness, fear, and despair) be suppressed "without mercy." In order to make the struggle against these humane impulses easier, the citizens of the Third Reich were offered an object to serve as the bearer of all these qualities that were abhorred because they had been forbidden and dangerous in their childhood—this object was the Jewish people. Freed from their "bad" (i.e., weak and uncontrolled) feelings, so-called Aryans could feel pure, strong, hard, clean, good, unambivalent, and morally right if everything they had feared in themselves since childhood could be attributed to the Jews and if, together with their fellow Germans, these "Aryans" were not only permitted but required to combat it relentlessly and ever anew among members of this "inferior race."

It seems to me that we are still threatened by the possible repetition of a similar crime unless we understand its origins and the psychological mechanism behind it.

The more insight I gained into the dynamics of perversion through my analytic work, the more I questioned the view advanced repeatedly since the end of the war that a handful of perverted people were responsible for the Holocaust. The mass murderers showed not a trace of the specific symptoms of perversion, such as isolation, loneliness, shame, and despair; they were not isolated but belonged to a supportive group; they were not ashamed but proud; and they were not despairing but either euphoric or apathetic.

The other explanation—that these were people who worshipped authority and were accustomed to obey—is not wrong, but neither is it adequate to explain a phenomenon like the Holocaust, if by obeying we mean the carrying out of commands that we consciously regard as being forced upon us.

People with any sensitivity cannot be turned into mass murderers overnight. But the men and women who carried out "the final solution" did not let their feelings stand in their way for the simple reason that they had been raised from infancy not to have any feelings of their own but to experience their parents' wishes as their own. These were people who, as children, had been proud of being tough and not crying, of carrying out all their duties "gladly," of not being afraid— that is, at bottom, of not having an inner life at all.

In *A Sorrow Beyond Dreams* Peter Handke describes his mother, who committed suicide at the age of fifty-one. His pity and concern for her permeate the book and help the reader understand why her son searches so desperately for his "true feelings" (*A Moment of True Feeling* is the title of another Handke book) in all his works. Somewhere in the graveyard of his childhood he had to bury the roots of these feelings in order to spare his unstable mother in difficult times. Handke depicts the atmosphere of the village in which he grew up:

No one had anything to say about himself; even in church, at Easter confession, when at least once a year there was an opportunity to reveal something of oneself, there was only a mumbling of catchwords out of the catechism, and the word "I" seemed stranger to the speaker himself than a chunk out of the moon. If in talking about himself anyone went beyond relating some droll incident, he was said to be "peculiar." Personal life, if it had ever developed a character of its own, was depersonalized except for dream tatters swallowed up by the rites of religion, custom, and good manners; little remained of the human individual, and indeed, the word "individual" was known only as a pejorative. . . .

All spontaneity . . . was frowned upon as something deplorable. . . . Cheated out of your own biography and feelings, you gradually became "skittish," as is usually said only of domesticated animals—horses, for example; you shied away from people, stopped talking, or, more seriously deranged, went from house to house, screaming.

Lack of feeling as an ideal manifested itself in many modern writers until approximately 1975 as well as in the geometric trend in painting. In Karin Struck's *Klassenliebe* (*Class Love*) (1973), we read:

Dietger can't cry. He was terribly upset by his grandma's death; he loved his grandma deeply. On the way back from the burial service, he said, I'm trying to decide if I should squeeze out a few tears—squeeze out, he said. . . . Dietger says, I don't need to have dreams. Dietger is proud of the fact that he doesn't dream. He says, I never dream, I sleep soundly. Jutta says Dietger is denying his unconscious perceptions and feelings as well as his dreams.

Dietger is a postwar child. And what feelings did Dietger's parents have? Little is known about that, for their generation was allowed to express its true feelings even less than the present one.

In *Suchbild*, Christoph Meckel quotes from the journal kept by his father, a poet and writer, during World War II:

A woman in my compartment on the train . . . is telling . . . about the . . . Germans' business dealings everywhere in the government. Bribery, high prices, and the like, and about the concentration camp in Auschwitz, etc. —As a soldier, you are so far removed from these things, which really don't interest you at all; you represent an entirely different Germany out there and you aren't looking for personal gain from the war but just want to keep a clear conscience. I have nothing but scorn for this civilian rubbish. Maybe I'm stupid, but soldiers are always the stupid ones who have to pay. At least we have a sense of honor, and no one can take that away from us.   (1/24/44)

On a roundabout way to have lunch I witnessed the public shooting of twenty-eight Poles on the edge of a playing field. Thousands line the streets and the river. A ghastly pile of corpses, all in all horrifying and ugly and yet a sight that leaves me altogether cold. The men who were shot had ambushed two soldiers and a German civilian and killed them. An exemplary modern folk-drama.   (1/27/44)

Once feelings have been eliminated, the submissive person functions perfectly and reliably even if he knows no one is going to check up on him:

I agree to see a colonel who wants something from me, and then he gets out of the car and approaches. With the help of a first lieutenant speaking broken German, he complains that it's not right to let them go for five days with almost no bread. I reply that it's not right for an officer to be a follower of Badoglio and am very curt. For another group of officers said to be Fascists, who thrust all kinds of papers at me, I have the car heated and am more polite.   (10/27/43)

This perfect adaptation to society's norms—in other words, to what is called "healthy normality"—carries with it the danger that such a person can be used for practically any purpose. It is not a loss of autonomy that occurs here, because this autonomy never existed, but a switching of values, which in themselves are of no importance anyway for the person in question as long as his whole value system is dominated by the principle of obedience. He has never gone beyond the stage of idealizing his parents with their demands for unquestioning obedience; this idealization can easily be transferred to a Führer or to an ideology. Since authoritarian parents are always right, there is no need for their children to rack their brains in each case to determine whether what is demanded of them is right or not. And how is this to be judged? Where are the standards supposed to come from if someone has always been told what was right and what was wrong and if he never had an opportunity to become familiar with his own feelings and if, beyond that, attempts at criticism were unacceptable to the parents and thus were too threatening for the child? If an adult has not developed a mind of his own, then he will find himself at the mercy of the authorities for better or worse, just as an infant finds itself at the mercy of its parents. Saying no to those more powerful will always seem too threatening to him.

Witnesses of sudden political upheavals report again and again with what astonishing facility many people are able to adapt to a new situation. Overnight they can advocate views totally different from those they held the day before—without noticing the contradiction. With the change in the power structure, yesterday has completely disappeared for them.

And yet, even if this observation should apply to many—perhaps even to most—people, it is not true for everyone. There have always been individuals who refused to be reprogrammed quickly, if ever. We could use our psychoanalytic knowledge to address the question of what causes this important, even crucial, difference; with its aid, we could attempt to discover why some people are so extraordinarily susceptible to the dictates of leaders and groups and why others remain immune to these influences.

We admire people who oppose the regime in a totalitarian country and think they have courage or a "strong moral sense" or have remained "true to their principles" or the like. We may also smile at their naïveté, thinking, "Don't they realize that their words are of no use at all against this oppressive power? That they will have to pay dearly for their protest?"

Yet it is possible that both those who admire and those who scorn these protesters are missing the real point: individuals who refuse to adapt to a totalitarian regime are not doing so out of a sense of duty or because of naïveté but because they cannot help but be true to themselves. The longer

I wrestle with these questions, the more I am inclined to see courage, integrity, and a capacity for love not as "virtues," not as moral categories, but as the consequences of a benign fate.

Morality and performance of duty are artificial measures that become necessary when something essential is lacking. The more successfully a person was denied access to his or her feelings in childhood, the larger the arsenal of intellectual weapons and the supply of moral prostheses has to be, because morality and a sense of duty are not sources of strength or fruitful soil for genuine affection. Blood does not flow in artificial limbs; they are for sale and can serve many masters. What was considered good yesterday can—depending on the decree of government or party—be considered evil and corrupt today, and vice versa. But those who have spontaneous feelings can only be themselves. They have no other choice if they want to remain true to themselves. Rejection, ostracism, loss of love, and name calling will not fail to affect them; they will suffer as a result and will dread them, but once they have found their authentic self they will not want to lose it. And when they sense that something is being demanded of them to which their whole being says no, they cannot do it. They simply cannot.

This is the case with people who had the good fortune of being sure of their parents' love even if they had to disappoint certain parental expectations. Or with people who, although they did not have this good fortune to begin with, learned later—for example, in analysis—to risk the loss of love in order to regain their lost self. They will not be willing to relinquish it again for any price in the world.

The artificial nature of moral laws and rules of behavior is most clearly discernible in a situation in which lies and deception are powerless, i.e., in the mother-child relationship. A sense of duty may not be fruitful soil for love but it undoubtedly is for mutual guilt feelings, and the child will forever be bound to the mother by crippling feelings of guilt and gratitude. The Swiss author Robert Walser once said: "There are mothers who choose a favorite from among their children, and it may be that they will stone this child with their kisses and threaten . . . its very existence." If he had known, had known on an *emotional* level, that he was describing his own fate, his life might not have ended in a mental institution.

It is unlikely that strictly intellectual attempts to seek explanations and gain understanding during adulthood can be sufficient to undo early childhood conditioning. Someone who has learned at his or her peril to obey unwritten laws and renounce feelings at a tender age will obey the written laws all the more readily, lacking any inner resistance. But since no one can live entirely without feelings, such a person will join groups that sanction or even encourage the forbidden feelings, which he or she will finally be allowed to live out within a collective framework.

Every ideology offers its adherents the opportunity to discharge their pent-up affect collectively while retaining the idealized primary object, which is transferred to new leader figures or to the group in order to make up for the lack of a satisfying symbiosis with the mother. Idealization of a narcissistically cathected group guarantees collective grandiosity. Since every ideology provides a scapegoat outside the confines of its own splendid group, the weak and scorned child who is part of the total self but has been split off and never acknowledged can now be openly scorned and assailed in this scapegoat. The reference in Himmler's speech to the "bacillus" of weakness which is to be exterminated and cauterized demonstrates very clearly the role assigned to the Jews by someone suffering from grandiosity who attempts to split off the unwelcome elements of his own psyche.

In the same way that analytic familiarity with the mechanisms of splitting off and projection can help us to understand the phenomenon of the Holocaust, a knowledge of the history of the Third Reich helps us to see the consequences of "poisonous pedagogy" more clearly. Against the backdrop of the rejection of childishness instilled by our training, it becomes easier to understand why men and women had little difficulty leading a million children, whom they regarded as the bearers of the feared portions of their own psyche, into the gas chambers. One can even imagine that by shouting at them, beating them, or photographing them, they were finally able to release the hatred going back to early childhood. From the start, it had been the aim of their upbringing to stifle their childish, playful, and life-affirming side. The cruelty inflicted on them, the psychic murder of the child they once were, had to be passed on in the same way: each time they sent another Jewish child to the gas ovens, they were in essence murdering the child within themselves.

In her book *Kindesmißhandlung und Kindesrechte (Mistreatment of Children and Children's Rights)*, Gisela Zenz tells about Steele and Pollock's psychotherapeutic work in Denver with parents who abuse their children. The children are treated along with their parents. The description of these children is useful in helping us to understand the origins of the behavior of the Nazi mass murderers, who undoubtedly were beaten as children:

> The children were virtually unable to develop object relationships commensurate with their age. Spontaneous and open reactions directed at the therapist were rare, as was the direct expression of affection or anger. Only a few of them took a direct interest in the therapist as a person. After six months of therapy twice weekly, a child was unable to remember the name of the therapist outside of the consulting room. In spite of apparently intense interaction with the therapist and a growing bond between therapist and child, the relationship always changed abruptly at the end of the hour, and when the children left, they gave the impression that their therapist meant nothing to them. The therapists attributed this partly to an adjustment on the child's part to the imminent return to the home environment and partly to a lack of object constancy, which was also observed when therapy was interrupted by vacation or illness. Almost uniformly, all the children denied the importance of the loss of object, which most of them had experienced repeatedly. Some of the children were gradually able to admit that the separation from the therapist over vacation had affected them, had made them sad and angry.

The authors were struck most by the children's inability to feel at ease and to experience pleasure. Some never laughed for months on end, and they entered the consulting room like "gloomy little adults," whose sadness or depression was only too obvious. When they played games, they seemed to be doing it more for the therapist's sake than for their own enjoyment. Many of the children seemed to be unfamiliar with toys and games and especially with playing with adults. They were surprised when the therapists took pleasure in the games and had fun playing with the children. By identifying with the therapist, the children were gradually able to experience pleasure in playing.

Most of the children saw themselves in an extremely negative light, describing themselves as "stupid," as "a child no one likes," who "can't do anything" and is "bad." They could never admit to being proud of something they obviously did well. They hesitated to try anything new, were terribly afraid of doing something wrong, and frequently felt ashamed. Several of them seemed to have developed scarcely any feeling of self. This can be seen as a reflection of the attitude of the parents, who did not regard their child as an autonomous person but entirely in relation to the gratification of their own needs. An important role also seemed to be played by frequent changes in the living situation. One six-year-old girl, who had lived with ten different foster families, couldn't understand why she kept her own name no matter whose house she was living in. The drawings the children made of people were exceedingly primitive, and many of them were unable to make a drawing of themselves although the pictures they drew of inanimate objects were appropriate for their age.

The children had a conscience—or rather, a system of values that was extremely rigid and punitive. They were highly critical of themselves as well as of others, became indignant or extremely agitated when other children overstepped their iron-clad rules for what was good and bad. . . .

The children were almost completely unable to express anger and aggression toward adults. Their stories and games, on the other hand, were full of aggression and brutality. Dolls and fictitious persons were constantly being beaten, tormented, and killed. Many children repeated their own abuse in their play. One child, whose skull had been broken three times as an infant, always made up stories about people or animals who suffered head injuries. Another child, whose mother had attempted to drown it when it was a baby, began the play therapy by drowning a doll baby in the bathtub and then having the police take the mother to prison. Although these real-life events played little part in the children's openly expressed fears, they were the basis of a strong unconscious preoccupation. The children were almost never able to express their anxieties verbally, yet they harbored intense feelings of rage and a strong desire for revenge, which, however, were accompanied by a great fear of what might happen if these impulses should erupt. With the development of transference during therapy, these feelings were directed against the therapist, but almost always in an indirect passive-aggressive form. For example, there was an increase in the number of accidents in which the therapist was hit by a ball or something "accidentally" happened to his belongings. . . .

In spite of minimal contact with the children's parents, the therapists had the strong impression that the parent-child relationship in these cases was characterized to a great degree by seductiveness and other sexual overtones. One mother got into bed with her seven-year-old son whenever she felt lonely or unhappy, and many parents, often in competition with each other, urgently sought out the affections of their children, many of whom were in the midst of the Oedipal stage. One mother described her four-year-old daughter as "sexy" and a flirt and said it was obvious she would have trouble in her relationships with men. It appeared as if those children who were forced to serve the needs of their parents in general were not spared having to serve the parents' sexual needs as well, which usually took the form of covert, unconscious advances toward their children.

It can be regarded as a stroke of genius on Hitler's part that for purposes of projection he offered the Jews to the Germans, who had been brought up to be self-controlled and obedient and to suppress their feelings. But the use of this mechanism is by no means new. It can be observed in most wars of conquest, in the Crusades, and in the Inquisition, as well as in recent history. Little attention has been given up to now, however, to the fact that what is called child-rearing is based for the most part on this mechanism and that, conversely, the exploitation of this mechanism for political purposes would be impossible without this kind of upbringing.

Characteristic of these examples of persecution is the presence of a strong narcissistic element. A part of the *self* is being attacked and persecuted here, not a real and dangerous enemy, as, for example, in situations when one's life is actually threatened.

Child-rearing is used in a great many cases to prevent those qualities that were once scorned and eradicated in oneself from coming to life in one's children. In his impressive book, *Soul Murder: Persecution in the Family,* Morton Schatzman shows the extent to which the child-rearing methods advocated by Daniel Gottlob Moritz Schreber, a renowned and influential pedagogue of the mid-nineteenth century, were based on the need to stifle certain parts of one's own self. What Schreber, like so many parents, tries to stamp out in his children is what he fears in himself:

> The noble seeds of human nature sprout upwards in their purity almost of their own accord if the ignoble ones, the weeds, are sought out and destroyed in time. This must be done ruthlessly and vigorously. It is a dangerous and yet frequent error to be put off guard by the hope that misbehavior and flaws in a child's character will disappear by themselves. The sharp edges and corners of one or the other psychic flaw may possibly become somewhat blunted, but left to themselves the roots remain deeply imbedded, continuing to run rampant in poisonous impulses and thus preventing the noble tree of life from flourishing as it should. A child's misbehavior will become a serious character flaw in the adult and opens the way to vice and baseness. . . . *Suppress everything* in the child, keep everything away from him that he should not make his own, and guide him perseveringly toward everything to which he should habituate himself. [Quoted by Schatzman]

The desire for "true nobility of soul" justifies every form of cruelty toward the fallible child, and woe to the child who sees through the hypocrisy.

The pedagogical conviction that one must bring a child into line from the outset has its origin in the need to split off the disquieting parts of the inner self and project them onto an available object. The child's great plasticity, flexibility, defenselessness, and availability make it the ideal object for this projection. The enemy within can at last be hunted down on the outside.

Peace advocates are becoming increasingly aware of the role played by these mechanisms, but until it is clearly recognized that they can be traced back to methods of child raising, little can be done to oppose them. For children who have grown up being assailed for qualities the parents hate in themselves can hardly wait to assign these qualities to someone else so they can once again regard themselves as good, "moral," noble, and altruistic. Such projections can easily become part of any Weltanschauung.

Is There a Harmless Pedagogy?

Gentle Violence

O VERT abuse is not the only way to stifle a child's vitality. I shall illustrate this by the example of a family whose history I was able to trace over several generations.

A young, nineteenth-century missionary and his wife went to Africa to convert people to Christianity. Through his work, this man was able to free himself of the tormenting religious doubts of his youth. At last *he* became a true Christian, who—like his father before him—gave his all to transmitting his faith to others. The couple had ten children, eight of whom were sent to Europe as soon as they were old enough to go to school. One of the children was the future father of A., and he always told his only son how lucky he, the son, was to grow up at home with his family. He himself, after being sent away to school as a little boy, had not seen his parents again until he was thirty years old. With trepidation he had waited at the train station for the parents he could not remember, and, sure enough, when they arrived, he had not recognized them. He often told this anecdote, not with any sign of sadness, but with amusement. A. described his father as kind, good-natured, understanding, appreciative, contented, and genuinely devout. All his family and friends also admired these qualities in him, and there was no ready explanation for why his son, having such a kindhearted father, should develop a severe obsessional neurosis.

Since childhood, A. had been burdened with disturbing obsessive thoughts of an aggressive nature, but he was unable to experience feelings of annoyance or dissatisfaction, to say nothing of anger or rage, in response to actual frustrations. He also had suffered since childhood because he had not "inherited" his father's "serene, natural, trusting" piety; he attempted to attain it by reading devotional literature, but "bad" (because critical) thoughts, which filled him with panic, always stood in the way. It took a long time in analysis before A. was able to express criticism without clothing it in alarming fantasies he then had to struggle to keep at bay. When his son joined a Marxist group at school, this came to his aid. It was easy for A. to locate contradictions, limitations, and intolerance in his son's ideology, and this subsequently enabled him to subject psychoanalysis to critical scrutiny as well and define it as the "religion" of his analyst. During the stages of transference he became increasingly aware of the tragedy of his relationship with his father. Examples of his disappointment with various ideologies multiplied, and he realized more and more how these ideologies served as defense mechanisms for their adherents. Intense feelings of indignation at all possible forms of mystification came to the surface. The newly awakened anger of the deceived child finally led him to be suspicious of all religious and political ideologies. His obsessions diminished, but they did not disappear entirely until these feelings could be experienced in connection with the long dead and internalized father of his childhood.

In his analysis A. was now able to acknowledge the helpless rage he felt at the terrible constrictions that had been imposed on him by his father's attitude. He was expected to be, like his father, good-natured, kind, appreciative, undemanding, not to cry, always to see everything "from the positive side," never to be critical, never to be dissatisfied, always to think of those who were "much worse off." A.'s previously unrecognized feelings of rebelliousness revealed to him the narrow confines of his childhood, from which everything had to be banished that was not suitable for his devout and "sunny" nursery. And only after he had been allowed to articulate his own revolt (which he had had to split off and project onto his son so that he could oppose it there) was his father's other side revealed to him. He had found it in his own rage and mourning; no one else could ever have convinced him of it, because his father's unstable side had found a home only in the psyche of the son, in his obsessional neurosis, where it had taken root in a remorseless way, crippling this son for forty-two years. By means of his illness, the son had helped preserve his father's piety.

Now that A. had found the way back to his childhood emotions, he was also able to empathize with the child that his father had once been. He asked himself how his father had dealt with the fact that his parents sent eight children so far away without ever visiting them, for the sake of promulgating the Christian idea of brotherly love in Africa. Wouldn't he necessarily have deep doubts about such a love and about the meaningfulness of work that required such cruelty toward one's own children? But he dared not have doubts, for fear his devout and strict aunt would not keep him. And how is a little six-year-old, whose parents are thousands of miles away, to fare all by himself? He has no choice but to believe in this God who demands such inconceivable sacrifices (for this makes his parents obedient servants of a good cause); he has no choice but to become devout and cheerful if he wants to be loved. In order to survive, he has to be content, appreciative, etc., and develop a sunny, happy disposition so that he will not be a burden to anyone.

If someone who has turned into this kind of a person becomes a father himself, he will be confronted with a situation that threatens the whole structure he has taken such pains to erect: he sees before him a child full of life, sees how a human being is meant to be, how *he* could have been if obstacles hadn't been placed in his way. But his fears are soon activated: this cannot be allowed to happen. If the child were allowed to stay as he is, wouldn't that mean that the father's sacrifices and self-denial weren't really necessary? Is it possible to have a child turn out well without forcing him to be obedient, without breaking his will, without combating his egotism and willfullness, as we have been told to do for centuries? Parents cannot permit themselves to ask these questions. To do so would cause no end of trouble, and they would be deprived of the sure ground provided by an inherited ideology that places the highest value on suppressing and manipulating vital spontaneity. A.'s father found himself in this same position.*

He tried to make his son control his bodily functions while still an infant, and he succeeded in having him internalize this control at a very early age. He helped the mother to toilet train him as an infant, and by distracting him "in a loving way" taught him to wait patiently to be fed, so that feedings were kept to an exact schedule. When A. was still very little and didn't like something he was given to eat or ate "too greedily" or "misbehaved," he was put in a corner, where he had to watch his parents calmly finish eating their meal. It may be that the child in the corner was serving as a surrogate for his father, who had been sent away to Europe as a child and who had wondered what sins he had committed to cause him to be taken so far away from his beloved parents.

A. did not remember ever being struck by his father. Nevertheless, without meaning to and without realizing it, the father treated his child just as cruelly as he treated the child within himself—in order to make a "contented child" out of him. He systematically tried to destroy everything that was vital in his firstborn. If the remnants of vitality had not taken refuge in an obsessional neurosis and from there sent out a call for help, then the son would indeed have been psychically dead, for he was only a pale shadow of his father, had no needs of his own, and no longer had any spontaneous feelings. All he knew were a depressing emptiness and fear of his obsessions. In analysis he learned for the first time, at the age of forty-two, what a vital, curious, intelligent, lively, and humorous child he had actually been. This child was now able to come alive in him and develop his creative powers. A. gradually

---

* The mother had also grown up with this ideology. I do not discuss her here because the faith A. was compelled to hold in spite of the doubts he felt was an important factor in his case and this was connected primarily with his father.

came to realize that his severe symptoms were, on the one hand, the result of the repression of important vital aspects of his self and, on the other, a reflection of his father's unlived, unconscious conflicts. The father's fragile piety and his split-off, unacknowledged doubts were revealed in the son's tormenting obsessions. If the father had been able to face his doubts consciously, come to terms with them, and integrate them, his son would have been freed of having to grow up with them and could have had a full life of his own at a much earlier age and without the help of analysis.

Pedagogy Fills the Needs of Parents, Not of Children

THE reader will have noticed long before now that all pedagogy is pervaded by the precepts of "poisonous pedagogy," no matter how well they may be concealed today. Since the books of Ekkehard von Braunmühl unmistakably expose the absurdity and cruelty of the pedagogical approach in today's world, I need only call attention to them here (see Bibliography). Perhaps the reason it is difficult for me to share his optimism is that I regard the idealization of one's own childhood as a major, unconscious obstacle to learning for parents.

My antipedagogic position is not directed against a specific type of pedagogical ideology but against all pedagogical ideology per se, even if it is of an anti-authoritarian nature. This attitude is based on insights that I shall describe shortly. For now, I should simply like to point out that my position has nothing in common with a Rousseauistic optimism about human "nature."

First of all, I do not see a child as growing up in some abstract "state of nature" but in the concrete surroundings of care givers whose unconscious exerts a substantial influence on the child's development.

Second, Rousseau's pedagogy is profoundly manipulative. This does not always seem to be recognized by educators, but it has been convincingly demonstrated and documented by Braunmühl. One of his numerous examples is the following passage from *Emile* (Book II):

> Take an opposite route with your pupil; always let him think he is the master, but always be it yourself. There is no more perfect form of subjection than the one that preserves the appearance of freedom; thus does the will itself become captive. The poor child, who knows nothing, can do nothing, and has no experience—is he not at your mercy? Are you not in control of everything in his environment that relates to him? Can you not control his impressions as you please? His tasks, his games, his pleasures, his troubles—is all this not in your hands without his knowing it? Doubtlessly, he may do as he wishes, but he may wish only what you want him to; he may not take a single step that you have not anticipated, he may not open his mouth without your knowing what he is going to say.

I am convinced of the harmful effects of training for the following reason: all advice that pertains to raising children betrays more or less clearly the numerous, variously clothed needs of the *adult*. Fulfillment of these needs not only discourages the child's development but actually prevents it. This also holds true when the adult is honestly convinced of acting in the child's best interests.

Among the adult's true motives we find:

1. The unconscious need to pass on to others the humiliation one has undergone oneself

2. The need to find an outlet for repressed affect

3. The need to possess and have at one's disposal a vital object to manipulate

4. Self-defense: i.e., the need to idealize one's childhood and one's parents by dogmatically applying the parents' pedagogical principles to one's own children

5. Fear of freedom

6. Fear of the reappearance of what one has repressed, which one reencounters in one's child and must try to stamp out, having killed it in oneself earlier

7. Revenge for the pain one has suffered

Since at least one of the points enumerated here is present in everyone's upbringing, the child-rearing process is at best suitable for making "good" pedagogues out of its objects. However, it will never be able to help its charges to remain vital. When children are trained, they learn how to train others in turn. Children who are lectured to, learn how to lecture; if they are admonished, they learn how to admonish; if scolded, they learn how to scold; if ridiculed, they learn how to ridicule; if humiliated, they learn how to humiliate; if their psyche is killed, they will learn how to kill—the only question is who will be killed: oneself, others, or both.

All this does not mean that children should be raised without any restraints. Crucial for healthy development is the respect of their care givers, tolerance for their feelings, awareness of their needs and grievances, and authenticity on the part of their parents, whose own freedom—and not pedagogical considerations—sets natural limits for children.

It is this last point that causes great difficulty for parents and pedagogues, for the following reasons:

1. If parents have had to learn very early in life to ignore their feelings, not to take them seriously, to scorn or ridicule them, then they will lack the sensitivity required to deal successfully with their children. As a result, they will try to substitute pedagogical principles as prostheses. Thus, under certain circumstances they may be reluctant to show tenderness for fear of spoiling the child, or, in other cases, they will hide their hurt feelings behind the Fourth Commandment.

2. Parents who never learned as children to be aware of their own needs or to defend their own interests because this right was never granted them will be uncertain in this regard for the rest of their life and consequently will become dependent on firm pedagogical rules. This uncertainty, regardless of whether it appears in sadistic or masochistic guise,

leads to great insecurity in the child in spite of these rules. An example of this: a father who was trained to be obedient at a very early age may on occasion take cruel and violent measures to force his child to be obedient in order to satisfy his own need to be respected for the first time in his life. But this behavior does not exclude intervening periods of masochistic behavior when the same father will put up with anything the child does, because he never learned to define the limits of his tolerance. Thus, his guilt feelings over the preceding unjust punishment will suddenly lead him to be unusually permissive, thereby awakening anxiety in the child, who cannot tolerate uncertainty about the father's true face. The child's increasingly aggressive behavior will finally provoke the father into losing his temper. In the end, the child then takes on the role of the sadistic opponent in place of the grandparents, but with the difference that the father can now gain the upper hand. Such situations, in which the child "goes too far," prove to the pedagogue that disciplining and punishment are necessary.

3. Since a child is often used as a substitute for one's own parents, he or she can become the object of an endless number of contradictory wishes and expectations that cannot possibly be fulfilled. In extreme cases, psychosis, drug addiction, or suicide may be the only solution. But often the child's feeling of helplessness leads to increasingly aggressive behavior, which in turn convinces parents and educators of the need for strict countermeasures.

4. A similar situation arises when it is drilled into children, as it was in the anti-authoritarian upbringing of the sixties,* to adopt certain ways of behavior that their parents wished had once been allowed them and that they therefore consider to be universally desirable. In the process, the child's real needs can be totally overlooked. In one case I know, for example, a child who was feeling sad was encouraged to shatter a glass when what she most wanted to do was to climb up

---

* This was a recent direction taken in German child-rearing methods, loosely based on permissive child-rearing in the United States.

onto her mother's lap. If children go on feeling misunderstood and manipulated like this, they will become genuinely confused and justifiably aggressive.

In contrast to generally accepted beliefs and to the horror of pedagogues, I cannot attribute any positive significance to the word *pedagogy*. I see it as self-defense on the part of adults, as manipulation deriving from their own lack of freedom and their insecurity, which I can certainly understand, although I cannot overlook the inherent dangers. I can also understand why criminals are sent to prison, but I cannot see that deprivation of freedom and prison life, which is geared wholly to conformity, subordination, and submissiveness, can really contribute to the betterment, i.e., the development, of the prisoner. There is in the word *pedagogy* the suggestion of certain goals that the charge is meant to achieve—and this limits his or her possibilities for development from the start. But an honest rejection of all forms of manipulation and of the idea of setting goals does not mean that one simply leaves children to their own devices. For children need a large measure of emotional and physical *support* from the adult. This support must include the following elements if they are to develop their full potential:

1. Respect for the child
2. Respect for his rights
3. Tolerance for his feelings
4. Willingness to learn from his behavior:
   a. About the nature of the individual child
   b. About the child in the parents themselves
   c. About the nature of emotional life, which can be observed much more clearly in the child than in the adult because the child can experience his feelings much more intensely and, optimally, more undisguisedly than an adult

There is evidence among the younger generation that this kind of willingness is possible even for people who were themselves victims of child-rearing.

But liberation from centuries of constraint can scarcely be expected to take place in a single generation. The idea that we as parents can learn more about the laws of life from a newborn child than we can from our parents will strike many older people as absurd and ridiculous. Younger people may also be suspicious of this idea, because many of them have been made insecure by a mixture of psychological literature and internalized "poisonous pedagogy." A very intelligent and sensitive father, for example, asked me if I didn't think it was taking advantage of children to try to learn from them. This question, coming from someone born in 1942 who had been able to rise above the taboos of his generation to an extraordinary degree, showed me that we must be mindful of the misunderstanding and new insecurity that can result from reading books on psychology.

Can an honest attempt to learn be considered an abuse? If we are not open to what the other person is telling us, genuine rapport is hardly possible. We need to hear what the child has to say in order to give our understanding, support, and love. The child, on the other hand, needs free space if he or she is to find adequate self-expression. There is no discrepancy here between means and ends, but rather a dialectical process involving dialogue. Learning is a result of listening, which in turn leads to even better listening and attentiveness to the other person. In other words, to learn from the child, we must have empathy, and empathy grows as we learn. It is a different matter for parents or educators who would like the child to be a certain way or think they must expect him to be that way. To reach their sacred ends, they try to mold the child in their image, suppressing self-expression in the child and at the same time missing out on an opportunity to learn something. Certainly, abuse of this sort is often unintentional; it is not only directed against children but—if we look more closely —pervades most human relationships, because the partners frequently were abused children and are now showing unconsciously what happened to them in childhood.

Antipedagogical writings (by Braunmühl and others) can be of great help to young parents as long as they do not interpret them as instructions on "how to be a parent" but use them to expand their knowledge; they can then find encouragement to abandon their prejudices and look at things in a new way.

The Last Act of the Silent Drama: The World Reacts with Horror

Introduction

IT is difficult to write about child abuse without taking on a moralizing tone. It is so natural to feel outrage at the adult who beats a child and pity for the helpless child that, even with a great deal of understanding of human nature, one is tempted to condemn the adult for being cruel and brutal. But where will you find human beings who are only good or only cruel? The reason why parents mistreat their children has less to do with character and temperament than with the fact that they were mistreated themselves and were not permitted to defend themselves. There are countless people like A.'s father who are kind, gentle, and highly sensitive and yet inflict cruelty on their children every day, calling it childrearing. As long as child beating was considered necessary and useful, they could justify this form of cruelty. Today such people suffer when their "hand slips," when an incomprehensible compulsion or despair induces them to shout at, humiliate, or beat their children and see their tears, yet they cannot help themselves and will do the same thing again next time. This will inevitably continue to happen as long as they persist in idealizing their own childhood.

Paul Klee is renowned as a great painter of magical and poetic canvases. His only child may have been the one person who was familiar with his other side. Felix Klee, the painter's son, told an interviewer (Brückenbauer; February 29, 1980): "He had two sides; he was full of fun, but he was also capable of playing his part in my upbringing by giving me an energetic whipping." Paul Klee made wonderful puppets, presumably for his son, of which thirty are still preserved. His son relates: "Papa constructed the stage in a doorway of our small apartment. He admitted that when I was in school he sometimes put on a performance for the cat. . . ." Yet the father performed not only for the cat but for his son as well. In view of this, could Felix hold against his father the beatings he was given?

I have used this example to help readers free themselves from clichés about good or bad parents. Cruelty can take a thousand forms, and it goes undetected even today, because the damage it does to the child and the ensuing consequences are still so little known. This section of the book is devoted to these consequences.

The individual psychological stages in the lives of most people are:

1. To be hurt as a small child without anyone recognizing the situation as such

2. To fail to react to the resulting suffering with anger

3. To show gratitude for what are supposed to be good intentions

4. To forget everything

5. To discharge the stored-up anger onto others in adulthood or to direct it against oneself

The greatest cruelty that can be inflicted on children is to refuse to let them express their anger and suffering except at the risk of losing their parents' love and affection. The anger stemming from early childhood is stored up in the unconscious, and since it basically represents a healthy, vital source of energy, an equal amount of energy must be expended in order to repress it. An upbringing that succeeds in sparing the parents at the expense of the child's vitality sometimes leads to suicide or extreme drug addiction, which is a form of suicide. If drugs succeed in covering up the emptiness caused by repressed feelings and self-alienation, then the process of withdrawal brings this void back into view. When withdrawal is not accompanied by restoration of vitality, then the cure is sure to be temporary. Christiane F., subject of an international bestseller and film, paints a devastatingly vivid picture of a tragedy of this nature.

The War of Annihilation against the Self

The Lost Opportunity of Puberty

PARENTS often have such success with the numerous methods they use to subdue their children that they don't encounter any problems until the children reach puberty. The "cooling off" of feelings and drives during the latency period abets parents in their desire to have model children. In the book *The Golden Cage* by Hilda Bruch, parents of anorexic daughters describe how gifted, well-mannered, successful, well-adjusted, and considerate these children had been. The parents cannot understand the sudden change; they are left helpless and uncomprehending by an adolescent who seems to be rejecting all norms and whose self-destructive behavior cannot be modified by logical arguments or by the subtle devices of "poisonous pedagogy."

At puberty, adolescents are often taken totally by surprise by the intensity of their true feelings, after having succeeded in keeping them at a distance during the latency period. With the spurt of biological growth, these feelings (rage, anger, rebelliousness, falling in love, sexual desire, enthusiasm, joy, enchantment, sadness) seek full expression, but in many cases this would endanger the parents' psychic balance. If adolescents were to show their true feelings openly, they would run the risk of being sent to prison as dangerous terrorists or put in mental institutions as insane. Our society would no doubt have nothing but a psychiatric clinic to offer Shakespeare's Hamlet or Goethe's Werther, and Schiller's Karl Moor would probably face the same fate. This is why drug addicts attempt to adapt to society by struggling against their authentic feelings, but since they cannot live entirely without them in the storm of puberty, they try to regain access to them with the help of drugs, which seem to do the trick, at least in the beginning. But society's views, which are represented by the parents and which the adolescent has long ago internalized, must prevail: the consequences of having strong, intense feelings are rejection, isolation, ostracism, and threat of death, i.e., self-destruction.

The drug addict punishes himself for seeking his true self —certainly a justifiable and essential goal—by destroying his own spontaneous feelings, repeating the punishment that was inflicted on him in early childhood when he showed the first signs of vitality. Almost every heroin addict describes having initially experienced feelings of hitherto unknown intensity, with the result that he becomes even more conscious of the vapidity and emptiness of his usual emotional life.

He simply can't imagine that this experience is possible without heroin, and he understandably begins to long for it to be repeated. For, in these out-of-the-ordinary moments, the young person discovers how he might have been; he has made contact with his self, and as might be expected, once this has happened, he can find no rest. He can no longer act as though his true self had never existed. Now he knows that it *does* exist, but he also knows that ever since early childhood this true self has not had a chance. And so he strikes a compromise with his fate: he will encounter his self from time to time without anyone finding out. Not even he will realize what is involved here, for it is the "stuff" that produces the experience; the effect comes "from outside" and is difficult to bring about. It will never become an integrated part of his self, and he will never have to or be able to assume responsibility for these feelings. The intervals between one fix and the next—characterized by total apathy, lethargy, emptiness, or uneasiness and anxiety—bear this out: the fix is over like a dream that one can't remember and that can have no effect on one's life as a whole.

Becoming dependent on an absurd compulsion is likewise comprehensible in terms of the addict's previous history: since dependence has typified his entire previous life, he is hardly aware of it as such. A twenty-four-year-old woman who has been addicted to heroin since age sixteen appears on TV and explains that she supports her habit by means of prostitution and has to take drugs to be able "to put up with those animals." She makes a very sincere impression, and we can appreciate and sympathize with everything she says. Only the matter-of-factness with which she regards this vicious circle as the only possible way of life for her puzzles us. This woman obviously cannot imagine a different life, free of her addiction, because she has never known anything like a free decision. The only life she has ever known has been one dominated by a destructive compulsion, and this is why she is unable to grasp the absurdity of such a path. It will not surprise us to learn that she continues to idealize both parents, as is frequently the case with drug addicts. She feels guilty for being so weak, for disappointing and disgracing her parents. She also says "society" is to blame—which of course cannot be denied. But the real predicament, the conflict between her search for her true self and the necessity of adapting to the needs of her parents, cannot be recognized as long as she continues to protect her parents from self-reproach. The concrete example of Christiane F.'s life story can help us to understand this predicament.

The Search for the Self and Self-destruction through Drugs

THE LIFE OF CHRISTIANE F.

For the first six years of her life, Christiane lived in the country on a farm, where she spent the whole day with the farmer, fed the animals, and "romped in the hay with the others." Then her family moved to Berlin, and she, her sister, who was a year younger, and her parents lived in a two-and-a-half-room apartment on the twelfth floor in Gropius City, a high-rise housing development. The sudden loss of a rural setting, of familiar playmates, and of all the free space that goes with living in the country is in itself hard enough for a child, but it is all the more tragic if the child must come to terms with this loss all by herself and if she is constantly faced with unpredictable punishment and beatings.

I would have been quite happy with my animals if things with my father hadn't kept getting worse. While my mother was at work, he sat around at home. Nothing had come of the marriage agency they wanted to open. Now he was waiting for a job to turn up that was to his liking. He sat on our worn-out sofa and waited. And his insane fits of rage became more frequent.

My mother helped me with my homework when she came home from work. For a while I had trouble telling the letters H and K apart. One evening my mother was taking great pains to explain the difference to me. I could scarcely pay attention to what she was saying because I noticed my father getting more and more furious. I always knew exactly when it was going to happen: he went and got the hand broom from the kitchen and gave me a trouncing. Now I was supposed to tell him the difference between H and K. Of course, by that time I didn't know anything anymore so I got another licking and was sent to bed.

That was his way of helping me with my homework. He wanted me to be smart and make something of myself. After all, his grandfather had had loads of money. He'd owned a printing company and a newspaper in East Germany, and more besides. After the war, it had all been expropriated by the GDR. Now my father flipped out whenever he got the idea I wouldn't make it in school.

There were some evenings I can still remember down to the last detail. One time I was assigned to draw houses in my arithmetic notebook. They were supposed to be six squares wide and four squares high. I had one house finished and was doing just fine when my father suddenly came and sat beside me. He asked me where the next house should go. I was so scared I stopped counting the squares and started guessing. Every time

I pointed to the wrong square, he pasted me one. All I could do was bawl and couldn't answer at all anymore, so he went over to the rubber plant. I knew very well what that meant. He pulled the bamboo stick supporting the plant out of the flowerpot. Then he thrashed my behind with the stick until you could literally peel off the skin.

I was even scared at mealtimes. If I spilled anything, I got smacked for it. If I knocked something over, he tanned my behind. I hardly dared to touch my glass of milk. I was so scared that I did something wrong at almost every meal.

After supper I'd ask my father quite sweetly if he wasn't going out. He went out quite often, and then we three females could finally breathe deep sighs of relief. Those evenings were marvelously peaceful. Of course, then when he came home late at night, there could always be another catastrophe. Usually he had had something to drink. Then any little thing sent him off on a rampage. It might be toys or clothes we had left lying around. My father always said the most important thing in life was to be neat and tidy. And if he found any untidiness when he came home, he'd drag me out of bed in the middle of the night and give me a beating. My little sister got the tail end of it, too. Then my father threw our things on the floor and ordered us to put them all away again neatly in five minutes. We usually didn't manage it in that short a time and so we got another licking.

My mother usually stood at the door crying while this was going on. She hardly ever dared to stand up for us, because then he would hit her, too. Only Ajax, my dog, often tried to intervene. He whined shrilly and had very sad eyes whenever one of us was being given a beating. He was the most likely one to bring my father to his senses, because he loved dogs, as we all did. He yelled at Ajax once in a while, but he never hit him.

I somehow loved and respected my father in spite of it all. He towered above other fathers in my eyes. But more than anything else I was afraid of him. At the same time I found it quite normal that he was always hitting us. It was no different at home for other children in Gropius City. Sometimes they even had a black eye, and so did their mothers. Some fathers would lie on the street or the playground in a drunken stupor. My father never got that drunk. And sometimes on our street, furniture would come flying out of the high-rise windows, women would cry for help and the police would come. So we didn't have it all that bad. . . .

Probably what my father loved more than anything else was his car, a Porsche. He polished it almost every day that it wasn't in the shop. I don't think anyone else in Gropius City had a Porsche. Anyway, there definitely wasn't anyone else with a Porsche who was out of work.

Of course, in those days I didn't have any idea of what was wrong with my father and why he was always going on a regular rampage. It only dawned on me later when I used to have talks with my mother about my father. I gradually figured out a thing or two. He simply wasn't making it. He kept trying to get ahead and was always falling flat on his face. His father despised him for it. Grandpa even warned my mother against marrying such a good-for-nothing. My grandpa had always had great plans for my father. . . . My most fervent wish was to grow up quickly, to be grown-up like my father, to have real power over other people. In the meantime I tested out what power I did have. . . .

Nearly every day [my girl friend and I], together with my little sister, played a game we had learned. When we got out of school we collected cigarette butts from ashtrays and trash cans. We smoothed them out, stuck them between our lips, and puffed on them. If my sister wanted to have a butt too, she got her hand slapped. We ordered her to do the housework—to do the dishes and dust and whatever else our parents had told us to do. Then we got out our doll carriages, locked the apartment door behind us, and went for a walk. We kept my sister locked in until she had finished the work. [*Christiane F.: Autobiography of a Girl of the Streets and Heroin Addict*]

Christiane, who is beaten often by her father for reasons she does not understand, finally begins to act in ways that give her father "good reason to beat her." By so doing, she improves his character by making an unjust and unpredictable father into one who at least punishes justly. This is the only way she has to rescue the image of a father she loves and idealizes. She also begins to provoke other men and turn them into punitive fathers—first the building superintendent, then her teachers, and finally, during her drug addiction, the police. In this way she can shift the conflict with her father onto other people. Because Christiane cannot talk with her father about their conflicts or settle them with him, she relegates her fundamental hatred for him to her unconscious, directing her hostility against surrogate male authority figures. Eventually, all the child's bottled-up rage at being humiliated, deprived of respect, misunderstood, and left alone is turned against herself in the form of addiction. As time goes by, Christiane does to herself what her father had done to her earlier: she systematically destroys her self-respect, manipulates her feelings with the use of drugs, condemns herself to speechlessness (this highly articulate child!) and isolation, and in the end ruins body as well as soul.

When I read Christiane's account of her childhood, I sometimes was reminded of descriptions of life in a concentration camp. The following scenes are two examples:

At first we did it to harass other kids: we'd grab a kid, shut him in an elevator, and push all the buttons. We held on to the second elevator so the first one had to jiggle its way up to the top, stopping at every floor. They often did the same thing to me, especially when I was coming back with the dog and had to get home for supper on time. Then they pushed all the buttons, so it took forever to get to the twelfth floor, and Ajax got terribly nervous.

It was mean to push all the buttons when someone was in a big hurry. He would end up peeing in the elevator. But it was even meaner to take a kid's wooden spoon away from him. All the little kids always took a long wooden soup ladle out with them, because that was the only way we could reach the elevator buttons. Without the ladle, you were completely helpless. If you lost it or the other kids took it away from you, you had to walk up the eleven flights of stairs. Of course, none of the other kids ever helped you out, and the grown-ups thought you just wanted to play in the elevator and make it break down.

One time one of my [pet] mice ran into the grass, which we weren't allowed to walk on. We couldn't find it again. I was a little sad, but I was comforted by the thought that the mouse would like it much better outside than in the cage.

My father picked that evening to come into my room and look into the mouse cage. He asked in a funny voice: "How come there are only two? Where's the third one?" I didn't even notice there was anything wrong when he asked in such a funny way. My father never did like the mice and he kept telling me I should give them away. I told him the mouse had run away outside on the playground.

My father looked at me as though he had gone crazy. Then I knew he was going to go on one of his wild rampages. He shouted and started right in hitting me. He kept on hitting me, and I was trapped on my bed and couldn't get away. He had never hit me like that before, and I thought he was going to kill me. Then, when he started letting my sister have it too, I had a few seconds to get free and I instinctively tried to get to the window. I think I really would have jumped from the twelfth floor.

But my father grabbed me and threw me back on the bed. My mother was probably crying in the doorway again, but I didn't even see her. I didn't see her until she threw herself between me and my father and started pummeling him.

He was beside himself. He knocked my mother down onto the floor. All of a sudden I was more afraid for her than for myself. I went over to them. She tried to escape into the bathroom and bolt the door. But my father was holding her by the hair. As usual, there was wash soaking in the bathtub, because so far we hadn't been able to afford a washing machine. My father stuck my mother's head into the tub full of water. Somehow or other, she managed to get loose. I don't know whether he let her go or whether she got herself free.

My father disappeared into the living room. He was white as a sheet. My mother went and got her coat. She left the apartment without saying a word.

That was without a doubt one of the most awful moments of my life when my mother simply walked out of the apartment without a word and left us alone. My first thought was, Now he's going to come back and start hitting me again. But everything was quiet in the living room except for the television, which was on.

No one seriously doubts that the inmates of a concentration camp underwent terrible suffering. But when we hear about the physical abuse of children, we react with astonishing equanimity. Depending on our ideology, we say, "That's quite normal," or "Children have to be disciplined, after all," or "That was the custom in those days," or "Someone who won't listen has to be made to feel it," etc. An elderly gentleman I once met at a party told me with amusement that when he was a little boy his mother had swung him back and forth over a fire she had lighted specially for the purpose of drying his pants and breaking him of the habit of wetting them. "My mother was the most wonderful person you'd ever want to meet, but that's the way things were done in our family in those days," he said. Such lack of empathy for the suffering of one's own childhood can result in an astonishing lack of sensitivity to other children's suffering. When what was done to me was done for my own good, then I am expected to accept this treatment as an essential part of life and not question it.

This kind of insensitivity thus has its roots in the abuse a person suffered as a child. He or she may be able to remember what happened, but in most cases the emotional content of the whole experience of being beaten and humiliated has been completely repressed.

This is where the difference lies between treating an adult and a child cruelly. The self has not yet sufficiently developed for a child to retain the memory of it or of the feelings it arouses. The knowledge that you were beaten and that this, as your parents tell you, was for your own good may well be retained (although not always), but the suffering caused by the way you were mistreated will remain unconscious and will later prevent you from empathizing with others. This is why battered children grow up to be mothers and fathers who beat their own offspring; from their ranks are recruited the most reliable executioners, concentration-camp supervisors, prison guards, and torturers. They beat, mistreat, and torture out of an inner compulsion to repeat their own history, and they are able to do this without the slightest feeling of sympathy for their victims because they have identified totally with the aggressive side of their psyche. These people were beaten and humiliated themselves at such an early age that it was never possible for them to experience consciously the helpless, battered child they once were. In order to do this, they would have needed the aid of an understanding, supportive adult, and no such person was available. Only under these circumstances would children be able to see themselves as they are at that moment—namely, as weak, helpless, downtrodden, and battered—and thus be able to integrate this part into the self.

Theoretically, a child beaten by his father could afterwards cry his heart out in the arms of a kind aunt and tell her what happened; she would not try to minimize the child's pain or justify the father's actions but would give the whole experience its due weight. But such good fortune is rare. The wife of a child-beating father shares his attitude toward child-rearing or is herself his victim—in either case, she is rarely the child's advocate. Such an "aunt" is therefore a great exception, because the battered child is very unlikely to have the inner freedom to seek her out and make use of her. A child is more likely to opt for a terrible inner isolation and splitting off of his feelings than he is to "tattle" to outsiders about his father or mother. Psychotherapists know how long it sometimes takes before a child's resentment, which has been repressed for thirty or forty or even fifty years, can be articulated and re-lived.

Thus, it may well be that the plight of a little child who is abused is even worse and has more serious consequences for society than the plight of an adult in a concentration camp. The former camp inmate may sometimes find himself in a situation where he feels that he can never adequately communicate the horror of what he has gone through and that others approach him without understanding, with cold

and callous indifference, even with disbelief,* but with few exceptions he himself will not doubt the tragic nature of his
experiences. He will never attempt to convince himself that the
cruelty he was subjected to was for his own good or interpret
the absurdity of the camp as a necessary pedagogical measure;
he will usually not attempt to empathize with the motives of
his persecutors. He will find people who have had similar experiences and share with them his feelings of outrage, hatred,
and despair over the cruelty he has suffered.

The abused child does not have any of these options.
As I have tried to show in the example of Christiane F., she is
alone with her suffering, not only within the family but also
within her self. And because she cannot share her pain with
anyone, she is also unable to create a place in her own soul
where she could "cry her heart out." No arms of a "kind aunt"
exist there; "Keep a stiff upper lip and be brave" is the watch-
word. Defenselessness and helplessness find no haven in the
self of the child, who later, identifying with the aggressor,
persecutes these qualities wherever they appear.

A person who from the beginning was forced, whether
subjected to corporal punishment or not, to stifle, i.e., to condemn, split off, and persecute, the vital child within himself
will spend his whole life preventing this inner danger that he
associates with spontaneous feelings from recurring. But psychological forces are so tenacious that they can rarely be
thoroughly suppressed. They are constantly seeking outlets
that will enable them to survive, often in very distorted forms
that are not without danger to society. For example, one person suffering from grandiosity will project his own childish
qualities onto the external world, whereas another will struggle
against the "evil" within himself. "Poisonous pedagogy" shows
how these two mechanisms are related to each other and how
they are combined in a traditional religious upbringing.

---

* William G. Niederland's book *Folgen der Verfolgung (The Results
of Persecution)* (1980) presents a penetrating analysis of the uncomprehending reception given former inmates as reflected in psychiatric
diagnoses.

In addition to the degree of maturity and those elements of loyalty and of isolation involved in the case of a child, there is another fundamental difference between abuse of children and of adults. The abused inmates of a concentration camp cannot of course offer any resistance, cannot defend themselves against humiliation, but they are inwardly free to hate their persecutors. The opportunity to experience their feelings, even to share them with other inmates, prevents them from having to surrender their self. This opportunity does not exist for children. They *must not* hate their father—this, the message of the Fourth Commandment, has been drummed into them from early childhood; they *cannot* hate him either, if they must fear losing his love as a result; finally, they do not even *want* to hate him, because they love him. Thus, children, unlike concentration-camp inmates, are confronted by a tormenter they love, not one they hate, and this tragic complication will have a devastating influence on their entire subsequent life. Christiane F. writes:

> I never hated him but was just afraid of him. I was always proud of him, too. Because he loved animals and because he had such a terrific car, his '62 Porsche.

These remarks are so moving because they are true: this is just the way a child feels. Her tolerance has no limits; she is always faithful and even proud that her father, who beats *her* brutally, never would do anything to hurt an animal; she is prepared to forgive him everything, always to take all the blame herself, not to hate him, to forget quickly everything that happens, not to bear a grudge, not to tell anyone about it, to try by her behavior to prevent another beating, to find out why her father is dissatisfied, to understand him, etc. It is rare for an adult to have this attitude toward a child unless the adult happens to be the psychotherapist, but for a dependent, sensitive child, what I have just described is almost the rule. And what happens to all this repressed affect? It cannot simply disappear from the face of the earth. It must be directed toward substitute objects in order to spare the father. Here again, Christiane's account gives us a concrete example when she describes life with her now divorced mother and her mother's boyfriend Klaus:

> [Klaus and I] got into fights with each other too. About little things. Sometimes I started it. Usually it was because of my playing my records. For my eleventh birthday my mother had bought me a record player, just a cheap little one, and I had a few records—Disco-Sound and teeny-bopper music. And evenings I would put one on and turn the thing up so loud it would break your eardrums. One night Klaus came into my room and said I should turn the record player down. I didn't do it. He came back again and snatched the arm off the record. I put it back on and stood in front of the record player so he couldn't get at it. Then he grabbed me and pushed me aside. When that man touched me, I freaked out.

The same child who submitted to the most incredible beatings from her father without any attempt to defend herself now immediately "freaks out" when "that man" touches her. Analysts often hear about similar situations from their patients. Women who suffer from frigidity, or who begin, during analysis, to have feelings of disgust when their husbands touch them, often rediscover very early memories of sexual abuse by their fathers or other men in the family. As a rule, when these feelings begin to emerge, they are accompanied by little show of feeling; for the time being, strong affect is reserved for the present partner. Only gradually does the patient experience the whole range of disappointment with her beloved father: shame, humiliation, rage, indignation.

It frequently occurs in analysis that just before the memory of being sexually molested by the father is allowed to break through into consciousness, the patient covers it up by remembering similar scenes with men less closely related.

Who are these men? If it was not her own father, why didn't the child resist? Why didn't she tell her parents about it? Is it because she has already gone through it with her father and as a result has automatically become practiced in keeping silent? The displacement of "bad" affect onto people she is indifferent to enables her to preserve a "good" relationship with her father on a conscious level. Once Christiane could have her fights with Klaus, her father seemed "like a different person." "He acted awfully nice. And he really was, too. He gave me another dog. A female." And somewhat later she writes:

> My father was terrific. I could tell that he loved me, too, in his way. Now he treated me almost like a grown-up. I was even allowed to go out at night with him and his girl friend.
>
> He had become really reasonable. Now he had friends his own age and he told them he'd been married before. I didn't have to call him Uncle Richard anymore. I was his daughter. And he seemed to be really proud of having me for a daughter. Of course, typical for him—he arranged his vacation to suit himself and his friends. At the tail end of my vacation. And I got back to my new school two weeks late. So I started skipping school from the beginning.

The resistance she never showed when her father beat her now emerges in the struggle with her teachers.

> I felt I wasn't accepted in school. The rest of them had that two weeks' head start. In a new school, that makes a big difference. I tried my routine from elementary school here, too. I interrupted my teachers and contradicted them. Sometimes because I was right, and sometimes just for the hell of it. I was back in the fray. Against the teachers and against the school. I wanted to be accepted.

Later the struggle extends to the police as well. This way Christiane can forget her father's rage—to the extent that she even writes:

> Building superintendents were really the only [!] authoritarian types I knew. You had to hate them because they were always bugging you when you were having fun. The police still represented an authority you didn't question, as far as I was concerned. Then I learned that the superintendents in Gropius City were really the same as cops. Only, the cops were much more dangerous. Whatever Piet and Kathi* said was the last word for me anyway.

---

* Here, a boy's nickname.

The others offered her hashish, and she realized that she "couldn't say no."

> Kathi began to fondle me. I didn't know what I ought to think of it.

A child conditioned to be well-behaved must not notice what she is feeling, but asks herself what she *ought* to feel.

> I didn't resist. It was like I was paralyzed. I was scared as hell of something. At one point I wanted to split. Then I thought, "Christiane, this is the price you have to pay for being one of the crowd now." I just let it all happen and didn't say anything. Somehow I had terrific respect for this guy.

Christiane was forced to learn at an early age that love and acceptance can be bought only by denying one's own needs, impulses, and feelings (such as hate, disgust, and aversion)—at the high price of surrender of self. She now directs all her efforts toward attaining this loss of self, i.e., to *being cool*. That is why the word *cool* occurs on nearly every page of the book. In order to reach this state and be free of unwanted feelings, she starts using hashish.

> The guys in our crowd weren't like the alchies, who were aggressive and tense even when they were at the club. Our guys could turn off completely. After work they changed into wild clothes, smoked dope, listened to cool music, and it was all perfectly peaceful. Then we forgot all the shit we had to put up with out there the rest of the day.
>
> I still didn't feel quite like the others. For that, I thought, I was still too young. But the others were my models. I wanted to be—or to become—as much like them as possible. I wanted to learn from them because I thought they knew how to be cool and not let all the assholes and all the shit get to you.

> I always had to find some way to get high. I was invariably totally spaced out. That's the way I wanted it, so I wouldn't have to face all the crap at school and at home.

> I wanted to look mysterious. I didn't want anyone to see through me. No one was supposed to notice that I wasn't at all the cool chick I wanted to be.

Problems didn't exist when the group was together. We never talked about our problems. We never bothered anyone else with our shit at home or at work. When we were together, the lousy world of the others didn't exist for us at all.

With great effort, Christiane is consciously developing and perfecting her false self, as illustrated by these sentences:

I thought the guys [at the Disco] must be incredibly cool. . . . Somehow [Micha] was even cooler than the guys in our crowd.

There wasn't any contact at all among the people.

It was a really cool group.

I met a guy on the stairs . . . he was unbelievably relaxed. . . .

Yet the ideal of being completely relaxed is least likely to be attained by someone in puberty. This is the very period when a person experiences feelings most intensely, and the use of a pill to aid the struggle against these feelings verges on *psychic murder*. In order to preserve something of her vitality and her capacity to feel, Christiane has to take another drug, not a tranquilizer this time, but just the opposite, one that arouses her, peps her up, and restores the feeling of being alive. The main thing, however, is that she can regulate, control, and manipulate everything herself. Just as her father previously succeeded in bringing the child's feelings under control, in keeping with his needs, by beating her, the thirteen-year-old girl now attempts to manipulate her mood by taking drugs:

At "The Sound" disco scene there was every kind of drug. I took everything except H[eroin]. Valium, Mandrax, Ephedrine, Cappis—that's Captagon—of course lots of shit and a trip at least twice a week. We took uppers and downers by the handful. The different pills tore your body apart, and that gave you a crazy feeling. You could give yourself whatever mood you felt like having. When I felt like dancing my head off at "The Sound," I swallowed more Cappis and Ephedrine; when I just wanted to sit quietly in a corner or in the Sound Cinema, I took a lot of Valium and Mandrax. Then I was happy again for a few weeks.

How does it continue?

> In the days that followed, I tried to deaden any feeling I had
> for others. I didn't take any pills or do a single trip. I drank tea
> with hashish in it all day and rolled one joint after another.
> After a few days I went back to being real cool again. I had
> gotten to the point where, except for myself, I didn't love or
> like anyone or anything. I thought, Now I have my feelings
> under control.

> I became very placid. That was because I was always taking
> downers, and uppers only once in a while. I wasn't wired any-
> more. I hardly ever went out on the dance floor anymore. I
> really only danced like crazy when I couldn't dig up any Valium.
> At home, I must have been a pleasure to have around for my
> mother and her boyfriend. I didn't talk back and I didn't fight
> with them anymore. I didn't complain about anything anymore
> either because I had given up trying to change things at home.
> And I realized that this made the situation easier. . . .
> I kept taking more pills.
> One Saturday when I had some money and the scene had
> all kinds of pills to offer, I OD'd. For some reason I was very
> low, so I washed down two Captagons, three Ephedrines and
> then a few caffies, that's caffeine pills, with a beer. Then, when
> I got totally high, I didn't like that either. So I took some Man-
> drax and a whole bunch of Valium.

Christiane goes to a David Bowie concert, but she doesn't
allow herself to get excited about it, and before going she has
to take a large amount of Valium, "not to turn on but to stay
cool at the David Bowie concert."

> When David Bowie began to sing, it was almost as fantastic as I
> had expected. It was terrific. But when he got to the song "It's
> Too Late," I came down with a thud. All of a sudden I was really
> out of it. Over the past few weeks, when I didn't know what
> life was all about anymore, "It's Too Late" had been getting to
> me. I thought the song described my situation exactly. Now "It's
> Too Late" really killed me. I sure could have used some Valium.

When the drugs Christiane has been using no longer give
her the desired control over her emotions, she switches to

heroin at the age of thirteen, and at first everything goes as
she had hoped.

> I was feeling too good to think about it. There aren't any with-
> drawal symptoms when you're just beginning. With me, the cool
> feeling lasted all week. Everything was going great. At home
> there were no more fights at all. I was completely relaxed about
> school, studied sometimes, and got good grades. In the weeks
> that followed, I raised my grades in a lot of subjects from D to
> B. I suddenly had the feeling that I could handle everybody and
> everything. I was floating through life in a really cool way.

Children who were unable to learn to recognize their
authentic feelings and to be comfortable with them will have
a particularly difficult time in puberty.

> I was always carrying my problems around with me but didn't
> really know what problems they were. I snorted H and the prob-
> lems were gone. But it had been a long time since one snort
> lasted for a whole week.

> I didn't have any connection with reality anymore. Reality was
> unreal for me. I didn't care about yesterday or tomorrow. I had
> no plans, all I had were dreams. What I liked best was to talk
> with Detlef about how it would be if we had a lot of money. We
> would buy a big house and a big car and some really cool fur-
> niture. The one thing that never appeared in these pipe dreams
> was heroin.

The first time she goes cold turkey, that ability she had
coveted to manipulate her feelings and be free of them collapses. We witness complete regression to the infantile stage:

> Now I was dependent on H and on Detlef. It upset me more to
> be dependent on Detlef. What kind of love is that if you are
> totally dependent? What if Detlef made me ask and beg for
> dope? I knew how junkies begged when they went cold turkey.
> How they demeaned themselves and allowed themselves to be
> humiliated. How they went to pieces. I didn't want to have to
> ask for it. Especially not Detlef. If he was going to make me
> beg, then it was all over between us. I had never been able to
> ask anyone for anything.

I remembered the way I had demolished junkies when they went cold turkey. I had never really figured out what was the matter with them. I only noticed that they were terribly sensitive, easily hurt, and completely powerless. A junkie gone cold turkey hardly dares to talk back, he's such a nothing. Sometimes I had made them the brunt of my power trips. If you really went about it the right way, you could tear them to pieces, scare the hell out of them. You just had to keep hammering away at their weakness, keep rubbing salt into their wounds, and they fell apart. When they were cold turkey, they were able to see what miserable meatheads they were. Then their whole cool junkie act was all over; then they didn't feel superior to everything and everyone anymore.

I said to myself, Now they'll demolish you when you go cold turkey. They'll find out how lousy you really are.

There is no one Christiane can talk to about her panic at the thought of going cold turkey. Her mother "would simply flip out if you tell her that." "I couldn't do that to her," Christiane says, and she perpetuates the tragic loneliness of her childhood in order to spare the adult, in this case her mother.

She doesn't think of her father again until the first time she goes out to "hustle" and tries to keep this a secret.

Me hustle? Before I do anything like that I'd stop shooting up. Honestly. No, my father finally remembered he has a daughter and gave me some pocket money.

Whereas hashish had still offered her hope of being free and "coolly" independent, it soon becomes clear that in the case of heroin she has to contend with total dependence. The "stuff," the hard drug, eventually takes over the function of the unpredictable, hot-tempered father of her childhood, who had her completely at his mercy just the way heroin does now. And just as her true self had to remain hidden from her parents in those days, now too her real life is lived secretly, underground, kept secret from her school and from her mother.

From week to week we all got more aggressive. The dope and all the excitement, the daily struggle for money and H, the eternal hassle at home, the concealment, and the lies we told to deceive our parents all wore us to a frazzle. We couldn't keep the aggressiveness that was building up under control anymore, not even among ourselves.

When Christiane describes her first meeting with Max the Stutterer, the return of the father in the psychological dynamics of the situation may not be obvious to Christiane, but it is to the outsider. Her simple and forthright report gives the reader a better understanding of the tragic nature of a perversion than do many theoretical psychoanalytical treatises.

I had heard the sad story of Max the Stutterer from Detlef. Max was an unskilled laborer in his late thirties and came from Hamburg. His mother was a prostitute. He had been beaten terribly as a child. By his mother and her pimps and in the homes where he had been put. They beat him to such a pulp that he was so scared he never learned to talk right, and he had to be beaten even now to get off sexually.

The first time I went to his place I asked for the money in advance, although he was a regular customer and you didn't need to be careful with him. He actually gave me 150 marks, and I was kind of proud that I was cool enough to take so much money from him.

I took off my T-shirt, and he handed me a whip. It was just like in the movies. It wasn't really me. At first I didn't hit him hard. But he whimpered that he wanted me to hurt him. Then at some point I really let him have it. He cried out, "Mommy," and I don't know what-all. I didn't listen, and I tried not to look. But then I saw how the welts on his body kept swelling, and then the skin actually burst in some places. It was simply disgusting, and it lasted nearly an hour.

When he was finally finished, I put my T-shirt back on and ran. I ran out the door, down the stairs, and barely made it. In front of the building I lost control of my goddamn stomach and had to throw up. After I vomited, that was it. I didn't cry, and I didn't feel the least bit sorry for myself either. Somehow I realized that I had brought this situation on myself, that I sure had screwed up. I went to the station. Detlef was there. I didn't tell him much. Just that I had done the job with Max alone.

Max the Stutterer was now a regular customer for both Detlef and me. Sometimes we both went to his place, sometimes just one of us. Max was really O.K. And he loved us both. Of course, with what he earned as a laborer he couldn't keep on paying 150 marks. But he always managed somehow to scrape together 40 marks, the cost of a fix. Once he even broke open his piggy bank and took some change from a bowl, then counted out exactly 40 marks. When I needed money in a hurry, I could always stop by his place and collect 20 marks. I'd tell him I would be back the next day at such and such a time and do it for him then for a twenty. If he still had twenty, he'd agree to it.

Max was always waiting for us. He always had peach juice, my favorite drink, for me. Detlef's favorite pudding was always in the refrigerator for him. Max made the pudding himself. In addition, he always offered me a choice of yogurt flavors and chocolate because he knew I liked to eat after the job. The whippings I gave him had become strictly routine for me, and afterwards I ate and drank and rapped with Max for a while.

He kept getting thinner. He was really spending his last cent on us and didn't have enough to buy food for himself. He had gotten so used to us and was so happy that he hardly stuttered anymore when he was with us.

Soon after that, he lost his job. He was completely down and out, even without ever having been on dope. Junkies had demolished him. Meaning us. He begged us to at least stop by once in a while. But friendly visits aren't part of the deal where junkies are concerned. Partly because they are incapable of that much feeling for someone else. But then mainly because they are on the go all day to hustle money for dope and honestly don't have time for anything like that. Detlef explained this to Max when Max promised to give us a lot of money as soon as he got some. "A junkie is like a businessman. Every day you have to see to it that you make ends meet. You just can't give credit out of friendship or sympathy."

Christiane and her boyfriend Detlef are behaving here like working parents who profit from their child's (in this case, their customer's) love and dependence and ultimately destroy him. Max the Stutterer's touching selection of yogurt flavors for Christiane, on the other hand, was probably a reenactment of his "happy childhood." It is easy to imagine that his mother was still concerned about what he ate even after she had given him a beating. As for Christiane, without her previous history with her father she might never have been able to "cope" with her first encounter with Max as well as she did. Now she had her father in her, and she whipped her customer not only because he told her to but also as an expression of all the pent-up misery of a battered child. In addition, this identification with the aggressor helps her to split off her weakness, to feel strong at someone else's expense, and to survive, whereas Christiane the human being, the alert, sensitive, intelligent, vital, but still dependent child, is being increasingly suffocated.

> When [Detlef or I] went cold turkey, then one of us could demolish the other to the point of not being able to go on anymore. It didn't really make things any better to know that at some point we would be lying in each other's arms again like two children. Not only for us girls but also for Detlef and me, it had gotten so you saw in the other person what a shit you were yourself. You hated your own rottenness and attacked this rottenness in the other person and tried to convince yourself that you weren't quite as rotten.
>
> This aggressiveness naturally took itself out on strangers too.

> Before I was on H, I used to be afraid of everything. Of my father, later of my mother's boyfriend, of the fucking school and my teachers, of building superintendents, traffic cops, and subway conductors. Now I felt as though nothing could touch me. I wasn't even scared of the plainclothes cops who sometimes were hanging around the station. So far, I had gotten away, cool as a cucumber, from every bust.

Her inner emptiness and numbed feelings eventually make life meaningless for her and awaken thoughts of death.

> Junkies die all alone. Usually in a stinking john. And I honestly wanted to die. That's really all I was waiting for. I didn't know why I was alive. I never quite knew that before either. But what the hell does a junkie have to live for? Just to ruin others after ruining yourself? That particular afternoon I thought I ought

to die if only for my mother's sake. I didn't know anymore anyway whether I was alive or not.

But the silly fear of dying was getting me down. I wanted to die, but before every fix I had this silly fear of dying. Maybe my cat [who was deathly ill] made me realize what a lousy thing dying really is if you haven't even had any kind of a life yet.

It was a great stroke of luck for Christiane that two journalists from *Der Stern*, Kai Hermann and Horst Rieck, got her to talk to them over an extended period of two months. It may be of great significance for her future that in the crucial stage of puberty this girl, after her horrifying experiences, had the good fortune to emerge from her boundless psychological isolation and find sympathetic, understanding, concerned people who listened to her and gave her the opportunity to express herself and tell her story.

The Hidden Logic of Absurd Behavior

CHRISTIANE'S story awakens such feelings of despair and helplessness in sympathetic readers that they probably would like most of all to forget about it as quickly as possible by passing it all off as a fabrication. But they are unable to, because they sense that she has told the unvarnished truth. If they go beyond the outer trappings of the story and permit themselves, as they read, to consider *why* it happened, they will find an accurate description of the nature not only of addiction but of other forms of human behavior as well that are conspicuous at times for their absurdity and that our logic is unable to explain. When we are confronted with adolescent heroin addicts who are ruining their lives, we are all too readily inclined to try to reach them with rational arguments or, still worse, with efforts to "educate" them. In fact, many therapeutic groups work in this direction. They substitute one evil for another instead of trying to help these young people see what function addiction actually has in their lives and how they are unconsciously using it to communicate something to the outside world. The following example illustrates this.

On a German television program shown on March 23, 1980, a former heroin addict, who has been off the drug for five years, talks about his present life. His depressive, almost suicidal frame of mind is apparent. He is around twenty-four, has a girl friend, and says that he is going to turn the attic of his parents' house into a private apartment for himself, which he wants to do over with all kinds of bourgeois fixings. His parents, who never understood him and who regarded his addiction as a kind of physical and fatal disease, are ailing now, and it is at their insistence that he is going to live in their house. This man is intensely preoccupied with the value of all sorts of little objects that he is now able to own and for which he must sacrifice his autonomy. From now on, he will live in a gilded cage, and it is very understandable that he keeps talking about the danger of returning to his heroin addiction. If this man had had therapy that enabled him to experience his bottled-up infantile rage at his restrictive, coldhearted, and authoritarian parents, he would have sensed what his actual needs were, would not have let himself be confined in a cage, and would probably have become a more genuine and sincere source of help to his parents. A person can offer this help freely to his parents if he does not make himself dependent on them like a child. But if he does, he is likely to punish them with his addiction or by committing suicide. Either of these enactments will tell the true story of his childhood, which he has had to keep to himself (and from himself) all his life.

In spite of its enormous resources, classical psychiatry is essentially powerless to help as long as it attempts to replace the harmful effects of early childhood training with new kinds of training. The whole penal setup in psychiatric wards, the ingenious methods of humiliating patients, have the ultimate goal—as does the disciplining of children—of silencing the patient's coded language. This is made very clear in the case of anorexia. What is someone with anorexia, who comes from an affluent family and has been spoiled with an abundance of material possessions and intellectual opportunities and who is now proud that her weight does not exceed sixty-five pounds, actually saying about herself? Her parents insist that they have a harmonious marriage, and they are horrified at their daughter's conscious and exaggerated efforts to go without food, especially since they have never had any trouble with this child, who always met their expectations. I would say that this young girl, under the onslaught of the feelings of puberty, is no longer able to function like an automaton, but in view of her background, she has no chance to express the feelings that are now erupting in her. By the manner in which she is enslaving herself, disciplining and restricting herself, even destroying herself, she is telling us what happened to her in early childhood. This is not to say that her parents were bad people; they only wanted to raise their child to be what she did indeed become: a well-functioning, high-achieving, widely admired girl. Often it wasn't even the parents themselves but governesses who were responsible for raising her. In any case, anorexia nervosa exhibits all the components of a strict upbringing: the ruthless, dictatorial methods, the excessive supervision and control, the lack of understanding and empathy for the child's true needs. To this is added overwhelming affection alternating with rejection and abandonment (orgies of gluttony followed by vomiting). The first law of this police system is: any method is good if it makes you the way we want and need you to be, and only if you are this way can we love you. This is later reflected in anorexia's reign of terror. Weight is monitored to the ounce, and the sinner is immediately punished if the boundary is overstepped.

Even the best of psychotherapists have to try to convince these patients, whose lives are in danger, to gain weight; otherwise, a dialogue cannot take place. But it makes a difference whether the therapist explains to the patient that she must gain weight, at the same time making it the aim of her therapy to reach an understanding of her self, or whether weight gain is regarded as the sole therapeutic goal. In the latter case the doctor merely assumes the methods of compulsion used in the patient's early training and will have to be prepared for a reversal or a new set of symptoms. If neither of these eventualities should occur, this simply means that the second training period has been a success, and once puberty is over, a permanent lack of vital energy is assumed.

All absurd behavior has its roots in early childhood, but the cause will not be detected as long as the adult's manipulation of the child's psychic and physical needs is interpreted as an essential technique of child-rearing instead of as the cruelty it really is. Since most professionals themselves are not yet free from this mistaken belief, sometimes what is called therapy is only a continuation of early, unintended cruelty. It is not unheard of for a mother to give her year-old baby Valium so he will sleep soundly if she wants to go out in the evening. This may be necessary on occasion. But if Valium becomes the means of insuring the child's sleep, a natural balance will be disturbed, and the autonomous nervous system will be undermined at a very early age. We can imagine that when the parents return home late at night they may want to play with the baby a while and may awaken it, since they no longer need to worry about him waking up alone. The Valium not only undermines the child's natural ability to fall asleep but also interferes with the development of his perceptive faculties. At this early age the child is not supposed to know that he has been left alone, is not supposed to be afraid, and perhaps later the adult will be unable to perceive inner danger signals as a result.

To prevent absurd, self-destructive behavior from developing in adulthood, parents do not need extensive psychological training. They need only refrain from manipulating their child for their own needs, from abusing him by undermining his vegetative balance, and then the child will find the best defense against inappropriate demands in his own body. He will be familiar from the beginning with the language of his body and with his body signals. If parents are also able to give their child the same respect and tolerance they had for their own parents, they will surely be providing him with the best possible foundation for his entire later life. His self-esteem as well as the freedom to develop his innate abilities depend on this respect. As I have said, we do not need books about psychology in order to learn to respect our children; what we need is a revision of the theories of child-rearing.

The way we were treated as small children is the way we treat ourselves the rest of our life. And we often impose our most agonizing suffering upon ourselves. We can never escape the tormentor within ourselves, who is often disguised as a pedagogue, someone who takes full control in illness; for example, in anorexia. Cruel enslavement of the body and exploitation of the will are the result. Drug addiction begins with an attempt to escape parental control and to refuse to perform, but the repetition compulsion ultimately leads the addict to a constant concern with having to come up with large sums of money to provide the necessary "stuff"; in other words, to a quite "bourgeois" form of enslavement.

When I read about Christiane's problems with the police and with drug dealers, I suddenly saw before me the Berlin of 1945: the many illegal ways of coming by food, fear of the occupation forces, the black market—the "dealers" of that day. Whether this is a strictly private association for me, I do not know. For many parents of today's junkies, this was the only world that existed for them as children. It is not inconceivable, seen against the background of the inner emptiness resulting from the repression of feelings, that the drug scene in Germany also has something to do with the black market of the forties. This idea, unlike much of the material in this book, is not based on verifiable scientific evidence but on intuition, on a subjective association that I have not pursued further. I mention it, however, because many psychological studies are being conducted that show the long-term effects of the war and the Nazi regime as they relate to the second generation. Time after time, the amazing fact is uncovered that sons and daughters are unconsciously reenacting their parents' fate— all the more intensely the less precise their knowledge of it. From the few bits and pieces they have picked up from their parents about early traumatization caused by the war, they come up with fantasies based on their own reality, which they then often act out in groups during puberty. For example, Judith Kestenberg tells about adolescents in the sixties who rejected their peacetime affluence and disappeared into the woods. It was later revealed in therapy that their parents had survived the war as partisans in Eastern Europe but had never spoken openly about it with their children. (Cf. *Psyche* 28, pp. 249–65, and Helen Epstein, *Children of the Holocaust* [New York, 1979].)

I was once consulted by a seventeen-year-old anorexic patient who was very proud of the fact that she now weighed the same as her mother had thirty years before when she was rescued from Auschwitz. During our conversation, she revealed that this detail, her mother's exact weight, was the only thing she knew about that period of her mother's past, for the mother refused to talk about it and asked her family not to question her. Children are made anxious by secretiveness, by their parents hushing things up, by whatever touches upon their parents' feelings of shame, guilt, or fear. An important way of dealing with these threats is by fantasizing and playing games. Using the parents' props gives the adolescent a feeling of being able to participate in their past.

Could it be that the ruined lives described by Christiane go back to the ruins of 1945? If the answer is yes, how did this repetition come about? We can assume that its roots lie in the psychic reality of parents who grew up during a period of extreme material deprivation and who therefore made it their first priority to have enough to live comfortably. By continually adding to their material well-being, they warded off their fear of ever again having to sit among the ruins like hungry, helpless children. But no amount of affluence can banish this fear; as long as it remains unconscious, it leads an existence of its own. And now their children leave their affluent homes where they do not feel understood, because feelings and fears are supposed to have no place there; they enter the drug scene and either become active as dealers, like their fathers in the larger economic world, or sit apathetically on the sidelines.

By so doing, they then resemble their parents, who once actually were helpless, vulnerable little children sitting among the ruins but who were later not permitted to talk about their experiences. These children of the ruins had been banished forever from the parents' luxurious homes, and now they reappear like specters in their unkempt sons and daughters with their shabby clothes, their apathetic faces, their hopelessness and alienation, their hatred for all the luxury accumulated around them.

It is not hard to understand that parents are impatient with these adolescents, for people would rather submit to the strictest laws, go to all kinds of trouble, achieve spectacular feats, and choose the most demanding careers than be expected to bring love and understanding to the helpless unhappy child they once were, whom they have subsequently banished forever. When this child suddenly reappears on the lovely parquet floor of their lavish living room in the guise of their own son or daughter, it is not surprising that the child cannot count on finding understanding. What he or she will find is resentment, indignation, warnings or prohibitions, perhaps even hatred—above all, a whole arsenal of child-rearing weapons with which the parents try to ward off every unhappy childhood memory from the war years that tries to come to the surface.

There are also instances in which our children can cause us to confront our unmastered past, with beneficial results for the entire family.

Brigitte, born in 1936, highly sensitive, married, and the mother of two children, went into analysis for the second time because of her depressions. Her fears of impending catastrophe were clearly connected with the air raids she lived through in her childhood. In spite of the analyst's efforts, her fears were not dispelled until the patient, with her child's help, was led to acknowledge an open wound, which had not been able to heal in all this time because it had not been noticed until now and therefore had never been treated.

When her son reached the age of ten, the same age the

patient was when her father returned from the Eastern Front, he and some of his friends at school started drawing swastikas and playing games inspired by the Hitler period. It was clear from the way these activities were kept secret on the one hand and invited discovery on the other that the child, whose distress was apparent, was calling for help. Nevertheless, his mother found it difficult to respond to his distress and try to understand it by having a heart-to-heart talk with the boy. She regarded these games as sinister and didn't want to have to deal with the subject; as a former member of an anti-Fascist student group, she felt hurt by her son's behavior and reacted, against her will, in an authoritarian and hostile way. The conscious, ideological reasons for her attitude were not sufficient to explain the intense feelings of rejection she felt toward her son. Deep inside, something was coming to the fore that until now—even in her first analysis—had been completely inaccessible. As a result of the ability to feel that had emerged in her second analysis, she was able to approach her earlier experiences on an emotional level.

In her present situation, the more intolerant and horrified she became and the more pains she took to "put a stop to" her son's games, the more frequently and intensely he played them. The boy gradually lost trust in his parents and became more attached to his group of friends, which led to despairing outbursts on the mother's part. Finally, with the help of transference, the roots of her rage were uncovered, and the whole family situation then changed for the better. It began with the patient suddenly falling prey to tormenting questions she felt impelled to address to her analyst about himself and his past. She desperately tried to keep herself from asking these questions out of a feeling of panic that she would lose him if she uttered them. Or perhaps she feared being given answers that would make her despise him.

The analyst patiently allowed her to formulate her questions, whose significance he respected, but he did not answer them; since he sensed that they were not actually directed at him, he did not have to ward them off with hasty interpretations. And then the ten-year-old girl—who had not been al-

lowed to ask any questions of her father, just back from the war
—clearly emerged. The patient said she had not given this any
thought at the time. And yet it would be only natural for a
ten-year-old who had waited for years for her father's return
to ask: "Where were you? What did you do? What did you see?
Tell me a story! A true one." Nothing of the sort happened,
Brigitte said; it was taboo in the family to speak of "these
things" with the children, and they realized that they were
not supposed to know anything about that portion of their
father's past. Brigitte's curiosity, which was consciously suppressed at the time but which had already been stifled at an
earlier stage, thanks to her so-called good upbringing, now
entered into her relationship with her analyst in all its
vitality and urgency. It had been frozen over, to be sure, but
not frozen solid. And now that it was allowed to come fully to
life, her depressions disappeared. For the first time in thirty
years, she could talk to her father about his war experiences,
which was a great relief for him, too. For now the situation
was different: she was strong enough to hear what he had to
say without having to lose her autonomy in the process; she
was no longer the dependent little child. When she was a girl,
these conversations would not have been possible. Brigitte
understood that her childhood fear of losing her father by
asking questions had not been unfounded, for at that time
her father could not have brought himself to talk about his
experiences in the East. He had constantly tried to rid himself
of every memory of that time. His daughter adapted herself
completely to his need to forget and managed to keep herself
very poorly informed about the history of the Third Reich; the
little she did know was of a purely intellectual nature. It was
her view that one must judge that period "unemotionally" and
objectively, like a computer that counts the dead on both
sides without evoking any images or feelings of horror.

Brigitte was definitely not a computer but a very sensitive
person with an intelligent mind. And because she tried to suppress her thoughts and feelings she suffered from depressions,
feelings of inner emptiness (she often felt as though she were
"in front of a black wall"), insomnia, and dependence on

medication meant to inhibit her natural vitality. The intelligent young girl's curiosity and need to know, which had been diverted to strictly intellectual problems, first became visible almost literally in the form of "the devil on her son's doorstep," whom she tried to chase away from him as well—and only because in her repetition compulsion she wanted to spare her introjected, emotionally insecure father. Every child's ideas of what is evil are formed according to the parents' defense mechanisms: "evil" can be anything that makes the parents more insecure. This situation can give rise to guilt feelings that will resist all later attempts to dispel them unless their history has been experienced on a conscious level. Brigitte was fortunate in that this "devil" in her, i.e., the vital, alert, interested, and critical child, was stronger than her effort to adapt, and she was able to integrate this quintessential part of her personality.

During this period, swastikas lost their fascination for her son, and it became clear that they had served more than one function. On the one hand, they had been an "acting out" of Brigitte's repressed desire to know, and on the other hand they had caused her disappointment with her father to be redirected to her child. Once she had the possibility of experiencing all these feelings with her analyst, she no longer needed the child for this purpose.

Brigitte told me her story after hearing a talk I gave. At my request, she gladly gave permission for it to be included here, because she has the need, as she put it, to communicate her experiences to others "and not to remain silent any longer."

We were both convinced that her predicament reflected the situation of an entire generation that had been raised to keep silent and that consciously or (more frequently) unconsciously suffered from this. Psychoanalysts in Germany devoted little attention to this problem prior to the Conference of German-Speaking Psychoanalytic Societies in Bamberg (1980). As a result, until now only a few people here and there have had the good fortune to liberate themselves emotionally as well as intellectually from the taboo of silence.

(Cf., for example, *Männerphantasien* [*Male Fantasies*] by Klaus Theweleit.)

This same second generation reacted strongly to the television film *Holocaust* when it was aired in Germany. It was like breaking out of prison for them: the prison of silence, of not being able to ask questions, of not being able to feel, of the mad idea that such horror could be "dealt with unemotionally." Would it be desirable to raise our children to be people who could hear about the gassing of a million children without ever giving way to feelings of outrage and pain? Of what use are historians to us if they are able to write books about it in which their only concern is to be historically and objectively accurate? What good is this ability to be coldly objective in the face of horror? Wouldn't our children then be in danger of submitting to every new Fascist regime that came along? They would have nothing to lose except their inner emptiness. Indeed, such a regime would give them the opportunity to find a new outlet for their unlived feelings that are now split in scientific objectivity; as members of a grandiose group, they would finally be able to discharge these feelings that are of an unbridled, archaic nature as a result of having been locked up.

The collective form of absurd behavior is no doubt the most dangerous because the absurdity is no longer apparent and because it is sanctioned as "normal." It was taken for granted by most postwar children in Germany that it was improper or at least uncalled for to ask their parents specific questions about the Third Reich; often it was even explicitly forbidden. Keeping silent about this period, which represented their parents' past, was just as much a part of the "good manners" expected of children as was the denial of sexuality around the turn of the century.

Even though it would not be difficult to demonstrate the impact of this new taboo on the development of current forms of neurosis, traditional theories are reluctant to acknowledge the empirical evidence because not only patients but analysts, too, are victims of the same taboo. It is easier for analysts to pursue with their patients the sexual compulsions and prohibitions uncovered by Freud long ago that are often no longer ours than to uncover the repressions of our own time, which also means of *their own* childhood. But the history of the Third Reich teaches us, among other things, that what is monstrous is not infrequently contained in what is "normal," in what is felt by the great majority to be "quite normal and natural."

Germans who experienced the victories of the Third Reich as children or during puberty and then later in life became concerned with the issue of their integrity necessarily ran into difficulties in this regard. As adults they learned the terrible truth about National Socialism and integrated this knowledge intellectually. And yet there still live on in these people— often untouched by all their later knowledge—the voices connected with the songs, the speeches, and the jubilant mass rallies that were heard at a very early age and were accompanied by the intense feelings of childhood. In most cases pride, enthusiasm, and joyful hope are linked in their minds with these impressions.

How is a person to bring these two worlds—the emotional experience of childhood and the later knowledge that contradicted it—into harmony without denying an important part of the self? To numb one's feelings, as Brigitte attempted to do, and to deny one's roots, often seem to be the only ways to avoid this conflict and the tragic ambivalence inherent in it.

I know of no work of art that expresses the ambivalence of a major portion of this generation in Germany more clearly than Hans-Jürgen Syberberg's seven-hour film *Hitler, a Film from Germany*. It was Syberberg's intention to present his own subjective truth, and because he surrendered to his feelings, fantasies, and dreams, he created a contemporary portrayal in which many people will find themselves reflected, for it unites both perspectives, that of the person who sees and that of the one who is misguided.

The sensitive child's fascination with the Wagnerian music, with the pomp of the parades, with the Führer's emotionally charged, incomprehensible shouting on the radio; the idea of Hitler as a powerful and at the same time insignificant and harmless puppet—all this is in the film. But it takes its place alongside the horror and, above all, alongside a genuine adult pain that has been barely perceptible in previous films on this subject because such pain presupposes liberation from the constricting pedagogical pattern of blame and exoneration. In several scenes in the film this pain of Syberberg's is palpable: he realizes the tragedy of both the victims of the persecution and the victims of the seduction that he himself succumbed to as a child. Last but not least, his film, in my view, demonstrates the absurdity of *all* ideologies, those continuations of pedagogical principles applied in early childhood.

Only someone who has come to terms with having been led astray without denying it will be able to depict this with the intensity of grief that Syberberg does. The experience of grief is an essential part of the film and conveys more to the audience on an emotional level—at least in several powerful scenes—about the emptiness of National Socialist ideology than many well-documented, objective books on the topic have succeeded in doing. Syberberg's film represents one of the few attempts that have been made to live with an incomprehensible past instead of denying its reality.

Adolf Hitler's Childhood: From Hidden to Manifest Horror

My pedagogy is hard. What is weak must be hammered away. In my fortresses of the Teutonic Order a young generation will grow up before which the world will tremble. I want the young to be violent, domineering, undismayed, cruel. The young must be all these things. They must be able to bear pain. There must be nothing weak or gentle about them. The free, splendid beast of prey must once again flash from their eyes. I want my young people strong and beautiful. That way I can create something new.   ADOLF HITLER

Introduction

MY desire to learn more about Adolf Hitler's childhood did not emerge until I began to write this book, and it took me quite by surprise. The immediate occasion was the realization that my belief, based upon my experience as an analyst, that human destructiveness is a reactive (and not an innate) phenomenon either would be confirmed by the case of Adolf Hitler or—if Erich Fromm and others are right—would have to be completely revised. This question was important enough for me to try to answer, although I was very skeptical at first that I would be able to summon up empathy for this human being, whom I consider the worst criminal I have ever known of. Empathy, i.e., in this case the attempt to identify with the perspective of the child himself and not to judge him through adult eyes, is my sole heuristic tool, and without it, the whole investigation would be pointless. I was relieved to discover that for the purposes of my study I was successful in keeping this tool intact and was able to regard Hitler as a human being.

To do this, I had to free myself from thinking of "what is human" in traditional and idealizing terms based on splitting off and projecting evil; I had to realize that human being and "beast" do not exclude each other (cf. the Erich Fromm quotation on page 177). Animals do not suffer from the tragic compulsion of having to avenge, decades later, traumata experienced at an early age—as was the case, for example, with Frederick the Great, who was driven to become a great conqueror after the terrible humiliation he suffered as a child. In any event, I am not familiar enough with an animal's unconscious or its degree of awareness of its past to make any statements on the subject. So far, it is only in the *human* realm that I have discovered extreme bestiality; only there can I trace it and search for its motives. And I cannot renounce this search unless I am willing to be made into an instrument of cruelty, i.e., its unsuspecting (and thus guiltless yet blind) perpetrator and propagator.

If we turn our backs on something because it is difficult to understand and indignantly refer to it as "inhuman," we will never be able to learn anything about its nature. The risk will then be greater, when we next encounter it, of once again aiding and abetting it by our innocence and naïveté.

Over the past thirty-five years, countless works dealing with the life of Adolf Hitler have appeared. No doubt, I heard more than once that Hitler was beaten by his father, and even read it several years ago in a monograph by Helm Stierlin without being particularly struck by the fact. Since I have become sensitive, however, to the demeaning treatment children are sometimes subjected to in the first years of life, this information has taken on much greater importance for me. I asked myself what the childhood of this person had been like, a person who was possessed by hatred all his life and for whom it became so easy to involve other people in his hatred. As a result of reading *Schwarze Pädagogik* and of the feelings it awakened in me, I was suddenly able to imagine and feel what it must have been like for a child growing up in the Hitler household. What had previously been a black-and-white film was now in color, and it gradually merged to such an extent with my own experiences of World War II that it ceased being a film and turned into real life. This was not only a life that had been lived at a certain time and place in the past but one whose consequences and whose likelihood of being repeated I believe concern us all here and now as well. For the hope that by means of rational agreements it might be possible in the long run to prevent nuclear annihilation of the human race is at bottom a form of irrational wishful thinking and contradicts all our experience. As recently as the Third Reich, not to mention countless times before that, we have seen that reason constitutes only a small part of the human being, and not the dominant part, at that. All it took was a Führer's madness and several million well-raised Germans to extinguish the lives of countless innocent human beings in the space of a few short years. If we do not do everything we can to understand the roots of this hatred, even the most elaborate strategic agreements will not save us. The stockpiling of nuclear weapons is only a symbol of bottled-up feelings of hatred and of the accompanying inability to perceive and articulate genuine human needs.

The example of Hitler's childhood allows us to study the genesis of a hatred whose consequences caused the suffering of millions. The nature of this destructive hatred has long been familiar to psychoanalysts, but psychoanalysis will be of little help as long as it interprets this hatred as an expression of the death instinct. The followers of Melanie Klein, who in spite of their very accurate description of infantile hatred still define it as innate (instinctual) and not reactive, are no exception. Heinz Kohut comes closest to interpreting the phenomenon with his concept of narcissistic rage, which I have related to the infant's reaction to the lack of availability of the primary care giver.

But we must go one step further if we are to understand the origins of a lifelong insatiable hatred such as consumed Adolf Hitler. We must leave the familiar territory of drive theory and address the question of what takes place in a child who is humiliated and demeaned by his parents on the one hand and on the other is commanded to respect and love those who treat him in this fashion and under no circumstances to give expression to his suffering. Although something so absurd would scarcely be expected of an adult (except in pronouncedly sadomasochistic relationships), this is exactly what parents expect of their children in most cases, and in previous generations they were rarely disappointed. In the earliest stage of life, it is possible for a child to forget about the extreme acts of cruelty he or she has endured and to idealize their perpetrator. But the nature of the subsequent enactment reveals that the whole history of early persecution was stored up somewhere; the drama now unfolds in front of the spectators with an amazing resemblance to the original situation but under another guise: in the reenactment, the child who was once persecuted now becomes the persecutor. In pyschoanalytic treatment, the story is enacted within the framework of transference and countertransference.

If psychoanalysis could only free itself of its stubborn belief in the death instinct, it would be able to begin to answer the question of why wars occur, on the basis of material available on early childhood conditioning. Unfortunately, however, most psychoanalysts are not interested in what parents did to their children, leaving this question to family therapists. Since the latter in turn do not work with transference but concentrate primarily on modifying interactions among family members, they seldom gain the access to events of early childhood possible in a thoroughgoing analysis.

In order to show how the early debasement, mistreatment, and psychological rape of a child expresses itself throughout later life, I would need only to recount the history of a single analysis down to the last detail, but considerations of discretion make this impossible. Hitler's life, on the other hand, was observed and recorded so exactly by so many witnesses up to the very last day that this material can easily be used to demonstrate the enactment of the early childhood situation. In addition to the testimony of witnesses and the historical events in which his deeds are documented, his thoughts and feelings were expressed, albeit in coded form, in his many speeches and in his book *Mein Kampf*. It would be a highly instructive and rewarding task to make Hitler's entire political career comprehensible from the perspective of the history of his persecution in early childhood. But to pursue this task is far beyond the scope of this book, since my sole interest here is in showing examples of the effects of "poisonous pedagogy." For this reason I shall restrict myself to a few highlights in his biography; in so doing, I shall attribute particular significance to certain childhood experiences that until now have received little attention from his biographers. Because historians by profession concern themselves with external facts, and psychoanalysts with the Oedipus complex, few seem to have seriously raised the question: What did this child *feel*, what did he *store up* inside when he was beaten and demeaned by his father every day from an early age?

On the basis of available documents, we can easily gain an impression of the atmosphere in which Adolf Hitler grew up. The family structure could well be characterized as the prototype of a totalitarian regime. Its sole, undisputed, often brutal ruler is the father. The wife and children are totally subservient to his will, his moods, and his whims; they must accept humiliation and injustice unquestioningly and gratefully. Obedience is their primary rule of conduct. The mother, to be sure, has her own sphere of authority in the household, where she rules over the children when the father is not at home; this means that she can to some extent take out on those weaker than herself the humiliation she has suffered. In the totalitarian state, a similar function is assigned to the security police. They are the overseers of the slaves, although they are slaves themselves, carrying out the dictator's wishes, serving as his deputies in his absence, instilling fear in his name, meting out punishment, assuming the guise of the rulers of the oppressed.

Within this family structure, the children are the oppressed. If they have younger siblings, they are provided with a place to abreact their own humiliation. As long as there are even weaker, more helpless creatures than they, they are not the lowest of slaves. Sometimes, however, as was the case with Christiane F., the child is ranked below the dog, for the dog need not be beaten if a child is available.

This hierarchy, which can be observed in the way concentration camps were organized (with their ranking of guards, etc.) and which is legitimized by "poisonous pedagogy," is probably still maintained in many families today. The possible consequences for a sensitive child can be traced in detail in the case of Adolf Hitler.

Hitler's Father

HIS HISTORY AND HIS RELATIONSHIP
WITH HIS SON

IN his biography of Adolf Hitler, Joachim Fest has this to say about Alois Hitler's background and his life before Adolf was born:

> At House No. 13 in Strones, the home of Johann Trummelschlager, an unmarried servant girl by the name of Maria Anna Schicklgruber gave birth to a child on June 7, 1837. That same day the child was baptized Alois. In the registry of births in Döllersheim parish the space for the name of the child's father was left blank. Nor was this changed five years later when the mother married the unemployed journeyman miller Johann Georg Hiedler. That same year she turned her son over to her

husband's brother, Johann Nepomuk Hüttler, a farmer in Spital —presumably because she thought she could not raise the child properly. At any rate the Hiedlers, the story has it, were so impoverished that "ultimately they did not even have a bed left and slept in a cattle trough."

These two brothers are two of the presumptive fathers of Alois Schicklgruber. The third possibility, according to a rather wild story that nevertheless comes from one of Hitler's closer associates, is a Graz Jew named Frankenberger in whose household Maria Anna Schicklgruber is said to have been working when she became pregnant. Such, at any rate, is the testimony of Hans Frank, for many years Hitler's lawyer, later Governor General of Poland. In the course of his trial at Nuremberg, Frank reported that in 1930 Hitler had received a letter from a son of his half-brother Alois. Possibly the intention of the letter was blackmail. It indulged in dark hints about "very odd circumstances in our family history." Frank was assigned to look into the matter confidentially. He found some indications to support the idea that Frankenberger had been Hitler's grandfather. The lack of hard evidence, however, makes this thesis appear exceedingly dubious—for all that, we may also wonder what had prompted Frank at Nuremberg to ascribe a Jewish ancestor to Hitler. Recent researches have further shaken the credibility of his statement, so that the whole notion can scarcely bear close scrutiny. In any case, its real significance is independent of its being true or false. What is psychologically of crucial importance is the fact that Frank's findings forced Hitler to doubt his own descent. A renewed investigation undertaken in August 1942 by the Gestapo, on orders from Heinrich Himmler, produced no tangible results. All the other theories about Hitler's grandfather are also full of holes, although some ambitious combinational ingenuity has gone into the version that traces Alois Schicklgruber's paternity "with a degree of probability bordering on absolute certainty" to Johann Nepomuk Hüttler. Both arguments peter out in the obscurity of confused relationships marked by meanness, dullness, and rustic bigotry. The long and short of it is that Adolf Hitler did not know who his grandfather was.

Twenty-nine years after Maria Anna Schicklgruber's death from "consumption in consequence of thoracic dropsy" in Klein-Motten near Strones, and nineteen years after the death of her husband, the brother Johann Nepomuk Hüttler appeared before parish priest Zahnschirm in Döllersheim, accompanied by three acquaintances. He asked for the legitimation of his "foster son," the customs official Alois Schicklgruber, now nearly forty years of age. Not he himself but his deceased brother Johann Georg was the father, he said; Johann had avowed this, and his companions could witness the facts.

The parish priest allowed himself to be deceived or persuaded. In the old registry, under the entry of June 7, 1837, he altered the item "illegitimate" to "legitimate," filled in the space for the name of the father as requested, and inserted a false marginal note: "The undersigned confirm that Georg Hitler, registered as the father, who is well known to the undersigned witnesses, admits to being the father of the child Alois as stated by the child's mother, Anna Schicklgruber, and has requested the entry of his name in the present baptismal register. XXX Josef Romeder, witness; XXX Johann Breiteneder, witness; XXX Engelbert Paukh." Since the three witnesses could not write, they signed with three crosses, and the priest put in their names. But he neglected to insert the date. His own signature was also missing, as well as that of the (long-since-deceased) parents. Though scarcely legal, the legitimation took effect: from January 1877 on, Alois Schicklgruber called himself Alois Hitler.

This rustic intrigue was without a doubt set in motion by Johann Nepomuk Hüttler, for he had raised Alois and was understandably proud of him. Alois had just received another promotion, he had married, and had accomplished more than any Hüttler or Hiedler before him: it was only natural that Johann Nepomuk felt a desire to give his own name to his foster son. But Alois may also have had an interest in a change of name, for he was an enterprising man who in the interval had made quite a career for himself. He may therefore have felt the need to provide himself with security and a firm footing by obtaining an "honorable" name. At the age of thirteen he had been apprenticed to a shoemaker in Vienna. But, by and by, he decided against being an artisan and instead entered the Austrian Finance Office. He advanced rapidly as a customs official and was ultimately promoted to the highest civil service rank open to a man of his education. He was fond of appearing as the representative of constituted authority on public occasions and made a point of being addressed by his correct title. One of his associates in the customs office called him "strict, precise, even pedantic," and he himself told a relation who asked his advice about a son's choice of occupation that working for the treasury demanded absolute obedience and sense of duty, and that it was not for "drinkers, borrowers, card players, and other people who go in for immoral conduct." The photographs that he usually had made on the occasion of his promotions show a portly man with the wary face of an official. Underneath that official mask, bourgeois competence and bourgeois pleasure in public display can be discerned. He presents himself to the viewer with considerable dignity and complacency, his uniform aglitter with buttons. [*Hitler*]

It should be added that, after the birth of her son, Maria Schicklgruber received child support for fourteen years from the Jewish businessman referred to by Fest. Fest does not quote verbatim the account of Hans Frank, Hitler's lawyer for many years, in the Hitler biography of 1973, but he does in his earlier book, *The Face of the Third Reich,* which first appeared in 1963.

> Hitler's father was the illegitimate child of a cook named Schickelgruber [*sic*] from Leonding, near Linz, employed in a household in Graz. . . . The cook, Adolf Hitler's grandmother, was working for a Jewish family named Frankenberger when she gave birth to her child [This should read "when she became pregnant"—J.F.]. At that time—this happened in the 1830s— Frankenberger paid Schickelgruber on behalf of his son [who presumably had made the cook pregnant—A.M.], then about nineteen, a paternity allowance from the time of her child's birth up to his fourteenth year. There was also a correspondence over the years between the Frankenbergers and Hitler's grandmother, the general tenor of which was the unexpressed common knowledge of the correspondents that Schickelgruber's child had been conceived in circumstances which rendered the Frankenbergers liable to pay a paternity allowance.

If these facts were so well known in the village that they were still being mentioned a hundred years later, it is inconceivable that Alois knew nothing of it. It is also scarcely conceivable that the villagers would believe such generosity was unmotivated. Whatever the truth actually was, a fourfold disgrace weighed upon Alois: being poor, being illegitimate, being separated from his real mother at the age of five, and having Jewish blood. There was certainty about the first three points; even if the fourth was nothing but a rumor, this did not make matters any easier. How is someone to defend himself against a rumor that is not acknowledged openly but only whispered behind his back? It is easier to live with certainties, no matter how negative their nature. One can, for example, climb so high up the professional ladder that not a trace of poverty remains; this, Alois managed to do. He also managed to make his second and third wives pregnant before he married them, replicating for his children his own fate as an illegitimate son and unconsciously avenging himself. But the question concerning his ethnic origins remained unanswered all his life.

If not consciously acknowledged and mourned, uncertainty about one's descent can cause great anxiety and unrest, all the more so if, as in Alois's case, it is linked with an ominous rumor that can neither be proven nor completely refuted.

Recently, I heard about an eighty-year-old man who had come from Eastern Europe and had been living in Western Europe for thirty-five years with his wife and children. A short time ago, to his great amazement, the man received a letter from his fifty-three-year-old illegitimate son in the Soviet Union. For fifty years he had believed his son dead, since the three-year-old child had been with his mother when she was shot to death. The child's father subsequently became a political prisoner, and it never occurred to him later to search for his son, so convinced was he of his death. The son, however, who had his mother's name, wrote in his letter that he had had no rest for fifty years; he had been led from one piece of information to the next and had kept finding new hope, only to see it repeatedly shattered. Yet he finally succeeded in finding his father after fifty years, although in the beginning he had not even known his name. We can imagine how much this man idealized his unknown father, what hopes he had attached to the possibility of seeing him again. For it must have required an enormous expenditure of energy to locate a man in Western Europe from a small provincial city in the Soviet Union.

This story demonstrates how crucial it can be for a person to clear up the unsolved question of his descent and to meet the unknown parent. It is unlikely that Alois Hitler could have experienced these needs consciously; besides, it was not possible for him to idealize his unknown father in view of the rumor that he was a Jew, which in Alois's surroundings meant disgrace and isolation. The fact that Alois's name was changed when he was forty—with all the highly significant "slips" described by Fest—shows how important but also how fraught with conflict the question of descent was for him.

Emotional conflict cannot be eliminated by means of official documents, however. Alois's children were to bear the brunt of his anxiety, which he tried to ward off with achievements, with a career as a civil servant, a uniform, and a pompous manner.

John Toland writes:

> [He] became quarrelsome and irritable. His main target was Alois Jr. For some time the father, who demanded absolute obedience, had been at odds with the son, who refused to give it. Later, Alois Jr. complained bitterly that his father frequently beat him "unmercifully with a hippopotamus whip," but in the Austria of those days severe beatings of children were not uncommon, being considered good for the soul. Once the boy skipped school for three days to finish building a toy boat. The father, who had encouraged such hobbies, whipped young Alois, then held him "against a tree by the back of his neck" until he lost consciousness. There were also stories that Adolf was whipped, if not so often, and that the master of the house "often beat the dog until the dog would cringe and wet the floor." The violence, according to Alois Jr., extended even to the docile Klara and, if true, must have made an indelible impression on Adolf.

Interestingly enough, Toland says "if true," even though he had corroborative information from Adolf's sister Paula that he did not include in his book. But Helm Stierlin, in his monograph *Adolf Hitler: A Family Perspective,* cites material from the Toland Collection. Paula told Toland in an interview:

> It was my brother Adolf who especially provoked my father to extreme harshness and who got his due measure of beatings every day. He was rather a nasty little fellow, and all his father's attempts to beat the impudence out of him and make him choose the career of a civil servant were in vain.

If Paula personally told John Toland that her brother Adolf was given "his due measure of beatings" every day, there is no reason to doubt her word. It is characteristic of biographers that they have difficulty identifying with the child and quite unconsciously minimize mistreatment by the parents. The following passage from Franz Jetzinger's book *Hitlers Jugend* (*Hitler's Youth*) is very indicative:

> It has been claimed that the boy was badly beaten by his father, using as a source something Angela is supposed to have said [to her half brother]: "Adolf, remember how Mother and I used to hold Father back by the coattails of his uniform when he was going to beat you?" This statement is highly suspect. The father had not worn a uniform since the Hafeld days; the last year he still wore it he wasn't living with the family. The beatings would have had to occur between 1892 and 1894 when Adolf was only four and Angela twelve. She would never have dared to hold such a strict father back by the coattails. That was fabricated by someone whose chronology was way off.
>
> The "Führer" himself told his secretaries, whom he liked to hoodwink anyway, that his father had once given him thirty lashes on the back, but the Führer told them many things that are demonstrably untrue. This remark in particular does not deserve credence because he made it in connection with stories about cowboys and Indians, boasting that he, in true Indian fashion, did not utter a sound during the beating. It may well be that the willful and recalcitrant boy was given an occasional thrashing—he richly deserved it—but he certainly could not be called a "battered child"; his father was a man of thoroughly progressive convictions. Such a contrived theory does nothing to solve the mystery of what made Hitler the way he was, indeed only complicates it!

It seems much more likely instead that Father Hitler, who after all was already over sixty when they lived in Leonding, closed an eye to the boy's behavior and did not take much interest in his upbringing.

If Jetzinger's facts are correct, and there is no reason to doubt they are, then his "evidence" corroborates my firm conviction that Adolf's father did not wait until his son was older to start beating him but began when the child was still very young, i.e., "only four." Actually, Jetzinger's proof is superfluous because Adolf's whole life is proof enough. It is no accident that he himself writes in *Mein Kampf* about a child of—"let us assume"—three (see page 160). Jetzinger apparently does not believe this. But why not? How often the evil warded off by a parent is projected onto the child!* After all, in the pedagogical works quoted in my first section and in the books by Dr. Schreber, which were extremely popular in their day, the physical chastisement of the infant is strongly recommended. It is emphasized repeatedly that wickedness cannot be driven out early enough so that "goodness may grow undisturbed." In addition, we know from newspaper accounts that mothers beat their babies, and perhaps we would know much more about this subject if pediatricians would speak out about what they observe every day. Until recently, however, their oath of professional secrecy (at least in Switzerland) explicitly forbade this, and now they still remain silent, perhaps out of habit, or "for reasons of propriety." If anyone doubts that Adolf Hitler was abused as a young child, the passage I have just quoted from Jetzinger's biography should furnish objective proof, although Jetzinger would actually like to prove the opposite—at least consciously. But he has perceived more than he is conscious of, as can be seen in the glaring paradox in his account. For if Angela had to be afraid of her "strict father," then Alois was not as good-natured as

---

* The collection of essays edited by Ray E. Helfer and C. Henry Kempe, with the title *The Battered Child*, 3rd ed. (Chicago, 1980), provides the reader with valuable insight into the motives for beating infants.

Jetzinger describes him, and if he was good-natured, then she had no need to fear him.

I have lingered over this passage because it serves as an example of how a biographer distorts the biography by exonerating the subject's parents. It is significant that Jetzinger uses the word *hoodwink* when Hitler is telling the bitter truth. He claims that Hitler "certainly" was not "a battered child" and that "the willful and recalcitrant boy" "richly deserved" his occasional thrashings. For "his father was a man of thoroughly progressive convictions." There is certainly room for argument about Jetzinger's concept of progressive convictions, but aside from this, there are fathers who do indeed think in progressive terms on the surface, repeating the history of their own childhood only when it comes to their children or even just one of them targeted for this purpose.

The strangest psychological interpretations result from the pedagogical position that sees its main task in protecting parents from the reproaches of their children. In contrast to my thesis that Hitler's justifiable childhood hatred of his father found an outlet in hatred of the Jews, Fest believes that Hitler did not start to hate his father until 1938, as a grown man, after learning of his Jewish ancestry from Frank. He writes:

> No one can say what effect it had on his son when he learned these facts just as he was setting out to win power in Germany; but there is some reason to suppose that the vague aggressiveness he had always felt towards his father now turned into distinct hatred. In May 1938, only a few weeks after the German annexation of Austria, he had the village of Döllersheim and its environs turned into an army training area. His father's birthplace and his grandmother's burial place were obliterated by the tanks of the Wehrmacht.

Such hatred for the father cannot spring full-blown in an adult from an "intellectual" anti-Semitic attitude. Hatred like this is deeply rooted in experiences lived through in the obscurity of childhood. It is significant that Jetzinger also thinks that after receiving Frank's report Hitler's political hatred for the Jews was transformed into personal hatred for his father and members of his family.

After Alois's death, the Linz *Tagespost* of January 8, 1903, published an obituary, as follows:

> The sharp word that fell occasionally from his lips could not belie the warm heart that beat beneath the rough exterior. At all times an energetic champion of law and order and universally well-informed, he was able to pronounce authoritatively on any subject that came under discussion. [Quoted by Toland]

> On the gravestone was attached an oblong picture of the former customs official, eyes fixed determinedly ahead. [Toland]

B. F. Smith even reports that Alois had "genuine respect for other people's rights and real concern for their welfare."

What appears as a "rough exterior" in someone held in high regard can be pure hell for one's own child. Toland gives an example of this:

> In a show of rebellion, Adolf decided to run away from home. Somehow Alois learned of these plans and locked the boy upstairs. During the night Adolf tried to squeeze through the barred window. He couldn't quite make it, so took off his clothes. As he was wriggling his way to freedom, he heard his father's footsteps on the stairs and hastily withdrew, draping his nakedness with a tablecloth. This time Alois did not punish with a whipping. Instead, he burst into laughter and shouted to Klara to come up and look at the "toga boy." The ridicule hurt Adolf more than any switch and it took him, he confided to Frau Hanfstaengl, "a long time to get over the episode."

> Years later he told one of his secretaries that he had read in an adventure novel that it was a proof of courage to show no pain. And so "I resolved not to make a sound the next time my father whipped me. And when the time came—I still can remember my frightened mother standing outside the door—I silently counted the blows. My mother thought I had gone crazy when I beamed proudly and said, 'Father hit me thirty-two times!'"

These and similar passages give us the impression that Alois was expressing his blind rage at the debasement he suffered in his own childhood by repeatedly beating his son. Apparently he had a compulsion to inflict his debasement and sufferings on this particular child.

An incident I heard about might help us to understand the roots of such a compulsion. An American television program showed some young mothers who were in group therapy, all of whom reported they had mistreated their babies. A mother told about one occasion when she couldn't bear to listen to her baby scream a moment longer; she suddenly snatched it from its crib and hurled it against the wall. The desperation she felt at the time became very obvious to the viewer. She went on to tell how, having reached her wits' end, she had called an emergency telephone number that offers assistance in such cases. The voice on the line asked her whom she had actually wanted to strike out at. To her astonishment, she heard herself saying, "Myself," whereupon she broke down sobbing.

This incident lends support to my interpretation of Alois's behavior toward his son as a form of self-punishment. But this circumstance does not change the fact that Adolf, who as a child of course could not know all this, lived in daily jeopardy, in a hell of continual fear and severe trauma. Nor does it change the fact that he was forced at the same time to repress these feelings in order to rescue his pride or that he did not show his suffering and had to split it off.

What irrepressible unconscious envy the little boy, by his mere existence, must have aroused in Alois! Born in wedlock as a "legitimate" child, in addition as the son of a customs official, with a mother who was not so poverty-stricken that she had to give him up, and with a father whom he knew (one whose presence he was forced to experience physically every day so intensely and with such lasting effect). Weren't these the very things whose lack had caused Alois so much suffering and which he had been unable to attain, in spite of all his efforts, during his whole life, since we can never alter the facts of our childhood? We can only accept them and learn to live with the reality of our past or totally deny it and make others suffer as a result.

For many people it is very difficult to accept the sad truth that cruelty is usually inflicted upon the innocent. Don't we learn as small children that all the cruelty shown us in our upbringing is a punishment for our wrongdoing? A teacher told me that several children in her class, after seeing the *Holocaust* film, said, "But the Jews must have been guilty or they wouldn't have been punished like that."

With this in mind, we can understand the attempts of all Hitler's biographers to attribute every possible sin, especially laziness, obstinacy, and dishonesty, to little Adolf. But is a child born a liar? And isn't lying the only way to survive with such a father and retain a remnant of one's dignity? Sometimes deception and bad grades in school provide the only means for secretly developing a shred of autonomy for a person so totally at the mercy of another's whims as was Adolf Hitler (and not he alone!). We can assume on this basis that Hitler's later descriptions of an open battle with his father over a choice of career were doctored versions, not because the son was a coward "by nature," but because his father was unable to permit any discussion. It is more likely that the following passage from *Mein Kampf* reflects the true state of affairs.

> I had to some extent been able to keep my private opinions to myself; I did not always have to contradict him immediately. My own firm determination never to become a civil servant sufficed to give me complete inner peace.

It is significant that when Konrad Heiden quotes this passage in his Hitler biography he remarks at the end, "In other words, a little sneak." We expect a child in a totalitarian setting to be open and honest but at the same time to obey implicitly, bring good grades home from school, not contradict his father, and always fulfill his duty.

Another biographer, Rudolf Olden, writing about Hitler's problems at school, says:

> Apathy and poor performance soon become more pronounced. With the loss of a stern guiding hand upon the sudden death of his father, a crucial stimulus disappears.

The beatings are here considered a "stimulus" to learning. This is written by the very same biographer who has just presented this picture of Alois:

> Even after he retired, he retained the typical pride of a bureaucrat and insisted on being addressed as "Herr," followed by his title, whereas the farmers and laborers used the informal form of address ["Du"] with one another. By showing him the respect he demanded, the local people were really making fun of this outsider. He was never on good terms with the people he knew. To make up for it he had established a nice little dictatorship in his own home. His wife looked up to him, and he treated the children with a hard hand. Adolf in particular he had no understanding for. He tyrannized him. If he wanted the boy to come to him, the former noncommissioned officer would whistle on two fingers.

This description, written in 1935 when many Braunau acquaintances of the Hitler family were still living and it was not yet so difficult to gather information of this sort, is not repeated, to my knowledge, in the postwar biographies. The image of a man who calls his child to him by whistling as though he were a dog is so strongly reminiscent of reports of the concentration camps that it is not surprising if present-day biographers have been reluctant to make the connection. In addition, all the biographies share the tendency to play down the father's brutality with the observation that beatings were quite normal in those days or even with complicated arguments against "vilifying" the father, such as those presented by Jetzinger. Sadly enough, Jetzinger's careful research provides an important source for later biographies, even though his psychological insights are not far removed from those of an Alois.

The way Hitler unconsciously took on his father's behavior and displayed it on the stage of world history is indicative of how the child must really have seen his father: the snappy, uniformed, somewhat ridiculous dictator, as Charlie Chaplin portrayed him in his film and as Hitler's enemies saw him, is the way Alois appeared in the eyes of his critical son. The heroic Führer, loved and admired by the German people, was the other Alois, the husband loved and admired by his subservient wife, Klara, whose awe and admiration Adolf no doubt shared when he was still very little. These two internalized aspects of his father can be identified in so many of Adolf's later enactments (in connection with the "heroic" aspect, we need only think of the greeting "Heil Hitler," of the adoration of the masses, etc.) that we receive the impression that throughout his later life his considerable artistic talents impelled him to reproduce his earliest—deeply imprinted, though unconscious—memories of a tyrannical father. His portrayal is unforgettable for everyone who was alive at the time; some of his contemporaries experienced the dictator from the perspective of the horror felt by a mistreated child, and others from the perspective of an innocent child's complete devotion and acceptance. Every great artist draws on the unconscious contents of childhood, and Hitler's energies could have gone into creating works of art instead of destroying the lives of millions of people, who would then not have had to bear the brunt of this unresolved suffering, which he warded off in grandiosity. Yet, in spite of his grandiose identification with the aggressor, there are passages in *Mein Kampf* that show the way Hitler experienced his childhood.

In a basement apartment, consisting of two stuffy rooms, dwells a worker's family of seven. Among the five children there is a boy of, let us assume, three. . . . The very narrowness and overcrowding of the room does not lead to favorable conditions. Quarreling and wrangling will very frequently arise. . . . But if this battle is carried on between the parents themselves, and almost every day, in forms which in vulgarity often leave nothing to be desired, then, if only very gradually, the results of such visual instruction must ultimately become apparent in the children. The character they will inevitably assume if the quarrel takes the form of brutal attacks by the father against the mother, of drunken beatings, is hard for anyone who does not know this milieu to imagine. At the age of six the pitiable little boy suspects the existence of things which can fill even an adult with nothing but horror. . . . All the other things that the little fellow hears at home do not tend to increase his respect for his dear fellow men.

It ends badly if the man goes his own way from the very beginning and the woman, for the children's sake, opposes him. Then there is fighting and quarreling, and as the man grows estranged from his wife, he becomes more intimate with alcohol. When at length he comes home on Sunday or even Monday night, drunk and brutal, but always parted from his last cent, such scenes often occur that God have mercy!
I have seen this in hundreds of instances.

Although the deep and lasting damage it would have done to his dignity prevented Hitler from admitting the situation of the "let us assume, three-year-old boy" to be his own in the first-person account of *Mein Kampf,* the content of his description leaves no doubt whose childhood is meant.

A child whose father does not call to him by name but by whistling to him as though the child were a dog has the same disenfranchised and nameless status in the family as did "the Jew" in the Third Reich.

Through the agency of his unconscious repetition compulsion, Hitler actually succeeded in transferring the trauma of his family life onto the entire German nation. The introduction of the racial laws forced every citizen to trace his or her descent back to the third generation and to bear the ensuing consequences. At first, the wrong ancestry, or an uncertain one, meant disgrace and degradation; later it meant death— and this during peacetime, in a country that called itself civilized. There is no other example of such a phenomenon in all of history. The Inquisition, for example, persecuted the Jews because of their religion, but they were offered the chance to survive if they accepted baptism. In the Third Reich, however, neither behavior nor merit nor achievement were of any avail; on the basis of descent alone a Jew was condemned, first to be demeaned and later to die. Is this not a twofold reflection of Hitler's fate?

1. It was impossible for Hitler's father, in spite of all his efforts, successes, and advances in career from shoemaker to chief customs inspector, to remove the "stain" in his past, just as it was later forbidden the Jews to remove the stigma of the yellow star they were forced to wear. The stain remained and oppressed Alois all his life. It may be that his frequent moves (eleven, according to Fest) had another cause beside a professional one—to obliterate his traces. This tendency is also very clear in Adolf's life. "When he was told in 1942 that there was a memorial marker in the village of Spital [in the region where his father was born] he went into one of his wild rages," Fest reports.

2. At the same time, the racial laws represented the repetition of the drama of Hitler's own childhood. In the same way that the Jew now had no chance to escape, the child Adolf at one time could not escape his father's blows, which were caused, not by the child's behavior, but by the father's unresolved problems, such as his resistance to mourning over his own childhood. It is fathers such as this who are likely to drag their sleeping child out of bed if they cannot come to terms with a mood (perhaps having just felt insignificant and insecure on some social occasion) and beat the child in order to restore their narcissistic equilibrium (cf. Christiane F.'s father).

The Jews fulfilled the same function in the Third Reich —which attempted to recover from the disgrace of the Weimar Republic at their expense—as this sleeping child. This was Adolf's function throughout his childhood; he had to accept the fact that at any moment a storm could break over his helpless head without his being able to find any way to avert or escape it.

Since there were no bonds of affection between Adolf and his father (it is significant that in *Mein Kampf* he refers to

Alois as "Herr Vater"), his burgeoning hatred was constant and unequivocal. It is different for children whose fathers have outbursts of rage and can then, in between times, play good-naturedly with their children. In this case the child's hatred cannot be cultivated in such a pure form. These children experience difficulties of another sort as adults; they seek out partners with a personality structure that, like their fathers', tends toward extremes. They are bound to these partners by a thousand chains and cannot bring themselves to leave them, always living with the hope that the other person's good side will finally win out; yet at every fresh outburst they are plunged into new despair. These sadomasochistic bonds, which go back to the equivocal and unpredictable nature of a parent, are stronger than a genuine love relationship; they are impossible to break, and signal permanent destruction of the self.

Little Adolf could be certain of receiving constant beatings; he knew that nothing he did would have any effect on the daily thrashings he was given. All he could do was deny the pain, in other words, deny himself and identify with the aggressor. No one could help him, not even his mother, for this would spell danger for her too, because she was also battered (cf. Toland).

This state of constant jeopardy is reflected very clearly in the fate of the Jews in the Third Reich. Let us try to imagine the following scene. A Jew is walking down the street, perhaps on his way home from buying milk, when a man wearing an SA armband attacks him; this man has the right to do anything to the Jew he wants, anything his fantasy happens to dictate and that his unconscious craves at the moment. The Jew can do nothing to alter this; he is in the same position as little Adolf once was. If the Jew tries to defend himself, there is nothing to prevent his being trampled to death. He is like the eleven-year-old Adolf, who in desperation once ran away from home with three friends, planning to float down the river on a homemade raft and thus flee from his violent father. Just for the very thought of trying to escape, he was nearly beaten to death (cf. Stierlin). It is just as impossible for the Jew to escape; all roads are cut off and lead to death, like the railroad tracks that simply came to an end at Treblinka and Auschwitz—signifying the end of life itself. This is the way any child feels who is beaten day in and day out and who is very nearly killed for daring to think of escape.

In the scene I have just described, which occurred countless times between 1933 and 1945 in many variations, the Jew has to endure everything like a helpless child. He must submit to having this creature with the SA armband, who has been transformed into a screaming, berserk monster, pour the milk over his head and summon others to the scene to share his amusement (the way Alois laughed at Adolf's "toga"). He must endure having the SA man feel big and strong alongside someone who is completely at his mercy, completely in his power. If this Jew loves his life, he will not risk it now just for the sake of proving to himself that he is tough and courageous. Instead, he will remain passive yet inwardly full of revulsion and scorn for this man, just as Adolf had been when he gradually came to see through his father's weakness and began to pay him back, at least a little, by doing poorly in school, which he knew upset his father.

Joachim Fest does not think that Adolf's poor performance in school had anything to do with his relationship with his father but feels it was a result of the increased academic demands he encountered in Linz, where he was no longer capable of competing with his classmates, who came from solid middle-class homes. On the other hand, Fest writes that Adolf was "a wide-awake, lively, and obviously able pupil" (*Hitler*). Why should a boy like this have difficulties in school if not for the reason that he himself gives but which Fest questions because he sees Adolf as having a "tendency to laziness" and "an incapacity for regular work . . . [which] appeared quite early." This is something Alois might have said, but the fact that Hitler's most thorough biographer, who himself adduces thousands of pages of proof of his subject's later capacity for work, identifies with the father against the child here would be astonishing if it were not the general rule.

Almost all biographers unquestioningly accept the standards of judgment of that pedagogical ideology according to which parents are always right and children lazy, spoiled, stubborn, and moody if they do not function as they are expected to at all times. When children say anything against their parents, they are often suspected of lying. Fest writes:

> Later, in order to introduce a few effective dark shadings into the picture [as though this were necessary!—A.M.] the son even tried to make Alois look like a drunkard. Hitler tells of scolding and pleading with his father in scenes "of abominable shame," tugging and pulling him out of "reeking, smoky taverns" to bring him home. [*Hitler*]

Why "effective dark shadings"? Because the biographers agree that although the father liked to drink at the inn and afterwards caused scenes at home, he "was not an alcoholic." With the diagnosis "not an alcoholic," everything the father did can be overlooked and the child can be completely dissuaded of the significance of his experience, i.e., the shame and disgrace connected with witnessing these terrible scenes.

Something similar occurs when people in analysis ask relatives questions about their deceased parents. The parents, faultless while they were alive, are automatically promoted to angels upon their death, leaving a hell of self-reproach as a legacy to their children. Since it is unlikely that anyone these children know will confirm their earlier negative impressions of their parents, they must keep these impressions to themselves and think themselves very wicked for having them. It would have been no different for the thirteen-year-old Hitler when he lost his father and from then on encountered nothing but an idealized father image on all sides. Who would have acknowledged to the boy his father's cruelty and brutality then, if even today biographers still attempt to describe those regular beatings as harmless? As soon as Hitler succeeded in transferring the evil he felt in himself to "the Jew per se," however, he succeeded in breaking out of his isolation.

There is probably no more reliable common tie among the peoples of Europe than their shared hatred of the Jews. Those in power have always been able to manipulate this hatred for their own purposes; for example, it seems to be remarkably well suited to unite conflicting interests, with the result that even groups extremely hostile to one another can be in complete agreement about how dangerous and obnoxious the Jews are. Hitler realized this and once said to Rauschning that "if the Jews didn't exist they would have to be invented."

Where does anti-Semitism's perpetual ability to renew itself come from? The answer is not difficult to find. A Jew is not hated for doing or being something specific. Everything Jews do or the way they are applies to other groups as well. Jews are hated because people harbor a forbidden hatred and are eager to legitimate it. The Jewish people are particularly well-suited objects of this need. Because they have been persecuted for two thousand years by the highest authorities of church and state, no one ever needs to feel ashamed for hating the Jews, not even if one has been raised according to the strictest moral principles and is made to feel ashamed of the most natural emotions of the soul in other regards (cf. pages 92–3). A child who has been required to don the armor of "virtue" at too early an age will seize upon the only permissible discharge; he will seize upon anti-Semitism (i.e., his right to hate), retaining it for the rest of his life. It is possible that Hitler did not have easy access to this discharge, however, because it would have touched upon a family taboo. Later, in Vienna, he was happy to shed this silent prohibition, and when he came to power he needed only to proclaim this one legitimate hatred in the Western tradition as the highest Aryan virtue.

I derive my suspicion that the question of descent was made taboo in Adolf's family from the great importance he later placed on the subject. His reaction to the report Frank gave him in 1930 only confirms my suspicion, for it reveals the combination of knowing and not knowing, so typical for a child, and reflects the family's confusion about the subject. Adolf Hitler, wrote Frank, knew that his father was not the child of [Maria Anna] Schickl-gruber by the Graz Jew; he knew it from what his father and his grandmother had told him. He knew that his father was the off-spring of the premarital relations between his grandmother and the man whom she later married. But they were both poor and the support money which the Jew paid over a number of years was an extremely desirable supplement to the poverty-stricken household. He was well able to pay and for that reason he was claimed to be the father, and the Jew paid, without going to court, probably because he could not face the publicity that a legal settlement would have entailed. [Quoted by Jetzinger]

Jetzinger has this to say about Hitler's reaction:

This paragraph obviously reproduced what Hitler said to Frank's revelation. Naturally he must have been terribly upset but of course did not permit himself to let on in front of Frank but acted as though the contents of the report were not entirely new to him; he said he knew on the basis of what he had been told by his father and his grandmother that his father was not the child of the Jew from Graz. But here Hitler, in his momentary confusion, really went too far! His grandmother had been dead for over forty years when he was born; she can't have told him anything! And his father? He would have had to tell him before Adolf turned fourteen because that is when the father died. Such things are not said to a boy that age, and especially not: "Your grandfather was not a Jew," if there was no question of there being a Jewish grandfather anyway! Hitler further re-sponded that he knew his father was the result of the pre-marital relations between his grandmother and the man she later married. Then why had he written in his book several years earlier that his father was the son of a poor little farm laborer? The miller, who was the only one the grandmother could have had premarital relations with—but only after she was living in Döllersheim again—was never a farm laborer in his life! And to accuse the grandmother, whether this was done by Hitler or Frank, of such underhandedness as to claim some-one with the ability to pay as the father of her child betrays a mentality that is common among immoral people but proves nothing in regard to parentage! Adolf Hitler knew absolutely nothing about his descent! Children are usually not told about such things.

Such intolerable confusion about a child's family background can be the cause of learning problems in school (because knowledge is forbidden and thus is threatening and
dangerous). In any case, Hitler later wanted to know from
every citizen with great accuracy whether a Jew was hiding
in the family tree, back to the third generation.

Fest has several things to say about Adolf's poor showing
in school; he states, for example, that his work did not improve
after his father's death and cites this as proof that his poor
performance had nothing to do with his father. The following
points refute Fest's contention.

1. The passages from *Schwarze Pädagogik* show very
clearly that teachers are only too happy to take over for the
father when it comes to disciplining the pupil and that they
have much to gain from it in the way of their own narcissistic
stabilization.

2. When Adolf's father died, he had already long since
been internalized by the son, and the teachers now provided
father substitutes against whom he could try to defend himself somewhat more successfully. Doing poorly in school is
one of the few ways a child has to punish the teacher-father.

3. When he was eleven, Adolf was nearly beaten to death
when he tried to free himself from an intolerable situation
by running away. His brother Edmund did die around this
time; although we have no information about this, it may
have been that Adolf had a certain amount of power over his
weaker brother. In any event, it is during this period that he
began to do poorly in school, in contrast to the good grades he
had earlier. Who knows, perhaps this bright and gifted child
might have found a different, more humane way of dealing
with his pent-up hatred if his curiosity and vitality had been
given more nourishment in school. But even an appreciation
of intellectual values was made impossible for him by his early,
deeply problematical relationship with his father, which was
then transferred to his teachers and school.

This child, who is subject to rages like those of his father,
grows up to order the burning of books by freethinking

authors. They are books that Hitler hated but had never read. Perhaps he could have read and understood them if he had been allowed from the beginning to develop his potential. The burning of books and the condemnation of artists are acts of revenge because this gifted child was prevented from enjoying school. Perhaps this story will illustrate what I mean:

Once I was sitting on a park bench in a strange city. An old man, who later told me he was eighty-two, sat down beside me. My attention was caught by the attentive and respectful way he spoke to some children playing nearby, and I struck up a conversation with him, in the course of which he told me about his experiences as a soldier in the First World War. "You know," he said, "I have a guardian angel who is always with me. It often happened that all my friends were hit by grenades or bombs and died, whereas I, although I was standing right there, came through without a scratch." It isn't important whether all this occurred exactly as he reported. What matters is that this man was conveying an expression of his self, of his complete trust in a benevolent fate. Thus, when I asked about his siblings, it didn't surprise me to hear him answer: "They are all dead; I was my mother's pet." His mother "loved life," he said. Sometimes in the spring she would wake him up in the morning to go with her and listen to the birds singing in the woods before he went to school. These were his happiest memories. When I asked whether he had ever been given beatings, he answered, "Hardly ever; my father's hand may have slipped occasionally. That made me angry every time, but he never did it in my mother's presence; she would never have permitted it. But you know," he went on, "once I was severely beaten by my teacher. In the first three grades, I was the best pupil, then in the fourth we got a new teacher. One time he accused me of something I hadn't done. Then he took me aside and started hitting me and kept on hitting, shouting like a madman the whole time, "Now will you tell the truth?' But how could I? After all, I would have had to lie to satisfy him, and I had never done that before because I had no reason to be afraid of my parents. So I endured the beating for a quarter of an hour, but I never cared for school after that and became a poor pupil. It often distressed me later that I never got my high-school diploma. But I don't think I had any choice at the time."

As a child, this man appeared to have been held in such esteem by his mother that he in turn was able to respect and express his feelings. He was therefore *aware* of being angry with his father when the latter's "hand slipped"; he was *aware* that his teacher was forcing him to tell a lie and demeaning him, and he also felt grief because he had to pay for his integrity by neglecting his education because there was no other way for him at the time. I noticed that he didn't say, like most people, "My mother loved me very much," but instead, "She loved life," and I recalled having once written that about Goethe's mother. This elderly man had known his happiest moments in the woods with his mother when he had sensed her delight in the birds and shared it with her. Their warm relationship still shone in his aging eyes, and her regard for him expressed itself unmistakably in the way he now was speaking to the children at play. There was nothing superior or condescending in his manner, but simply attentiveness and respect.

I have dwelt so long on Hitler's problems at school because their causes and their later ramifications are typical of millions of other cases as well. The fact that Hitler had so many enthusiastic followers proves that they had a personality structure similar to his, i.e., that they had had a similar upbringing. The contemporary biographies demonstrate how far we still are in our thinking from the realization that a child has a right to be respected. Fest, who took immense and exhaustive pains to depict Hitler's life, cannot believe the son's claim that he suffered greatly because of his father and thinks Adolf is only "dramatizing" these difficulties—as if anyone were more qualified to judge the situation than Adolf Hitler himself.

Fest's tendency to spare the parents is scarcely surprising when we consider the extent to which psychoanalysis itself is captive to this approach. Insofar as its followers still consider it their main goal to fight for the free expression of sexuality, they are overlooking other crucial matters. We can see what a child who has not been shown respect and therefore lacks self-respect does with "liberated" sexuality when we consider child prostitution and the current drug scene. Here we can learn, among other things, about the disastrous dependency (on other people and on heroin) that can result from children's "liberation," which does not deserve the name if it is accompanied by self-degradation.

Both child abuse and its consequences are so well integrated into our lives that we are scarcely struck by their absurdity. Adolescents' "heroic willingness" to fight one another in wars and (just as life is beginning!) to die for someone else's cause may be a result of the fact that during puberty the warded-off hatred from early childhood becomes reintensified. Adolescents can divert this hatred from their parents if they are given a clear-cut enemy whom they are permitted to hate freely and with impunity. This may be why so many young painters and writers volunteered for the front in World War I. The hope of freeing themselves from the constraints imposed by their family enabled them to take pleasure in marching to the music of a military band. One of heroin's roles is to replace this function, with the difference that in the case of drugs the destructive rage is directed against one's own body and self.

Lloyd de Mause, who as a psychohistorian is particularly interested in motivation and in describing the group fantasies underlying it, once did a study of the dominant fantasies among aggressor nations. Looking through his material, he noticed that again and again statements by the leaders of these nations employed images relating to the birth process. With striking frequency they speak of their nation as being strangled, a situation they hope the war will finally rectify. De Mause believes that this fantasy reflects the actual situation of the infant during birth, which results in a trauma for every human being and thus is subject to the repetition compulsion.

The observation can be made, in support of this thesis, that the feeling of being strangled and having to get free does not occur in nations that are genuinely threatened—as, for example, Poland was in 1939—but in nations where this was not true—e.g., in Germany in 1914 and 1939 or in the United States during the Vietnam War. A declaration of war, therefore, is no doubt an attempt to escape *fantasies* of being threatened, constricted, and debased. On the basis of what I now know about childhood and what I am trying to demonstrate with the example of Adolf Hitler, I would definitely be inclined to draw the conclusion that it is not the birth trauma (as de Mause assumes) but other experiences that are reactivated in an eagerness for war. Even the most difficult birth is a unique, delimited trauma that, despite our smallness and weakness, we have usually overcome either on our own or with the help of a third party who comes to our rescue. In contrast to this, beatings, psychological humiliation, and other cruel treatment are recurrent experiences; there is no escape from them and there is no helping hand available, because no one considers this hell to be a hell. It is a continuous condition, or one that is repeatedly reencountered. There can be no ultimate liberating cry here, and these experiences can be forgotten only with the aid of splitting off and repression. Now, it is precisely those events that have never been come to terms with that must seek an outlet in the repetition compulsion. The jubilation characteristic of those who declare war is the expression of the revived hope of finally being able to avenge earlier debasement, and presumably also of relief at finally being permitted to hate and shout. The former child seizes the first opportunity to be active and to break its enforced silence. If the mourning process has not been possible, a person will use the repetition compulsion to try to undo the past and to banish former tragic passivity by means of activity in the present. Since this can't succeed, because of the impossibility of changing the past, wars of this kind do not bring liberation to the aggressor but ultimately lead to catastrophe, even when there are initial victories.

In spite of these considerations, it is possible to imagine that the birth fantasy does play a role here. For children who are beaten every day and must remain silent about it, birth may be the only childhood event where they emerged the victor, not only in fantasy but in actuality; otherwise, they would not have survived. They fought their way through a narrow passage and were allowed to scream afterwards, in spite of which they were taken care of by helping hands. Can this bliss be compared to what came later? It would not be surprising if we wanted to use this great triumph to help ourselves get over the defeats and loneliness of later years. Seen from this perspective, associations between the birth trauma and the declaration of war could be interpreted as a denial of the actual, hidden trauma, which is never taken seriously by society and therefore requires enactment. In Hitler's life, the "Boer wars" of his schooldays, *Mein Kampf,* and World War II belong to the visible tip of the iceberg. The hidden explanation for why he developed the way he did cannot be sought in the experience of emerging from the womb, an experience Hitler shares with all human beings. Not all human beings, on the other hand, were tormented the way he was as a child.

What didn't the son do to forget the trauma of the beatings his father gave him: he subjugated Germany's ruling class, won over the masses, and bent the governments of Europe to his will. He possessed nearly limitless power. At night, however, in his sleep, when the unconscious lets us know about our early childhood experiences, there was no escape: then his father came back to frighten him, and his terror was boundless. Rauschning writes:

> Hitler, however, has states that approach persecution mania and a dual personality. His sleeplessness is more than the mere result of excessive nervous strain. He often wakes up in the middle of the night and wanders restlessly to and fro. Then he must have light everywhere. Lately he has sent at these times for young men who have to keep him company during his hours of manifest anguish. At times his condition must have been

dreadful. A man in the closest daily association with him gave me this account: Hitler wakes at night with convulsive shrieks. He shouts for help. He sits on the edge of his bed, unable to stir. He shakes with fear, making the whole bed vibrate. He mutters confused, totally unintelligible phrases. He gasps, as if imagining himself to be suffocating.

My informant described to me in full detail a remarkable scene—I should not have credited the story if it had not come from such a reliable source. Hitler stood swaying in his room, looking wildly about him. "It was he! It was he! He's been here!" he gasped. His lips were blue. Sweat streamed down his face. Suddenly he began to reel off figures, and odd words and broken phrases, entirely devoid of sense. It sounded horrible. He used strangely constructed and entirely un-German word formations. Then he stood quite still, only his lips moving. He was massaged and offered something to drink. Then he suddenly burst out—

"There, there! In the corner! Who's that?"

He stamped and shrieked in the familiar way. He was shown that there was nothing out of the ordinary in the room, and then he gradually grew calm. After that he lay asleep for many hours, and then for some time things were endurable again.

Although (or because) most of the people surrounding Hitler had once been battered children themselves, no one grasped the connection between his panic and the "unintelligible" numbers. The feelings of fear he had repressed in his childhood when counting his father's blows now overtook the adult at the peak of his success in the form of nightmares, sudden and inescapable, in the loneliness of the night.

Had he made the entire world his victim, he still would not have been able to banish his introjected father from his bedroom, for one's own unconscious cannot be destroyed by destroying the world. Yet, in spite of this fact, the world would still have had to pay dearly if Hitler had lived any longer, for the springs of his hatred flowed unceasingly—even in his sleep.

Those who have never experienced the power of the unconscious may find it naïve to try to explain Hitler's deeds as an outgrowth of his childhood experiences. There are still many men and women who are of the opinion that "childhood matters are merely childish matters" and that politics is something serious, something for adults, and not child's play. These people think connections between childhood and later life farfetched or ridiculous, since they would like, for good reason, to forget completely the reality of those early years. A life such as Hitler's is especially instructive here because in it the continuity between earlier and later can be traced so clearly. Even as a small boy he expressed his longing to be free from his father's yoke in the war games he played. First he led the Indians and then the Boers into battle against the oppressors. "It was not long before the great heroic struggle [the Franco-German War of 1870–71] had become my greatest inner experience," he writes in *Mein Kampf*, and in the same passage we can detect the fateful connection between those games that reflected his childhood unhappiness and the deadly seriousness to come: "From then on, I became more and more enthusiastic about everything that was in any way connected with war or, for that matter, with soldiering."

Hitler's French and German teacher, Dr. Huemer, reports that during puberty Hitler "reacted with ill-concealed hostility to advice or reproof; at the same time, he demanded of his fellow pupils their unqualified subservience" (cf. Toland). As a result of his early identification with a tyrannical father, Adolf—according to a witness from Braunau—would stand on a hill when still very little and "deliver long and passionate speeches."* Since Hitler spent only the first three years of his life in Braunau, this indicates how early his career as Führer began. In these speeches the child was imitating the way he had seen his imposing father hold forth and at the same time was also seeing himself, the awestruck admiring child of those first three years, as the audience.

The same situation was repeated in his appearances at organized mass rallies, those later reenactments of the Führer's childish self. The narcissistic, symbiotic unity be-

---

* This information was given to me orally by Paul Moor.

tween Führer and Volk is shown very clearly in the words of his boyhood friend August Kubizek, "for [whose] benefit alone" Hitler gave many speeches. Toland writes:

> These orations, usually delivered when they were walking through the fields or on some deserted woodland path, reminded Kubizek of an erupting volcano. It was like a scene on the stage. "I could only stand gaping and passive, forgetting to applaud." It took some time before Kubizek realized his friend was not acting but was "in dead earnest." He also discovered that Hitler expected only one thing of him: approval; and Kubizek, enthralled more by Adolf's oratory than by what he said, readily gave it. . . . Adolf seemed to know exactly how Kubizek felt. "He always sensed my reactions as intensely as if they were his. Sometimes I had the feeling that he was living my life as well as his own."

Perhaps no better commentary can be found to illustrate Hitler's legendary powers of seduction: whereas the Jews represented the humiliated, defeated side of his childhood self that he tried with all his might to do away with, the adoring German Volk, played here by Kubizek, were his good and beautiful side that loved his father and was loved by him. The German Volk and his friend Kubizek assume the role of Adolf, the good child. Hitler as father protects the child's pure soul from danger by driving out and destroying "the wicked Jews," i.e., "wicked thoughts" as well, so that undisturbed oneness between father and son can finally prevail.

Of course, this interpretation is not written for people who consider dreams "airy nothings" and the unconscious the invention of "a sick mind." But I could imagine that even those who do know something about the unconscious might look with misgivings or indignation upon my attempt to try to understand Hitler's actions on the basis of his childhood experiences, because they would rather not be forced to think about the whole "inhuman story." Yet can we really assume that the dear Lord suddenly conceived the idea of sending down to earth a "necrophilic beast," as Hitler is described by Erich Fromm, who wrote:

How can we explain that these two well-meaning, stable, very normal, and certainly not destructive people gave birth to the future "monster," Adolf Hitler? [*The Anatomy of Human Destructiveness*]

I have no doubt that behind every crime a personal tragedy lies hidden. If we were to investigate such events and their backgrounds more closely, we might be able to do more to prevent crimes than we do now with our indignation and moralizing. Perhaps someone will say: But not everyone who was a battered child becomes a murderer; otherwise, many more people would be murderers. That is true. However, humankind is in dire enough straits these days that this should not remain an academic question. Moreover, we never know how a child will and must react to the injustice he or she has suffered—there are innumerable "techniques" for dealing with it. We don't yet know, above all, what the world might be like if children were to grow up without being subjected to humiliation, if parents would respect them and take them seriously as persons. In any case, I don't know of a single person who enjoyed this respect* as a child and then as an adult had the need to put other human beings to death.

We are still barely conscious of how harmful it is to treat children in a degrading manner. Treating them with respect and recognizing the consequences of their being humiliated are by no means intellectual matters; otherwise, their importance would long since have been generally recognized. To empathize with what a child is feeling when he or she is defenseless, hurt, or humiliated is like suddenly seeing in a mirror the suffering of one's own childhood, something many people must ward off out of fear while others can accept it with mourning. People who have mourned in this way understand more about the dynamics of the psyche than they could ever have learned from books.

---

* By respect for a child, I don't mean a "permissive" upbringing, which is often a form of indoctrination itself and thus shows a disregard for the child's own world.

The persecution of people of Jewish background, the necessity of proving "racial purity" as far back as one's grandparents, the tailoring of prohibitions to the degree of an individual's demonstrable "racial purity"—all this is grotesque only at first glance. For its significance becomes plain once we realize that in terms of Hitler's unconscious fantasies it is an intensified expression of two very powerful tendencies. On the one hand, his father was the hated Jew whom he could despise and persecute, frighten and threaten with regulations, because his father would also have been affected by the racial laws if he had still been alive. At the same time—and this is the other tendency—the racial laws were meant to mark Adolf's final break with his father and his background. In addition to revenge, the tormenting uncertainty about the Hitler family was an important motive for the racial laws: the whole nation had to trace its "purity" back to the third generation because Adolf Hitler would have liked to know with certainty who his grandfather was. Above all, the Jew became the bearer of all the evil and despicable traits the child had ever observed in his father. In Hitler's view, the Jews were characterized by a specific mixture of Lucifer-like grandeur and superiority (world Jewry and its readiness to destroy the entire world) on the one hand and ugliness and ludicrous weakness and infirmity on the other. This view reflects the omnipotence even the weakest father exercises over his child, seen in Hitler's case in the wild rages of the insecure customs official who succeeded in destroying his son's world.

It is common in analysis for the first breakthrough in criticizing the father to be signaled by the surfacing of some insignificant and ludicrous trait of his that the patient's memory has repressed. For example, the father—big out of all proportion in the child's eyes—may have looked very funny in his short nightshirt. The child had never been close to his father, had been in constant fear of him, but with this memory of the skimpy nightshirt, the child's imagination provides a weapon, now that ambivalence has broken through in the analysis, which enables him to take revenge on a small scale against the godlike, monumental paternal figure. In similar fashion, Hitler disseminates his hatred and disgust for the "stinking" Jew in the pages of the Nazi periodical *Der Stürmer* in order to incite people to burn books by Freud, Einstein, and innumerable other Jewish intellectuals of great stature. The breakthrough of this idea, which made it possible for him to transfer his pent-up hatred of his father to the Jews as a people, is very instructive. It is described in the following passage from *Mein Kampf*.

> Since I had begun to concern myself with this question and to take cognizance of the Jews, Vienna appeared to me in a different light than before. Wherever I went, I began to see Jews, and the more I saw, the more sharply they became distinguished in my eyes from the rest of humanity. Particularly the Inner City and the districts north of the Danube Canal swarmed with a people which even outwardly had lost all resemblance to Germans. . . .
>
> All this could scarcely be called very attractive; but it became positively repulsive when, in addition to their physical uncleanliness, you discovered the moral stains on this "chosen people." . . .
>
> Was there any form of filth or profligacy, particularly in cultural life, without at least one Jew involved in it?
>
> If you cut even cautiously into such an abscess, you found, like a maggot in a rotting body, often dazzled by the sudden light—a kike!
>
> Gradually I began to hate them.

Once he succeeds in directing all his bottled-up hatred toward an object, the first reaction is one of great relief ("Wherever I went, I began to see Jews"). Forbidden, long-avoided feelings can now be given free rein. The more they had filled and pressed in upon one, the happier one feels at having finally found an ersatz object. Now there is no need to hate his own father; now Adolf can allow the dam to burst without being beaten for it.

Yet this ersatz satisfaction merely whets the appetite—nothing illustrates this better than the case of Adolf Hitler.

Although there probably had never before been a person with Hitler's power to destroy human life on such a scale with impunity, all this still could not bring him peace. His last will and testament, which calls for the continued persecution of the Jews, is impressive proof of this.

When we read Stierlin's description of Hitler's father, we see how closely the son resembled his father in personality.

> It appears, however, that his social rise was not without cost to himself and others. While he was conscientious and hard-working, he was also emotionally unstable, inordinately restless, and perhaps at times mentally disturbed. According to one source, he possibly once entered an asylum. Also, in the opinion of at least one analyst, he combined an overriding determination with a flexible conscience, shown especially in how he manipulated rules and records to his own ends, while maintaining a façade of legitimacy. (For example, in applying for papal approval to marry his legal cousin Klara, he stressed his two small motherless children, needing Klara's care, but failed to mention her pregnancy.)

Only a child's unconscious can copy a parent so exactly that every characteristic of the parent can later be found in the child. This phenomenon, however, is one that usually escapes the attention of biographers.

Hitler's Mother

HER POSITION IN THE FAMILY AND HER ROLE IN ADOLF'S LIFE

ALL the biographers agree that Klara Hitler loved her son very much and spoiled him. It must be stated at the outset that this view is a contradiction in terms if we take love to mean that the mother is open and sensitive to her child's true needs. This is precisely what is lacking if a child is spoiled, i.e., if his every wish is granted and he is showered with things he does not need—all this simply as ersatz for that which parents are unable to give their child because of their own problems. Therefore, if a child is spoiled, this points to a serious deficiency, which is then confirmed in later life. If Hitler had really been loved as a child, he would also have been capable of love. His relationships with women, his perversions (cf. Stierlin, page 194), and his whole aloof and basically cold relationships with people in general reveal that he never received love from any quarter.

Before Adolf was born, Klara had three children, all of whom died of diphtheria within a month of one another. The first two were perhaps already ill when the third child was born, who then died when he was only three days old. Thirteen months later, Adolf was born. I reproduce here Stierlin's very useful chart:

	BORN	DIED	AGE AT DEATH
1. Gustav (diphtheria)	5/17/1885	12/8/1887	2 yr. 7 mos.
2. Ida (diphtheria)	9/23/1886	1/2/1888	1 yr. 4 mos.
3. Otto (diphtheria)	1887	1887	approx. 3 days
4. Adolf	4/20/1889		
5. Edmund	3/24/1894	2/2/1900	almost 6 yrs.
6. Paula	1/21/1896		

The prettified legend depicts Klara as a loving mother who, after the death of her first three children, showered all her affection on Adolf. It is probably no accident that all the biographers who paint this lovely Madonna-like portrait are men. A candid contemporary woman who is herself a mother will perhaps have a somewhat more realistic picture of the events preceding Adolf's birth and a more accurate one of the sort of emotional atmosphere surrounding his first year of life, so crucial for a child's sense of security.

When she is sixteen, Klara Pötzl moves into the home of her "Uncle Alois," where she is to take care of his sick wife and two children. There she is later made pregnant by the master of the house even before his wife is dead, and when she is twenty-four the forty-eight-year-old Alois marries her. Within a period of two and a half years she gives birth to three children and loses all three in the space of four or five weeks. Let us try to imagine what actually happened. The first child, Gustav, comes down with diphtheria in November; Klara can scarcely take care of him because she is about to give birth to her third child, Otto, who probably catches the disease from Gustav and dies after three days. Soon after, before Christmas, Gustav dies and three weeks later the second child, Ida, as well. Thus, within a period of four to five weeks, Klara has lived through the birth of one child and the death of three. A woman need not be especially sensitive for such a shock to make her lose her equilibrium, especially if, like Klara, she is confronted with a domineering and demanding husband while still practically an adolescent. Perhaps as a practicing Catholic she regarded these three deaths as punishment for her adulterous relations with Alois; perhaps she reproached herself because the birth of her third child prevented her from taking good care of Gustav. In any case, a woman would have to be made of stone to remain untouched by these blows of fate, and Klara was not made of stone. But no one could help her to experience her grief; her marital duties toward Alois continued, and in the same year as her daughter Ida's death Klara became pregnant once again. In April of the following year, she gave birth to Adolf. It was because she could not deal adequately with her grief under these circumstances that the birth of a new child must have reactivated her recent shock, mobilizing her deepest fears and a feeling of great insecurity regarding her ability as a mother. What woman with these experiences behind her would not have been fearful during her new pregnancy of a repetition of the past? It is scarcely conceivable that her son, in his early period of symbiosis with his mother, imbibed feelings of peace, contentment, and security along with her milk. It is more likely that his mother's anxiety, the fresh memories of her three dead children reactivated by Adolf's birth, and the conscious or unconscious fear that this child would die too were all communicated directly to her baby as if mother and child were one body. It was also of course impossible for Klara to experience her anger toward her self-centered husband, who left her to her anguish. All the more, then, did her baby—who, after all, did not have to be feared like her domineering husband—come to feel the force of these negative emotions.

All this is destiny; it would be futile to try to find the guilty person. Many people have had a similar fate. For example, Novalis, Hölderlin, and Kafka were also strongly influenced by the loss of several siblings, but they were all able to express their sorrow. In Hitler's case there was an additional factor: he was unable to tell anyone about his feelings or about the deep anxiety stemming from the disturbed early relationship with his mother. He was forced to repress all this in order not to attract his father's attention and thus provoke fresh beatings. The only remaining possibility was to identify with the aggressor.

Something else resulted from this unusual family constellation: mothers who after losing one child have another often idealize the dead child (the way unhappy people frequently fantasize about the missed opportunities in their lives). The living child then feels impelled to make a special effort and to accomplish something extraordinary in order not to be overshadowed by the dead sibling. But the mother's real love is usually directed toward the idealized dead child, whom she imagines as possessing every virtue—if only it had lived. The same thing happened to van Gogh, for instance, although only one of his brothers had died.

A patient who once consulted me spoke of his happy and harmonious childhood with exaggerated enthusiasm. I am accustomed to idealizations of this nature, but in this case I was struck by something in his tone that I could not understand at first. In the course of our session the man revealed that he had had a sister who died when she was barely two

years old and who apparently had superhuman abilities for
her age: she supposedly took care of her mother when she was
ill, sang to her "to soothe her," could recite entire prayers by
heart, and so on. When I asked the man if he thought this
was possible at her age, he looked at me as though I had just
committed a terrible sacrilege, and said, "Not normally, but
with this child it was—it was simply extraordinary, a miracle."
I said to him that mothers very often idealize their dead
children, told him the story of van Gogh, and said it was
sometimes very difficult for the living child to be constantly
compared to such a magnificent image, which one can never
live up to. The man resumed speaking mechanically about his
sister's abilities and how terrible it was that she had to die.
Then, all of a sudden, he broke off and was overcome by
grief over his sister's death—or so he believed—which had
occurred almost thirty-five years before. I had the impression
that this was the first time he had ever shed tears over his own
childhood, for these tears were genuine. Only now did I also
understand the strange, artificial tone of voice that had struck
me at the beginning of the hour. Perhaps he had been unconsciously compelled to show me how his mother had spoken
of her firstborn. He spoke as effusively about his childhood
as his mother had about her dead child, but at the same time
he was communicating to me by his unnatural tone of voice
the truth about his childhood fate.

I often thought of this story when patients came to me
who had a similar family constellation. When I explored this
with them, time and again I heard of the cult connected with
the graves of dead children, a cult that is often practiced
for decades. The more precarious the mother's narcissistic
equilibrium, the more glowing the picture she paints of the
rich promise that died with her child. This child would have
made up for all her deprivation, for any pain caused her by
her husband, and for all her troubles with her difficult living
children. It would have been the ideal "mother" protecting
her from all harm—if only it had not died.

Since Adolf was the first child born after three other children had died, I cannot imagine how his mother's feeling toward him can be interpreted solely as one of "devoted love," as described by his biograpers. They all claim that Hitler received *too much* love from his mother (they see being spoiled or, as they put it, "oral spoiling," as the result of an excess of love), and *that* is supposed to be why he was so avid for admiration and recognition. Because he is thought to have had such a good and long symbiosis with his mother, he is supposed to have sought it again and again in his narcissistic merging with the masses. Statements such as these are sometimes found even in psychoanalytic case histories.

It seems to me that a pedagogical principle deeply rooted in all of us is at work in these interpretations. Child-rearing manuals often contain the advice not to "spoil" children by giving them too much love and consideration (which is called "doting" or "pampering"), but to steel them for real life right from the beginning. Psychoanalysts express themselves differently here; they say, for example, that "one must prepare the child to bear frustration," as if a child could not learn that on his or her own in life. In fact, exactly the reverse is true: a child who has been given genuine affection can get along without it as an adult better than someone who has never had it. Therefore, if a person craves or "is greedy for" affection, this is *always* a sign that he is looking for something he never had and not that he doesn't want to give up something because he had too much of it in childhood.

It can appear from the outside that someone's every wish is being granted without this being the case. Thus, a child can be spoiled with food, toys, and excessive concern without ever being seen or heeded for what he or she really is. If we take Hitler as an example, it is easy to imagine that he would never have been loved by his mother if he had appeared to hate his father, which in fact he did. His mother was not capable of love but only of meticulously fulfilling her duties. The condition she must have imposed on her son was that he be a good boy and "forgive and forget" his father's cruelty toward him. An instructive detail pointed out by B. F. Smith shows how little able Adolf's mother would have been to give him her support in his problems with his father:

> [T]he old man's dominance made him a permanent object of respect, if not of awe, to his wife and children. Even after his death his pipes still stood in a rack on the kitchen shelf, and when his widow wished to make a particularly important point she would gesture toward the pipes as if to invoke the authority of the master. [Quoted by Stierlin]

Since Klara extended her "reverence" for her husband, even after his death, to his pipes, we can scarcely imagine that her son would ever have been allowed to confide his true feelings to her, especially since his three dead siblings had surely "always been good" in his mother's mind, and now that they were in heaven were unable to do anything bad anyway.

Thus, Adolf could receive affection from his parents only at the expense of completely disguising and denying his true feelings. This gave rise to a whole mental outlook that Fest discovers to be a continuous pattern in Hitler's life. Fest's biography begins with the following sentences, which underscore this relevant and central point:

> All through his life he made the strongest efforts to conceal as well as to glorify his own personality. Hardly any other prominent figure in history covered his tracks so well as far as his personal life was concerned. He stylized his persona with forceful and pedantic consistency. The image he had of himself was more that of a monument than of a man. From the start he endeavored to hide behind it. [*Hitler*]

Someone who has experienced his mother's love will never need to disguise himself in this way.

Hitler systematically tried to cut off all contact with his past: he did not allow his half brother Alois to come near him, and he made his sister Paula, who kept house for him, change her name. But on the stage of world politics he unconsciously enacted the true drama of his childhood—under another guise. *He*, like his father before him, was now the dictator, the only one who had anything to say. It was the place of all the others to be silent and to obey. He was someone who aroused fear, but he also commanded the love of his people, who prostrated themselves at his feet just as the subservient Klara had once done at the feet of her husband.

The special fascination Hitler held for women is well known. For the shy little girl in them, he embodied the admired father, who knew exactly what was right and wrong and who could in addition offer them an outlet for the hatred they had bottled up since childhood. This combination gave Hitler his great following among both women and men. For all these people had once been raised to be obedient, had grown up in an atmosphere of duty and Christian virtues; they had to learn at a very early age to repress their hatred and their needs.

And now along came a man who did not question the underpinnings of this bourgeois morality of theirs, someone who on the contrary could put the obedience that had been instilled in them to good use, who never confronted them with searching questions or inner crises, but instead provided them with a universal means for finally being able to live out in a thoroughly acceptable and legal way the hatred they had been repressing all their lives. Who would not take advantage of such an opportunity? The Jews could now be blamed for everything, and the actual erstwhile persecutors—one's own, often truly tyrannical parents—could be honored and idealized.

I know a woman who never happened to have any contact with a Jew up to the time she joined the Bund Deutscher Mädel, the female equivalent of the Hitler Youth. She had been brought up very strictly. Her parents needed her to help out in the household after her siblings (two brothers and a sister) had left home. For this reason she was not allowed to prepare for a career even though she very much wanted to and even though she had the necessary qualifications. Much later she told me with what enthusiasm she had read about "the crimes of the Jews" in *Mein Kampf* and what a sense of relief it had given her to find out that it was permissible to hate someone so unequivocally. She had never been allowed to envy her siblings openly for being able to pursue their careers. But the Jewish banker to whom her uncle had to pay interest on a loan—*he* was an exploiter of her poor uncle, with whom she identified. She herself was actually being exploited by her parents and was envious of her siblings, but a well-behaved girl was not permitted to have these feelings. And now, quite unexpectedly, there was such a simple solution: it was all right to hate as much as she wanted; she still remained (and perhaps for this very reason was) her parents' good girl and a useful daughter of the fatherland. Moreover, she could project the "bad" and weak child she had always learned to despise in herself onto the weak and helpless Jews and experience herself as exclusively strong, exclusively pure (Aryan), exclusively good.

And Hitler himself? This is where the whole process of enactment had its start. It was also true for him that in the Jew he was mistreating the helpless child he once was in the same way his father had mistreated him. And just as the father was never satisfied and whipped him every day, nearly beating him to death when he was eleven, Hitler also was never satisfied; he wrote in his will, after he had already had six million Jews put to death, that it was still necessary to exterminate the last remnants of Jewry.

What is revealed here, as in the case of Alois and the other parents who beat their children, is the fear of a possible resurrection and return of the split-off parts of the self. This is why beating is a never-ending task—behind it hovers fear of the emergence of one's own repressed weakness, humiliation, and helplessness, which one has tried to escape all one's life by means of grandiose behavior: Alois with his position as a high-level customs official, Adolf as the Führer, someone else as a psychiatrist who swears by electric-shock treatment or as a research doctor who conducts experiments by transplanting monkey brains, as a professor who prescribes what his students should believe, or simply as a parent rearing a child. None of these endeavors is directed at other human beings (or at monkeys)—what is really at issue in everything these people do to others when they despise and demean them is the attempt to exterminate their own former weakness and to avoid sorrow.

Helm Stierlin's interesting study of Hitler proceeds from the premise that Adolf's mother unconsciously "delegated" him to come to her rescue. According to this view, oppressed Germany would then be a symbol for the mother. This may be correct, but there can be no doubt that deep-seated, intensely personal, and unconscious problems also find expression in the savage fanaticism of Hitler's later actions, which represent a gigantic struggle to purge his self—for which Germany is a symbol—of all traces of his boundless degradation.

One interpretation does not exclude the other, however: rescuing the mother also implies a struggle for the child's own existence. To put it another way: if Adolf's mother had been a strong woman, she would not—in the child's mind—have allowed him to be exposed to these torments and to constant fear and dread. But because she herself had been degraded and was a total slave to her husband, she was not able to shield her child. Now he had to save his mother (Germany) from the enemy in order to have the kind of good, pure, strong mother, free of Jewish contamination, who could have given him security. Children very often fantasize that they must save or rescue their mother so that she can finally be the mother to them whom they needed from the beginning. This can become a full-time occupation in later life. But since it is not possible for children to save their mothers, the compulsion to repeat this situation of powerlessness inevitably leads to failure or even to catastrophe if its underlying roots are not recognized and experienced. Stierlin's ideas could be carried even further along these lines and, put in symbolic terms, might lead to the following horrendous conclusion: the liberation of Germany and the destruction of the Jewish people down to the last Jew, i.e., the *complete* removal of the bad father, would have provided Hitler with the conditions that could have made him a happy child growing up in a calm and peaceful situation with a beloved mother.

This unconscious symbolic goal is of course a delusion, for the past can never be changed; yet every delusion has its own meaning, which is very easy to understand once the childhood situation is known. This meaning is frequently distorted by case histories and by information given us by biographers, who overlook precisely the most essential data because defense mechanisms are involved. For example, a great deal of research and writing has been done on the question of whether Alois Hitler's father was really Jewish and whether Alois could be called an alcoholic.

Often, however, the child's psychic reality has very little to do with what the biographers later "prove" to be facts. The mere *suspicion* of Jewish blood in the family is much more difficult for a child to bear than the certainty. Alois himself must have suffered from this uncertainty, and there can be little doubt that Adolf knew of the rumors even though no one wanted to speak openly about the matter. The very thing that parents try to hide is what will preoccupy a child the most, especially if a major parental trauma is involved (cf. page 166).

The persecution of the Jews "made it possible" for Hitler to "correct" his past on the level of fantasy. It permitted him:

1. To take *revenge* on his father, who was suspected of being half Jewish

2. To *liberate* his mother (Germany) from her persecutor

3. To *attain his mother's love* with fewer moral sanctions, with more true self-expression (the German people loved Hitler for being a shrieking Jew-hater, not for being the well-behaved Catholic boy he had to be for his mother)

4. To *reverse roles*—*he* has now become the dictator, *he* must now be obeyed and submitted to as his father once was; *he* organizes concentration camps in which people are treated the way he was as a child. (A person is not likely to conceive something monstrous if he does not know it somehow or other from experience. We simply tend to refuse to take a child's suffering seriously enough.)

5. Moreover, the persecution of the Jews permitted him to *persecute* the weak child in his own self that was now projected onto the victims. In this way he would not have to experience grief over his past pain, which had been especially hard to bear because his mother had not been able to prevent it. In this, as well as in his unconscious revenge on his early childhood persecutor, Hitler resembled a great number of Germans who had grown up in a similar situation.

In the portrait of Adolf Hitler's family as drawn by Stierlin, we still are shown the loving mother who, while she delegates the function of rescuer to her child, protects him at the same time from the violent father. In Freud's version of the Oedipus legend, we also find this beloved and loving idealized mother figure. In his book on male fantasies, Klaus Theweleit comes somewhat closer to the truth about these mothers, although he too hesitates to draw the logical consequences from his material. He ascertains that the image of a strict, punitive father and a devoted, protective mother keeps occurring in the cases he analyzes of representatives of Fascist ideology. The mother is referred to as "the best wife and mother in the world," as a "good angel," as "clever, of strong character, helpful, and deeply religious." The Fascists Theweleit analyzes admire qualities in the mothers of their comrades or in their mothers-in-law that they apparently do not want to attribute to their own mothers: severity, love of the fatherland, a Prussian attitude ("Germans do not cry")—the mother of iron who "doesn't bat an eyelash at the news of the death of her sons."

Theweleit quotes a case:

> Still, it was not this news that turned out to be the last straw for the mother. Four sons were killed in the war; this she survived. It took something ridiculous in comparison to devastate her. The province of Lorraine became French and with it the company mines. [*Männerphantasien*]

But what if these two sides were two halves of one's own mother? Hermann Ehrhardt relates in the same book:

Once on a winter's night I stood sullenly outside in the snow for
four hours before my mother finally said now I had been punished enough.

Before the mother "rescues" her son by saying he "had
been punished enough," she sees to it that he stands in the
snow for four hours. A child cannot understand why the
mother he loves hurts him so, cannot comprehend why the
woman who in his eyes is a giantess in actuality fears her
husband as if she were a little girl and unconsciously passes
on her own childhood humiliation to her little boy. A child
cannot help but suffer from this harsh treatment. But he dare
not live out this suffering or show it. There is no choice but to
split it off and project it onto others, i.e., to ascribe his
mother's harsh qualities to other mothers and even come to
admire these qualities in them.

Could Klara Hitler help her son as long as she was herself
her husband's dependent, submissive serving maid? While he
was alive, she timidly called her husband "Uncle Alois," and
after his death she would gesture toward his pipes, which
were on display in the kitchen, to emphasize a point she was
making.

What happens to a child when he must repeatedly see the
same mother who tells him of her love, who carefully prepares
his meals and sings lovely songs to him, turn into a pillar of
salt and look on without lifting a finger when this child is
given a brutal beating by his father? How must he feel when
time after time he hopes in vain that she will help him, will
come to his rescue; how must he feel when in his suffering he
waits in vain for her finally to use her power, which in *his*
eyes is so great, on his behalf? The mother watches her child
being humiliated, derided, and tormented without coming to
his defense, without doing anything to save him. Through her
silence she is in complicity with his persecutor; she is abandoning her child. Can we expect a child to understand this?
Should we be surprised if his bitterness, although repressed,
is also directed against the mother? Perhaps this child will
love his mother dearly on a conscious level; later, in his rela-

tionships with other people, he will repeatedly have the feeling of being abandoned, sacrificed, and betrayed.

Hitler's mother is surely no exception but rather the rule, if not even the ideal of many men. But can a mother who is only a slave give her child the respect he needs to develop his vitality? We can gather from the following depiction of the masses in *Mein Kampf* what Hitler's ideal of femininity was:

> The psyche of the great masses is not receptive to anything that is halfhearted and weak.
>
> Like a woman, whose psychic state is determined less by grounds of abstract reason than by an indefinable emotional longing for a force which will complement her nature, and who, consequently, would rather bow to a strong man than dominate a weakling, likewise the masses love a commander more than a petitioner and feel inwardly more satisfied by a doctrine, tolerating no other beside itself, than by the granting of liberalistic freedom with which, as a rule, they can do little, and are prone to feel that they have been abandoned. They are equally unaware of their shameless spiritual terrorization and the hideous abuse of their human freedom, for they absolutely fail to suspect the inner insanity of the whole doctrine. All they see is the ruthless force and brutality of its calculated manifestations, to which they always submit in the end.

In his description of the masses, Hitler accurately portrays his mother and her subservience. His political guidelines are based on very early experiences: brutality always wins out.

Hitler's scorn for women, understandable given his family background, was reinforced by the theories of Lanz von Liebenfels,

> [whose] race theory was permeated by sexual-envy complexes and deep-seated antifemale emotions; woman, he maintained, had brought sin into the world, and her susceptibility to the lecherous wiles of bestial subhuman men was the chief cause for the infection of Nordic blood. [Fest, *Hitler*]

Perhaps Klara called her husband "Uncle Alois" out of sheer timidity, but whatever the reason, he found this acceptable. Did he even require it, just as he wished to be addressed by his neighbors with the formal "Sie," not the usual familiar "Du"? Even Adolf refers to him in *Mein Kampf* as "Herr Hitler," which possibly goes back to a wish of his father's that was introjected at a very early age. It is quite likely that by insisting on these forms of address Alois was attempting to compensate for the misery of his early childhood (being given away by his mother, illegitimate, poor, of dubious parentage) and finally perceive himself as *Herr*. From this conjecture it is only one step to the possibility that it was for this very reason that for twelve years the Germans had to greet one another with the salutation "Heil Hitler." All of Germany had to bow to even the most eccentric, entirely personal demands of its Führer, just as Klara and Adolf had once had to bow to their omnipotent master.

Hitler flattered the "German, Germanic" woman because he needed her homage, her vote, and her other services. He had also needed his mother, but he never had a chance to achieve a truly warm, intimate relationship with her. Stierlin writes:

> N. Bromberg (1971) has written about Hitler's sexual habits: ". . . the only way in which he could get full sexual satisfaction was to watch a young woman as she squatted over his head and urinated or defecated in his face." He also reports ". . . an episode of erotogenic masochism involving a young German actress at whose feet Hitler threw himself, asking her to kick him. When she demurred, he pleaded with her to comply with his wish, heaping accusations on himself and groveling at her feet in such an agonizing manner that she finally acceded. When she kicked him, he became excited, and as she continued to kick him at his urging, he became increasingly excited. The difference in age between Hitler and the young women with whom he had any sexual involvement was usually close to the twenty-three-year difference between his parents."

It is totally inconceivable that a man who as a child received love and affection from his mother, which most Hitler biographers claim was the case, would have suffered from these sadomasochistic compulsions, which point to a very early childhood disturbance. But our concept of mother love obviously has not yet wholly freed itself from the ideology of "poisonous pedagogy."

SUMMARY

Readers who interpret my treatment of Hitler's early childhood as sentimental or even as an attempt to excuse his deeds naturally have every right to construe what they have read as they see fit. People who, for example, had to learn at a very early age "to keep a stiff upper lip" identify with their parents to the extent that they consider any form of empathy with a child as emotionalism or sentimentality. As for the question of guilt, I chose Hitler for the very reason that I know of no other criminal who is responsible for the death of so many human beings. But nothing is gained by using the word *guilt*. We of course have the right and the duty to lock up murderers who threaten our life. For the time being, we do not know of any better solution. But this does not alter the fact that the need to commit murder is the outcome of a tragic childhood and that imprisonment is the tragic sequel to this fate.

If we stop looking for new facts and focus on the significance within the total picture of what we already know, we will come upon sources of information in our study of Hitler that have thus far not been properly evaluated and therefore are not readily or widely accessible. As far as I know, for example, little attention has been paid to the important fact that Klara Hitler's hunchbacked and schizophrenic sister, Adolf's Aunt Johanna, lived with the family throughout his childhood. At least in the biographies I have read, I have never found a connection made between this fact and the Third Reich's euthanasia law. To find any significance in this connection, a person must be able and willing to comprehend the feelings that arise in a child who is exposed daily to an extremely absurd and frightening form of behavior and yet at the same time is forbidden to articulate his fear and rage or his questions. Even the presence of a schizophrenic aunt can be positively dealt with by a child, but only if he can communicate freely with his parents on the emotional level and can talk with them about his fears.

Franziska Hörl, a servant in the Hitler household when Adolf was born, told Jetzinger in an interview that she had not been able to put up with this aunt any longer and left the family on her account, stating simply that she refused to be around "that crazy hunchback" any longer.

The child of the family is not allowed to say such a thing. Unable to leave, he must put up with everything; not until he has grown up can he take any action. When Hitler was grown and came to power, he was finally able to avenge himself a thousandfold on this unfortunate aunt for his own misfortune. He had all the mentally ill in Germany put to death, because he felt they were "useless" for a "healthy" society (i.e., for him as a child). As an adult, Hitler no longer had to put up with anything; he was even able to "liberate" all of Germany from the "plague" of the mentally ill and retarded and was not at a loss to find ideological embellishments for this throughly personal act of revenge.

I have not gone into the background of the euthanasia law in this book because it has been my main concern to describe the consequences of actively humiliating a child, by presenting a striking example. Since such humiliation, combined with prohibiting a child's verbal expression, is a constant and universally encountered factor in child-rearing, the influence of this factor in the child's later development is easily overlooked. The claim that child beating (including spanking) is common, to say nothing of the conviction that it is necessary in order to spur the child on to learn, completely ignores the dimensions of childhood tragedy. Because the relationship of child beating to subsequent criminality is not perceived, the world reacts with horror to the crimes it sees committed and overlooks the conditions giving rise to them, as if murderers fell out of a clear blue sky.

I have used Hitler as an example to show that:

1. Even the worst criminal of all time was not born a criminal.

2. Empathizing with a child's unhappy beginnings does not imply exoneration of the cruel acts he later commits. (This is as true for Alois Hitler as it is for Adolf.)

3. Those who persecute others are warding off knowledge of their own fate as victims.

4. Consciously experiencing one's own victimization instead of trying to ward it off provides a protection against sadism; i.e., the compulsion to torment and humiliate others.

5. The admonition to spare one's parents inherent in the Fourth Commandment and in "poisonous pedagogy" encourages us to overlook crucial factors in a person's early childhood and later development.

6. We as adults don't get anywhere with accusations, indignation, or guilt feelings, but only by understanding the situations in question.

7. True emotional understanding has nothing to do with cheap sentimental pity.

8. The fact that a situation is ubiquitous does not absolve us from examining it. On the contrary, we must examine it for the very reason that it is or can be the fate of each and every one of us.

9. Living out hatred is the opposite of experiencing it. To experience something is an intrapsychic reality; to live it out, on the other hand, is an action that can cost other people their lives. If the path to experiencing one's feelings is blocked by the prohibitions of "poisonous pedagogy" or by the needs of the parents, then these feelings will have to be lived out. This can occur either in a destructive form, as in Hitler's case, or in a self-destructive one, as in Christiane F.'s. Or, as in the case of most criminals who end up in prison, this living out can lead to the destruction both of the self and of others. The history of Jürgen Bartsch, which I shall treat in the next chapter, is a dramatic example of this.

Jürgen Bartsch: A Life
Seen in Retrospect

*But another question will forever remain unanswered,
quite aside from any considerations of guilt: Why do there
have to be people who are this way? Are they usually born
like this? Dear God, what crime did they commit before
they were even born?*
(FROM A LETTER WRITTEN BY JÜRGEN BARTSCH IN PRISON)

Introduction

THOSE who swear by statistical studies and gain their psychological knowledge from those sources will see my efforts to understand the children Christiane and Adolf as unnecessary and irrelevant. They would have to be given statistical proof that a given number of cases of child abuse later produced almost the same number of murderers. This proof cannot be provided, however, for the following reasons:

1. Child abuse usually takes place in secret and often goes undetected. The child conceals and represses these experiences.

2. Although abundant testimony is presented, people can always be found who will substantiate the opposite. Even if the latter evidence is contradictory, as in Jetzinger's case (cf. pages 153–4), it is more likely to be given credence than the child is, because this helps to protect the parents.

3. So far, the connection between abuse of children and infants and later acts of murder has scarcely been noted by criminologists or even by the majority of psychologists. As a

result, little statistical data on the subject have been collected. Relevant studies do exist, however.

Even if statistical data confirm my own conclusions, I do not consider them a reliable source because they are often based on uncritical assumptions and ideas that are either meaningless (such as "a sheltered childhood"), vague, ambiguous ("received a lot of love"), or deceptive ("the father was strict but fair"), or that even contain obvious contradictions ("he was loved and spoiled"). This is why I do not care to rely on conceptual systems whose gaps are so large that the truth escapes through them, but rather prefer to make the attempt, as I did in the Hitler chapter, to take a different route. I am not searching for statistical objectivity but for the subjectivity of the victim in question, to the degree that my empathy permits. In the process I have discovered the interplay between hatred and love: on the one hand, lack of respect, lack of interest in the unique being dependent on his parents' needs, abuse, manipulation, curtailment of freedom, humiliation, and mistreatment; and on the other hand caresses, spoiling, and seductive behavior to the extent that the child is experienced as a part of the parents' self. My observations are lent scientific validity by the fact that they can be made repeatedly, can proceed with a minimum of theoretical assumptions, and can be verified or refuted even by nonprofessionals. Among nonprofessionals in the field of psychology, we can certainly point to members of the legal profession.

Statistical studies are hardly the thing to make disinterested jurists into empathic and perceptive human beings. And yet every crime, by virtue of being an enactment of a childhood drama, cries out for understanding. The newspapers carry these stories every day, but unfortunately usually report only the last act. Can knowledge of the underlying causes of a crime bring about a change in the way justice is administered? Not as long as the primary concerns are to assign guilt and impose punishment. But someday it may be possible to gain understanding for the fact that emerges so clearly in the case of Jürgen Bartsch: the accused never bears all the guilt by himself but is a victim of a tragic chain of circumstances.

Even so, a prison sentence is unavoidable if society is to be protected. But there is a difference between prison being used to *punish* a dangerous criminal according to the principles of "poisonous pedagogy" and a human tragedy being perceived, with the result that the person in question receives psycho- therapy during confinement. For example, prisoners could be allowed to paint or sculpt in groups, at no great financial cost. In this way they might have a chance to express creatively that crucial portion of their earliest years which has remained hidden from them, the mistreatment they suffered, and their ensuing feelings of hatred. Then the need to transform all this into brutally lived-out actions could be reduced.

To be receptive to an attitude such as this, we must first realize that merely pronouncing a person guilty accomplishes nothing. We are so caught up in the habit of assigning guilt that we have difficulty understanding any other approach. This is why my views are sometimes interpreted to mean that the parents are "to blame" for everything and why at the same time I am accused of dwelling on the plight of the victims and of letting the parents off too lightly, of forgetting that every human being must be responsible for his or her own actions. These accusations are also symptoms of "poisonous pedagogy" and are a sign of how effective the inculcation of the idea of guilt at a very early age is. It must be very difficult to learn to understand that a person can see the tragedy of a persecu- tor or a murderer without minimizing the cruelty of the crime or the dangerousness of the criminal. If I were to abandon one of these two sides of my position, it would fit better into the framework of "poisonous pedagogy." But it is my intention to escape this framework by limiting myself to disseminating information and by refraining from moralizing.

Pedagogues in particular are disturbed by the way I pre- sent my views, because, as they write, they "can find nothing to hold on to." If it is the rod or their particular method of child-rearing they have been holding on to, this turn of events would signal no great loss. By renouncing their principles of child-rearing, pedagogues might be able to experience the fears and guilt feelings that were once beaten into them or subtly instilled in them, for they would then no longer discharge these feelings onto others, onto the children. Experiencing these previously warded-off feelings would give them something more authentic and substantial to hold on to than do the principles of child-rearing (cf. my *Prisoners of Childhood: The Drama of the Gifted Child*).

A patient's father, who himself had had a very difficult childhood that he never talked about, often treated his son, in whom he kept seeing himself, in an extremely cruel way. Neither he nor his son was conscious of this cruelty; they both regarded it as a "disciplinary measure." When the son, who had severe symptoms, began his analysis, he was, as he said, "very grateful" to his father for the strict upbringing and "severe punishment" he had received. While in analysis, my patient, who had at one point been studying education at the university, discovered Ekkehard von Braunmühl and his anti-pedagogical writings and was strongly impressed by them. During this period he went home for a visit and for the first time experienced with great clarity the way his father continually hurt his feelings, either by not listening at all to what he was saying or by ridiculing everything he said. When his son pointed this out to him, the father, who was a professor of education, said in all seriousness: "You ought to thank me for that. You'll have to put up with people all your life who won't pay any attention to you or won't take what you say seriously. This way you're already used to it, having learned it from me. What you learn when you're young, you know for the rest of your life." The twenty-four-year-old son was taken aback by this reply at first. How often he had heard his father make similar statements without ever questioning their validity! This time, however, he became indignant, and on the basis of something he had read in Braunmühl, he said: "If you intend to continue treating me according to these principles, to be consistent you would then actually have to kill me, for someday I will have to die too. That would be the best way you could prepare me for it." His father accused him of being impertinent and acting as though he knew all the answers, but this was a very decisive experience for the son. From that point on, his studies took an entirely different direction.

It is difficult to decide whether this story serves as an example of "poisonous" or so-called harmless pedagogy. It occurred to me here because it provides a transition to the case of Jürgen Bartsch. My gifted twenty-four-year-old patient was so tormented in his analysis by cruel and sadistic fantasies that he sometimes thought in his panic that he might become a child murderer. But as a result of working through his fantasies in analysis and experiencing his early relationship with his father and mother, these fears disappeared along with his other symptoms, and he could begin to develop in a free and healthy way. His recurrent fantasies of revenge, in which he wanted to murder a child, were in my interpretation a compressed expression of hatred for his father, who was repressing his vitality, and of identification with this aggressor who was murdering a child (i.e., the patient himself). I have given this example before presenting Bartsch's case because I am struck by a similarity in the psychodynamics of the two men even though the outcome of their stories is so different.

"Out of the Clear Blue Sky?"

I HAVE spoken with many people who have read Katharina Rutschky's *Schwarze Pädagogik* and were shocked at the cruel way children "used to be" raised. It was their impression that "poisonous pedagogy" was definitely a thing of the past, its practice having been discontinued around the time when their grandparents were children.

In the late 1960s the trial of a so-called sex offender by the name of Jürgen Bartsch caused a great stir in West Germany. Between the ages of sixteen and twenty this young man had murdered a number of children in an indescribably cruel manner. In *Das Selbstporträt des Jürgen Bartsch* (*The Self-Portrait of Jürgen Bartsch*), which appeared in 1972 and is now unfortunately out of print, Paul Moor presents the following facts.

Born November 6, 1946, the illegitimate son of a tubercular war widow and a Dutch seasonal worker, Karl-Heinz Sadrozinsky—later Jürgen Bartsch—was abandoned by his mother in the hospital, which she surreptitiously left ahead of schedule; she died a few weeks later. Several months thereafter, Gertrud Bartsch, the wife of a well-to-do butcher in Essen, entered the same hospital to have major surgery. She and her husband decided to take the abandoned baby, in spite of the reservations voiced by the adoption officials in the welfare office on account of the child's dubious background—such strong reservations that the actual adoption did not take place until seven years later. The new parents raised the child very strictly and isolated him completely from other children because they didn't want him to find out that he was adopted. When the father opened a second butcher shop (with the idea of setting Jürgen up with a business of his own as soon as possible) and Frau Bartsch had to work there, the child was taken care of first by his grandmother and then by a series of maids.

When Jürgen was ten, his parents put him in a Children's Home in Rheinbach, where approximately twenty children were living. At the age of twelve he was taken out of this relatively pleasant atmosphere and put in a Catholic school in which three hundred boys, problem children among them, were subjected to strict military discipline.

Between 1962 and 1966 Jürgen Bartsch murdered four boys, and he estimated that in addition he made more than a hundred unsuccessful attempts. There were minor deviations in each murder, but the basic procedure was the same: after he had lured a boy into a former air-raid shelter, now empty, on Heeger Street, not far from the Bartsch home in Langenberg, he beat the child into submission, tied him up with butcher's string, manipulated his genitals while he himself sometimes masturbated, killed the child either by strangulation or by blows, cut open the body, completely emptied out the stomach and breast cavities, and buried the remains. The variations included:

cutting the corpse up into little pieces, cutting off the limbs, decapitation, castration, putting out the eyes, slicing sections of flesh (which he then smelled) from buttocks and thighs, and unsuccessful attempts at anal intercourse. In the extraordinarily detailed descriptions he gave during preliminary questioning and during the trial, Bartsch emphasized that the climax of his sexual arousal did not occur during masturbation but while he was cutting up the corpses, which gave him a kind of continuous orgasm. With the fourth and last murder he finally attained what he had always had in mind as his ultimate goal: he tied his victim to a post and butchered the screaming child without killing him first.

When deeds such as these are brought to light, they understandably elicit a wave of outrage, indignation, even horror. People are also amazed that such cruelty is possible at all, especially in the case of a youth who was friendly, likable, intelligent, and sensitive and who did not show any signs of being a vicious criminal. In addition, his entire background and childhood did not at first glance reveal any special indications of cruelty. He grew up in a conventional middle-class home like many others, with his share of stuffed animals, in a family it is easy to identify with. People could well say, "Things were not all that different for us; that's all very normal. Everyone would become a criminal if a childhood like his is supposed to be responsible for what he became." There scarcely seemed to be any other explanation than that this youth had been born "abnormal." Even the neurological experts stressed again and again that Bartsch had not been neglected as a child but came from a "sheltered background," from a family that had taken good care of him, and he therefore bore full responsibility for his actions.

Thus, we have here again, as in the case of Adolf Hitler, a portrait of innocent, respectable parents whom, for inexplicable reasons, the good Lord or the devil himself presented with a monster. But monsters are not sent into decent middle-class homes from heaven or from hell. Once we have become familiar with the mechanisms that turn child-rearing into a form of persecution—identification with the aggressor, splitting off and projection, and the transference of one's own childhood conflicts to the child—then we can no longer be satisfied with antiquated explanations. Moreover, when we realize the powerful effect these mechanisms have on the individual, the intense and compulsive hold they can exert, we see in the life of every such "monster" the logical consequences of childhood. I shall attempt to illustrate this in the life of Jürgen Bartsch.

But first I must address the question of why it is so difficult to make psychoanalytical findings about the human being accessible to the public. Paul Moor, who grew up in the United States and then lived in West Germany for thirty years, was very surprised at the view of human nature held by the officials participating in Bartsch's first trial. He could not understand why the people involved were not aware of all those aspects of Bartsch's case that immediately struck him, a foreigner. Naturally, the norms and taboos of a given society are reflected in every courtroom. What a society is not supposed to see will not be seen by its judges or prosecutors either. But it would be too easy to speak only of "society" here, for the experts and judges are, after all, human beings as well. Perhaps their upbringing was similar to Jürgen's; they idealized this system from the time they were little and found appropriate methods of discharge. How could they be expected to notice the cruelty of this upbringing without having the whole edifice of their beliefs come tumbling down? It is one of "poisonous pedagogy's" main goals to make it impossible from the very beginning to see, perceive, and evaluate what one has suffered as a child. Over and over in the testimony of the experts we find the characteristic statement that, after all, "other people" were brought up similarly without becoming sex criminals. In this way the existing system of child-rearing is justified if it can be shown that only a few "abnormal" people who are its product become criminals.

There are no objective criteria that would permit us to designate one childhood as "especially bad" and another as "not so bad." The way children experience their situation depends in part on their sensitivity, and this varies from person to person. Furthermore, in every childhood there are tiny saving as well as shattering circumstances that can be overlooked by an outside observer. Little can be done to alter these fateful factors.

What can and must be changed, however, is our state of awareness of the consequences of our actions. Protecting the environment is no longer a matter of altruism or "do-goodism" now that we know that air and water pollution affect our very survival. Only as a result of this knowledge can laws be implemented that will put a stop to the reckless polluting of our environment. This has nothing to do with morality; it is a matter of self-preservation.

The same can be said for the findings of psychoanalysis. As long as the child is regarded as a container into which we can safely throw all our "emotional garbage," little will be done to bring about any change in the practice of "poisonous pedagogy." At the same time we will be struck by the rapid increase in psychosis, neurosis, and drug addiction among adolescents; we will be outraged and indignant at acts of sexual perversion and violence and will become accustomed to regard mass murders as an unavoidable aspect of our present world.

But if analytic insights become part of public consciousness—and this will certainly happen someday, thanks to a new generation that has grown up with fewer constraints— then, in the interest of all humanity, the subjugation of the child implicit in the law of the "parental powers" can no longer be justified. It will no longer be acceptable for parents to vent their fury and rage freely on their children while the children are required to control their emotions from an early age.

There will surely also be some change in parents' behavior when they learn that what they have previously practiced in good faith as "necessary disciplining" is in reality a history of humiliating, hurting, and mistreating the child. Further, with increasing public understanding of the relationship between criminality and the experiences of early childhood, it is no longer a secret known only to the experts that every crime contains a concealed story, which can then be deciphered from the way the misdeed is enacted and from its specific details. The more closely we study this relationship, the more quickly we will break down the protective walls behind which future criminals have heretofore been bred with impunity. The ensuing acts of revenge can be traced back to the fact that the adult can freely take out his or her aggressions on the child, whereas the child's emotional reactions, which are even more intense than the adult's, must be suppressed by force and by the strongest sanctions.

Once we realize, on the basis of psychoanalytic findings, how many pent-up feelings and aggressions people who function *well* and who behave unobtrusively must live with and the toll this takes on their health, we might well regard it as fortunate—and by no means a matter of course—that everyone does not become a sex offender. There are, to be sure, other ways of learning to live with these pent-up feelings, such as psychosis, addiction, or a perfect adjustment that still enables parents to pass on their bottled-up feelings to their child (cf. the example on pages 201–2), but behind every sexual offense there are specific factors that occur much more frequently than we are usually ready to admit. They often come to the surface in analysis in the form of fantasies that do not have to be translated into actions for the simple reason that experiencing these impulses permits their integration and maturation.

What Does a Murder Tell Us about the Childhood of the Murderer?

THROUGH a lengthy correspondence, Paul Moor made an effort to understand Jürgen Bartsch as a human being; he also spoke with many people who knew something about Bartsch and were willing to talk about him. Moor's inquiries about the boy's first year of life brought the following to light.

Jürgen Bartsch found himself in pathogenic surroundings the very day he was born: November 6, 1946. Immediately after the delivery, he was taken away from his tubercular mother, who died a few weeks later. There was no ersatz mother for the baby. In Essen I found a nurse named Anni, still working in the same maternity ward, who remembers Jürgen very clearly: "It was so unusual to keep children in the hospital longer than two months. But Jürgen stayed with us for eleven months." Modern psychology knows that the first year in the life of a human being is the most important one. Maternal warmth and body contact are of irreplaceable value for the child's later development.

While the baby was still in the hospital nursery, the economic and social attitudes of his future adoptive parents were already beginning to influence his life. Nurse Anni: "Frau Bartsch paid extra so he could stay here with us. She and her husband wanted to adopt him, but the authorities were hesitant because they had reservations on account of the baby's background. His mother was illegitimate like him. She had also been raised by the state for a time. No one was sure who the father was. Normally, we sent children without parents to another ward after a certain amount of time, but Frau Bartsch didn't want that to happen. In the other ward there were all sorts of children, including some from lower-class parents. I still remember today how the baby's eyes shone. He smiled at a very early age, followed objects with his eyes, raised his head, all at a very, very early age. At one point he discovered that the nurse would come when he pushed a button, and that amused him greatly. He didn't have any problems eating then. He was a thoroughly normal, well-developed baby who related well to those around him."

On the other hand there were some early pathological developments. The nurses on the ward had to devise special methods for caring for him, since it was an exception to have such a big baby there. To my astonishment I learned that the nurses had toilet trained him before he was eleven months old. Anni obviously found my astonishment strange. "Please don't forget the way things were then, just one year after a lost war. We didn't even have shifts." With some impatience, she answered my questions about how she and the other nurses had managed that. "We simply put him on the potty, beginning at six or seven months.

We had children here in the hospital who were already walking at eleven months, and they were nearly toilet trained too." Under the circumstances, a German nurse of her generation, even as kind a one as she . . . could hardly be expected to use more enlightened methods of child training.

After eleven long months of this pathogenic existence the child, now called Jürgen, was taken by his adoptive parents. Everyone who knows Frau Bartsch more than slightly says that she is a "demon for cleanliness." Shortly after being released from the hospital, the baby regressed in the matter of his abnormally early toilet training. This disgusted Frau Bartsch.

Acquaintances of the Bartsch family noticed around that time that the baby was always black and blue. Frau Bartsch had a different explanation for the bruises each time, but it was never very convincing. At least once during this period the downcast father, Gerhard Bartsch, confessed to a friend that he was considering divorce: "She beats the baby so badly I simply can't stand it anymore." Another time, when he was taking his leave, Herr Bartsch excused himself for being in such a hurry: "I have to get home or she will beat the child to death."

Jürgen, of course, is unable to report about this period, but we can assume that the frequent anxiety attacks he tells of are the result of these beatings. "When I was very little, I was always terribly afraid of my father's lumbering way. And I have hardly ever seen him laugh, which I noticed even way back then."

"Why this fear I wrote about? It was not so much of confession as it was of the other children. You don't know that I was the scapegoat in the early grades or all the things they did to me. Defend myself? Just try it if you are the smallest one in the class! I was too afraid even to sing in school or to do gymnastics! A few reasons why: classmates who aren't seen outside of school aren't accepted, in line with the idea, 'He doesn't want to bother with us!' Children don't make a distinction between whether he doesn't want to or he can't. I couldn't. A couple of afternoons with my teacher Herr Hünnemeier, a couple of days in Werden at my grandma's, where I slept on the floor, the rest of the afternoons in Katernberg in the shop. The end result: at home everywhere and nowhere, no pals, no friends, because I didn't know anyone. Those are the main reasons, but there's something else that's very important. Until I started going to school I was locked up, most of the time, in the old underground prison [his grandmother's cellar] with barred windows and artificial light. Walls ten feet high. All that. I was allowed out only if my grandma had me by the hand; wasn't allowed to play with another child. For *six years*. I might get dirty, 'and anyway so-and-so is no one for you!' So I resign myself to it, but I'm only in the way there and pushed from one corner to another, get a beating when I don't deserve it and get away with it when I deserve one. My parents don't have any time. I'm afraid of my father because he starts yelling right away, and my mother was hysterical even then. But more than anything else: no contact with others of the same age because, as I said, it's forbidden! So how do you fit in? Get rid of my shyness, which sometimes happens when I'm playing? After six years it's too late!"

Being locked up is an important factor. Later, Bartsch will lure little boys into an underground shelter and murder them there. Because he had no one as a child who understood his unhappiness, he was unable to experience it and had to repress his pain, "not letting anyone see [his] misery."

"I wasn't a coward about everything, but I would have been one if I had let anyone notice how I suffered. Maybe that was wrong, but that's what I thought anyway. Because every boy has his pride, you surely know that. No, I didn't cry every time I got a licking—I thought that was being a 'sissy'—and so at least I was brave about one thing, not letting anyone see my misery. But in all seriousness now, whom should I have gone to, whom should I have poured my heart out to? My parents? As fond as I am of them, I am sorry to say that they never, but really never, could come up with even a tiny fraction of an ounce of understanding in this regard. Never 'could,' I say, not never 'did'; please notice my good intentions! And—this is not a reproach, it's a simple fact—I am firmly convinced—yes, I even experienced it at first hand—that my parents never knew how to deal with children."

Not until he is in prison does Jürgen reproach his parents for the first time:

"You never should have kept me apart from other children, then I wouldn't have been so chicken in school. You never should have sent me to those sadists in their black cassocks, and after I ran away because the priest mistreated me, you shouldn't have brought me back to that school. But you didn't know that. Mama shouldn't have thrown into the stove the book about reproduction that I was supposed to get from Aunt Martha when I was eleven or twelve. Why didn't you play with me one single time in twenty years? But maybe other parents would have been the same way. At least I was a wanted child. Even though I didn't know it for twenty years, only today when it's too damned late.

"Whenever my mother flung the curtain in the doorway to one side and came charging out of the shop like an amazon and I was in the way, then slap! slap! slap! I got it in the face. Simply because I was in the way, often enough that was the only reason. A few minutes later I was suddenly the dear boy you put your arm around and kissed. Then she was surprised that I resisted and was afraid of her. I was already afraid of that woman when I was very little, just the same as I was of my father, except that I saw less of him. Today I ask myself how he ever stood it. Sometimes he was at work from four in the morning till ten or eleven at night without a break, usually in the kitchen where he made his sausages. For days at a time I didn't see him at all, and if I did hear or see him it was only when he went rushing around shouting. But when I was a baby and made a mess in my diapers, he was the one who tended to me. He would say himself: 'I was the one who always had to wash and change the diapers. My wife never did it. She couldn't; she couldn't bring herself to do it.'

"I don't mean to run my mother down. I'm fond of my mother, I love my mother, but I don't believe she is a person who is capable of the slightest understanding. My mother must love me very much. I find it really astonishing, otherwise she wouldn't be doing everything for me that she is. I used to get it in the neck a lot. She's broken coat hangers on me, like when I didn't get my homework right or didn't do it fast enough.

"It got to be a routine with my bath. My mother always bathed me. She never stopped doing it, and I never griped about it, although sometimes I would have liked to say, 'Now, for heaven's sake . . .' But I don't know, it's also possible that I accepted it as a matter of course till the very end. In any case, my father wasn't allowed to come in. If he had, I would have yelled.

"Until I was arrested when I was nineteen, it went like this: I washed my hands and feet myself. My mother washed my head, neck, and back. That might have been normal, but she also went over my stomach, all the way down, and my thighs too, practically everything from top to bottom. You can certainly say that she did much more than I did. Usually I didn't do anything at all, even though she said, 'Wash your hands and feet.' But usually I was pretty lazy. Neither my mother nor my father ever told me I should keep my penis clean under the foreskin. My mother didn't do that when she washed me either.

"Did I find the whole thing peculiar? It was the kind of feeling that wells up periodically for seconds or minutes and perhaps is close to breaking through, but it doesn't quite come to the surface. I felt it, but never directly. I felt it only indirectly, if it's even possible to feel something indirectly.

"I can't remember ever being affectionate with my mother in a spontaneous way, ever putting my arm around her and trying to hug her. I can vaguely remember her doing that when I was lying in bed between my parents, watching television in the evening, but that may have happened twice in four years, and I resisted it. My mother was never especially happy about that, but I always had a sort of horror of her. I don't know what to call it, perhaps an ironic twist of fate, or even sadder than that. When I dreamed about my mother when I was a little boy, either she was selling me or she was coming at me with a knife. Unfortunately, the latter really came true later on.

"It was in 1964 or 1965. I think it was a Tuesday; at that time my mother was in the shop in Katernberg only on Tuesdays and Thursdays. At noontime the meat was removed so the counters could be washed off. My mother washed one half and I the other. The knives, which were kept in a pail, were also washed off. I said I was finished, but she was having a bad day and she said, 'You're not finished by a long shot!' 'Yes, I am,' I said. 'Take a look.' She said, 'You take a look at the mirrors, you'll have to do all of them over again.' I said, 'I won't do them over again because they're already nice and shiny.' She was standing in the back by the mirror. I was standing three or four yards away from her. She bent over to the pail. I thought to myself, what's going on? Then she took a nice long butcher knife out and threw it at me, at about shoulder height. I don't remember whether it bounced off a scale or what, but it landed on a shelf in any case. If I hadn't ducked at the last moment, she would have hit me with it.

"I just stood there stiff as a board. I didn't even know where I was. It was so unreal somehow. That was something you simply couldn't believe. Then she came up to me, spit in my face, and began yelling that I was a piece of shit. Then she yelled, 'I'm going to call up Herr Bitter'—the head of the Essen Welfare Office—'and have him come right over and get you so you can go back where you came from, because that's where you belong!' I ran into the kitchen to Frau Ohskopp, who worked in the shop. She was washing the things from lunch. I stood next to the cupboard and held on to it. I said, 'She threw a knife at me.' 'You're crazy,' she said, 'you don't know what you're talking about.' I ran downstairs to the toilet and sat down and cried like a baby. When I went back upstairs, my mother was running around in the kitchen and had the telephone book open. Probably she really was looking for Herr Bitter's number. For a long time she didn't speak to me. I guess she thought, 'He's a bad fellow who lets someone throw a knife at him and simply jumps aside,' I don't know.

"You should hear my father sometime! He has a pretty extraordinary pair of lungs, a regular drill sergeant's voice. Awful! There can be different reasons for it—his wife or some little thing that displeases him. Sometimes the shouting was something awful, but I'm sure he didn't think of it that way at all. He can't help it, but it was horrible for me as a child. I remember a lot of things like that.

"He was always one for issuing military commands and blaming me for something. He simply can't help it, I've often said that. But he has a hell of a lot on his mind, and so we won't hold it against him.

"In the first trial the lawyer said, 'Herr Bartsch, what was it like in the school in Marienhausen? Your son is supposed to have been given so many beatings. Conditions are supposed to have been so brutal there.' My father answered, in these very words, 'Well, after all, he wasn't beaten to death.' That was a straightforward answer.

"As a rule my parents were never available during the day.

Of course my mother rushed past me from time to time like
greased lightning, but it was understandable that she had no
time for a child. I hardly dared open my mouth because wherever I was, I was in the way, and what's called patience is something my mother never had any of. I often got hit for the simple
reason that I got in her way because I wanted to ask her something.

"I never was able to understand what was going on inside
her. I know how much she loved me and still loves me, but a
child, I always thought, should be able to sense that as well.
Just one example (this is by no means an isolated case; it
happened often): my mother thought absolutely nothing of it
to put her arm around me and kiss me one minute and the next
minute, if she saw that I had left my shoes on by mistake, she
took a coat hanger from the closet and hit me with it till it broke.
Things like that happened often, and every time something inside
me broke too. I've never been able to forget those things or the
way I was treated and I never will be able to. I'm sorry but I just
can't help it. Some people would say I'm ungrateful. That's
hardly the case, because all this is nothing more and nothing
less than an impression I have, an impression based on my
experiences, and the truth is really supposed to be better than
pious lies.

"My parents never should have gotten married in the first
place. If two people who are scarcely capable of showing their
feelings start a family, in my opinion it can only lead to some
sort of trouble. All I heard was, 'Shut up, you're the youngest,
you've got nothing to say anyway. You're just a child, don't
speak until you're spoken to.'

"I feel the saddest when I'm at home, where everything is so
antiseptic you think you have to walk around on tiptoe. On
Christmas Eve everything is sooo clean. I go down to the living
room, and there are lots of presents there for me. It's really
fantastic, and at least on this evening my mother somewhat
controls her temper that otherwise blows hot and cold, so you
think maybe tonight you can forget a little your (I mean my)
own wickedness for once, but somehow there's tension crackling
in the air so you know there'll be hell to pay again. If we could
at least sing a Christmas carol. My mother says, 'Now go ahead
and sing a Christmas carol,' and I say, 'Oh, go on, I can't, I'm
much too big for that,' but I think, 'A child murderer singing

Christmas carols, that's enough to drive you crazy.' I unwrap my presents and am 'pleased,' at least I act that way. Mother unwraps her presents, the ones from me, and really is pleased. In the meantime, supper is ready, chicken soup with the chicken in it, and Father comes home, two hours after me. He's been working till now. He tosses some kind of household appliance at Mother, and she's so touched she has tears in her eyes. He mutters something that sounds like 'Merry Christmas'; then he sits down at the dining table: 'Well, what is it, are you coming or not?' The soup is eaten in silence. We don't even touch the chicken.

"Not a word is spoken the whole time, there's just the radio playing softly as it has been for hours. 'Hope and steadfastness bring strength and consolation in these times. . . .' We're finished eating. Father straightens up and bellows at us, 'Excellent! And what are we going to do now?' as loud as he can. It sounds really awful. 'We're not going to do anything now!' my mother screams and runs crying into the kitchen. I think, 'Who's punishing me, fate or the good Lord?' but I know immediately that that can't be it, and I'm reminded of a scene I saw on television: 'The same as last year, Madame?' — 'The same as *every* year, James!'

"I ask softly, 'Don't you at least want to look at your presents?' — 'No!' — He just sits there staring at the tablecloth with an empty gaze. It's not even eight o'clock yet. There's nothing to keep me down here anymore, so I head up to my room. I pace up and down and I seriously ask myself, 'Are you going to jump out the window now or not?' Why am I living in hell, why would I be better off dead instead of going through something like this? Because I'm a murderer? That can't be all there is to it because today was no different from every other year. This day was always the worst, mostly of course in recent years when I was still at home. Then everything, but really everything, came together all at once on one day.

"Of course my father (and of course my mother too) is one of those people who are convinced that the Nazis' ways of 'educating' had their good side too. 'No doubt about it,' I would almost say. I even heard my father say (in conversation with other older people, who almost *all* think that way!): 'Then we still had discipline, we had order; they didn't get stupid ideas when they were harassed,' etc. I think most young people feel the same way I do and would rather not look into their family history under the Third Reich because every one of us is afraid something or other might come out in the process that we would rather not have to know about.

"I'm sure the episode in the shop with her and the butcher knife happened after the third murder, but similar things, only not quite so bad, happened (of course only with my mother) before that. Every half year or so, even before the first murder. Always when she hit me. She always got furious when I warded off the blows. I was supposed to stand more or less at attention and accept the blows. From about sixteen and a half to nineteen, when she was about to hit me with something she had in her hand, I simply took it away from her. That was just about the worst thing for her. She took that as rebelliousness, although it was only self-defense, because she's by no means weak. And at such moments she had no qualms about injuring me. You can just tell about something like that.

"Those were always times when I had either offended her love of order ('The front room has been cleaned, I don't want anyone going in there today!') or talked back to her." [Moor]

I have let Jürgen Bartsch tell his story for a while without interrupting him, in order to give the reader an idea of the atmosphere of an analytic session. You sit there, you listen, and if you believe the patient and don't tell him what to think or offer him any theories, sometimes a hell will open up right in the midst of a sheltered home, a hell whose existence neither parents nor patient suspected till now.

Could we say that Jürgen's parents would have been better parents if they had known that their son's subsequent behavior would bring their own before the public eye? It's possible, but it is also conceivable that for reasons of their own unconscious compulsions they could not have treated him any differently than they did. But we can assume that if they had known better they would not have taken him out of the good Children's Home and put him in the private school in Marienhausen, would not have forced him to return there after he ran away. Everything that Jürgen tells about Marienhausen in his letters to Paul Moor, everything that came to light in the testimony of witnesses during the trial shows the degree to which "poisonous pedagogy" still prevails today. A few examples:

"In comparison, Marienhausen was a hell—even though a Catholic one; that doesn't make it any better—and not just on [Pater Pülitz's] account. I only have to think of the constant beatings given by the priests in their cassocks when we were in school, at choir, or—and they didn't think twice about it—in church. Of the sadistic punishments (having to stand in a circle in the courtyard in our pajamas for hours at a time until the first one collapsed), of the illegal child labor in the fields every afternoon for weeks in extreme heat (pitching hay, harvesting potatoes, pulling turnips, a thrashing for children who were slow), the merciless way they demonized the oh so wicked 'nastiness' among the boys (necessary for one's development!), the unnatural 'silentium' during meals and after a certain time of day, etc., and the confusing, unnatural things they said to children, such as, 'Anyone who so much as *looks at* one of the girls working in the kitchen will be given a thrashing!'

"One evening Deacon Hamacher gave me such a wallop in our sleeping quarters (I had said something, and in the evening there was a rule of strict silence) that it sent me sliding under the length of several beds. Just before that, 'Pater Catechist' had broken a yardstick on my behind and said in all seriousness that I would have to pay for it.
"Once in the sixth grade I had the flu and was in the infirmary, where the Catechist was on duty. He was not only the religion teacher but in charge of the infirmary as well. A boy with a high fever was in the bed next to mine. The Catechist came in, stuck a thermometer in him, went out, came back after a few minutes, took the thermometer out, looked at it, and then thrashed him mercilessly. The boy, who after all had a bad fever, whimpered and bawled. I don't know if he had any idea of what was going on. Anyway, the Catechist ranted and raved, and then he roared, 'He held the thermometer against the heat!' —forgetting that it wasn't even winter and the heat wasn't even on.' "

Here we see how a child must learn to accept the absurdities and whims of the educators without any opposition and without any feelings of hatred and at the same time condemn

and stifle any desire for the physical or emotional closeness
of another human being, which would have eased the burden.
This is a superhuman accomplishment that is demanded only
of children, never expected of adults.

"First PaPü [Pater Pülitz] said, 'If we ever catch two of you
together!' And when that did happen, then first came the usual
thrashing, only probably even worse than usual, and that's really
saying something. Then of course, first thing the next day, expulsion. God, we were less afraid of being expelled than of those
thrashings. And then the usual clichés about how you could tell
boys like that, etc.; something like—anyone who has damp
hands is homosexual and does nasty things, and whoever does
those nasty things is a criminal. That's pretty much what they
told us and, above all, that these criminal offenses were second
only to murder—yes, in those very words: second only to murder.

"PaPü talked about it almost every day, as though he couldn't
possibly have the temptation himself sometimes. He said that it
was actually natural for 'the blood to back up,' as he put it. I
always thought that was a terrible expression. . . . He said he
had never given in to Satan, and he was proud of the fact. We
heard that practically every day, not in class, but always in-
between times.

"We always got up in the morning at six or half past. Strictest
rule of silence. Then getting ready in silence, always in very
orderly rows of two, to go downstairs and into church, then
the celebration of mass. Back from mass, still in silence and in
rows of two.

"Personal contact, friendships as such were forbidden. It was
forbidden to play with another boy too frequently. To a certain
extent you could get around that because they couldn't have
their eyes everywhere at once, but it was still forbidden. They
thought friendship was suspicious because someone who made
a real friend would be sure to reach inside his pants. They immediately sensed something sexual behind every glance.

"You can hammer some things into children by beating them,
that's clear. And it stays in there. Today it's often denied, but if
it's done under the right conditions, if you know you have to
retain it, then it stays in there, and a lot has stayed in there till
today.

"When PaPü wanted to find something out, like who had done something, he herded us down into the school courtyard and made us keep running until some of us got completely out of breath and collapsed.

"He told us very often (actually even more often than that) in great detail about the horrible mass murders of the Jews in the Third Reich and also showed us a lot of pictures of it. He seemed to enjoy doing this.

"In choir PaPü liked to strike indiscriminately at anyone he could reach and at the same time he would foam at the mouth. His stick would often break when he hit us, and then too this incomprehensible frenzy and foaming at the mouth."

The same man who always warns the boys against sexuality and threatens them with punishment for it lures Jürgen into his bed when the boy is ill:

"He wanted to have his radio back. The beds were quite far apart. I got out of bed with my fever and took the radio over to him. And all of a sudden he said, 'As long as you're here, you might as well get into bed with me!'

"I still didn't realize what was going on. First we just lay next to each other for a while, and then he pulled me up against him and put his hand down inside the back of my pants. That was something new, but really not so new after all. I don't remember how often it happened, it may have been four times, it can also have been seven times, mornings when we were sitting side by side in the choir, he kept making certain movements so he could reach my shorts.

"There in bed he pushed his hand down inside the back of my pajamas and 'stroked' me. He did the same thing in front and tried to masturbate me, but it didn't work, probably because I had a fever.

"I don't remember the words he used but he told me he would finish me off if I opened my trap."

How difficult it is for a child to extricate himself from a situation like this without help. And yet Jürgen summons the courage to run away, which makes him sense even more clearly than before how hopeless his situation is, how altogether lonely he is.

"In Marienhausen, before the thing with PaPü, I really never felt homesick, but when my parents brought me back to Marienhausen, all of a sudden I got terribly homesick. I was around PaPü a lot, and I couldn't imagine having to stay there. Now I was gone from Marienhausen and couldn't imagine going back there again. On the other hand, I figured, if you go home now you'll get a terrible beating. That's why I was afraid. I couldn't move in either direction.

"Near the grounds there's a big woods, and I went in there. I wandered around there practically all afternoon. Then at dusk, all of a sudden my mother was in the woods. Someone had probably seen me. I saw her from behind a tree. She was calling, 'Jürgen? Jürgen? Where are you?' And so I went with her. Of course she started right in scolding and yelling in a big way.

"My parents telephoned Marienhausen immediately. I didn't tell them anything. They kept telephoning Marienhausen for days. Then they came to me and said: 'Well, they've given you another chance! You're going back again!' Naturally, I yammered and wailed, 'Please, please, I don't want to go back.' But anyone who knew my parents would know it was no use.

Jürgen not only tells about Marienhausen from his own perspective; he describes, for example, the fate of a friend.

"He was a good pal. He had been at Marienhausen much longer than I. He came from Cologne, and he was the shortest one in our class. He didn't let anybody say anything bad about his hometown. I can't count the times he got into a fight because someone had insulted his city. Because there's no such thing as a 'city' but just human beings who mean something to a person, that's probably why he always suffered from homesickness.

"He stayed on there longer than I did, too. Because he really was the shortest one, he could never get out of having to stand in the front row at choir, and that way practically every time we rehearsed he got his share of blows in the stomach and in the face. God, *more* than his share because the last row was relatively protected. I can't begin to say how often he got kicked and hit. This isn't supposed to be some kind of hero worship— he would never forgive us for that. For he wasn't a hero and didn't want to be one. If PaPü or the fat Catechist had him in their clutches, then he screamed bloody murder, bellowing out his pain so you would think those hated holy walls would come tumbling down.

"One summer evening in 1960 while we were camping out in Rath near Niedeggen, Pater Pülitz had him 'kidnapped.' It was meant to be a game, a lot of fun. But Herbert didn't know that because nobody told him. He was dragged off deep into the woods at evening, tied up and gagged, stuck into a white sleeping bag, and left lying there. He was there till midnight. Fear, entreaties, despair, loneliness—it's futile, I can't say what he felt. After midnight they razzed him, taunts and jeers, a game, a lot of fun.

"A few years later he left Marienhausen, but when he was still a boy, he plunged to his death in the mountains. He was born to be beaten and tormented and then to die. He was the shortest boy in our class. His name was Herbert Grewe. And he was a good pal."

Marienhausen is only one example of many such places.

"In early 1970 the press and radio reported a scandal of sorts connected with the Don Bosco Home in Cologne. The conditions that no one got excited about in Marienhausen now moved the Welfare Office in Cologne to remove all its children from the Don Bosco Home in Cologne because they claimed they could no longer be responsible for leaving their children in such a place. The teachers were supposed to have knocked children down the stairs, trampled on them, put their heads into the toilet, etc., the same fun they had with us in Marienhausen. Exactly the same, and this was even a Don Bosco Home, run by the good Salesian Fathers. The reports also said that four teachers had repeatedly assaulted their charges. Sometime after 1960 Pater Pülitz taught in this same Home in Cologne for several years."

Even in the hell of his school, Jürgen also experienced something positive for which he is thankful: for the first time he was not the only scapegoat the way he had been at home and in his local school. Here there was a feeling of solidarity "against the sadistic teachers."

"The good part meant so much to me that I might even have been willing to put up with much worse. The main thing was to have the wonderful experience of for once not being excluded. There was a rare solidarity among all the boys against the sadistic teachers. I once read an Arabian proverb: The enemy of my enemy is my friend. You ought to have seen it, the tremendous feeling of solidarity, the way we stuck together. Memory is supposed to exaggerate some things, but I really don't think I'm doing that. For once I *wasn't* an outsider. We would all rather have been beaten to shreds than betray a pal. That was simply unthinkable."

Psychiatry went along with the persecution of Bartsch's "evil drives." On the basis of the argument that he could not control his "excessive sex drive," and in the hope of helping him, the medical authorities prescribed castration, to which he agreed.* This idea borders on the grotesque when we consider that Jürgen was already toilet trained at eleven months. He must have been an especially gifted child to have accomplished this so early, especially in a hospital where there was not a regular care giver. Jürgen proved by this that he was capable of "controlling his drives" to a very great degree. But that was his undoing. If he had not controlled himself so well and for such a long time, then his foster parents might not have adopted him at all or might have given him to someone else who had more understanding for him.

Jürgen's gifts helped him primarily to adapt to his situation in order to survive: to suffer everything in silence, not to rebel against being locked up in the cellar, and even to do well in school. But the eruption of feelings in puberty proved too much for his defense mechanisms. (We can observe something similar in the drug scene.) It would be tempting to say "fortunately," if the consequences of this eruption had not led to a continuation of the tragedy.

---

* Mysteriously, he died while the surgery was being performed—perhaps his unconscious answer to the authorities' total misunderstanding of his true personality.

"Naturally, I often said to my mother, 'Just wait till I'm twenty-one!' That much I dared to say. Then of course my mother would say: 'Yes, yes, I can just imagine. In the first place you're too stupid to get by anywhere except with us. And then, if you really did go out into the world, you'd see, after two days you'd be back here again.' The minute she said it, I knew it was true. I wouldn't have trusted myself to get by alone out there for more than two days. Why I don't know. And I knew for sure that when I turned twenty-one I would *not* go away. That was crystal clear to me, but I had to let off a little steam once in a while. But to think that I might have had any really serious intentions about it is completely absurd. I never would have done it.

"When I started my job I didn't say, 'I like it'; I didn't say, 'It's horrible' either. I didn't actually think that much about it."

Thus, any hope for a life of his own was nipped in the bud. How else can this be described but as soul murder? So far, criminology has never concerned itself with this kind of murder, has never even been able to acknowledge it, because as a part of child-rearing it is perfectly legal. Only the last link in a long chain of actions is punishable by the court. Often this link reveals in minute detail the crime's entire sorrowful prehistory without the perpetrator being aware of it.

The exact descriptions of his "deeds" that Bartsch gives Paul Moor show how little these crimes actually had to do with the "sex drive," although Bartsch was convinced of the opposite and eventually decided for this reason to have himself castrated. From Bartsch's letters, the analyst can learn something about the narcissistic origins of a sexual perversion, something that has not yet been adequately treated in the professional literature.

Bartsch didn't actually understand this himself and wonders repeatedly why his sex drive was separate from what he did. There were boys his age whom he was attracted to, whom he loved, and whom he would have liked to have as close friends, but he distinctly separated all that from what he did to the little boys. He hardly even masturbated in front of them, he writes. He was acting out here the deep humiliation,

intimidation, destruction of dignity, loss of power, and torment of the little boy in lederhosen he had once been. It particularly excited him to look into his victim's frightened, submissive, helpless eyes, in which he saw himself reflected. With
great excitement he repeatedly went through the motions of
destroying his self in his victims—now *he* is no longer the
helpless victim but the mighty persecutor!

Since Paul Moor's shattering book is out of print, I shall
quote here some longer passages from Bartsch's descriptions
of his deeds. His first attempts were with Axel, a boy in the
neighborhood:

"Then, a few weeks later, it was exactly the same. 'Come to the
woods with me,' I said, and Axel replied, 'No, then you'll start
acting crazy again!' But I took him with me anyway because I
promised not to do anything to him. But then I did act crazy
again. Again I stripped the boy naked by force, and then sudden
as a flash I had a devilish idea. I yelled at him again: 'Just
the way you are now, lie down on my lap, with your behind
facing up! It's all right to kick your legs if it hurts, but your
arms and everything else must stay perfectly still! Now I'm
going to hit your behind thirteen times, and each time harder
than the last! If you don't want to go along with it, I'll kill
you! 'Killing' was still an empty threat then, at least that's what
I believed myself. 'Do you want to?'

"He wanted to—what choice did he have? After he had lain
down on my lap with his behind facing up, I did exactly as I
had said. I kept on hitting him, harder and harder, and the boy
kicked his legs like mad but otherwise didn't resist. I didn't
stop at thirteen but only when my hand hurt so much that I
couldn't go on hitting him anymore.

"Afterwards the same thing: I calmed down completely and
felt incredibly humiliated for myself and for someone I liked so
much, abject misery personified, so to speak. Axel didn't cry
and afterwards he wasn't even overly upset. He was only very,
very quiet for a long time.

"I offered to let him hit me. He could have beaten me to
death, I wouldn't have tried to stop him, but he didn't want to.
In the end I was the one who bawled. 'Now you're sure not to

want to have anything more to do with me,' I said to him on the
way home. No answer.

"The next afternoon he came to my door again after all, but
somehow more quietly, more cautiously than before. 'Please—
no more,' was all he said. You won't believe it, I didn't believe
it myself at first, but he didn't even bear me a grudge! For
some time after that, we often played together, until he moved
away, but as far as I can tell, this incident I've just told you
about made me so afraid of myself that I had some peace for a
while. 'A short while,' as it says in the Bible."

"All I can say about the worst things is that from a certain age
(around thirteen or fourteen) I always had the feeling of no
longer having any control over what I was doing, of really
not being able to help it. I prayed, and I hoped at least that would
do some good, but it didn't.

"They were all so little, much littler than I. They were all so
afraid that they didn't resist at all."

"Until 1962 it was only a matter of undressing them and feeling
them and like that. Later, when killing became part of it, I
started cutting them up pretty much right away. At first I
always thought of razor blades, but then after the first time I
started thinking of knives, our knives."

It is important to note what Jürgen says in passing:

"If I love a certain person, the way a boy would love a girl,
then he doesn't correspond at all to my ideal of a victim. It's
not as though I would have to make an effort to hold myself
back somehow, that's ridiculous. In a case like that, the drive
simply disappeared automatically."

It was an entirely different matter with the little boys:

"At the crucial moment I would have liked it if the boy had
offered some resistance, even though the children's helplessness
generally excited me. But I was honestly convinced that the boy
wouldn't have had a chance against me.

"I tried kissing Frese, but that didn't belong to any plan. That
somehow emerged from the situation. I don't know why, from
one moment to the next the desire was there. I thought doing
that between times would be terrific. That was something new

for me. Victor and Detlef I hadn't ever kissed. If I said today that he wanted to be kissed, everyone would say, 'You pig, who do you expect to believe that?'—but it was actually true. In my opinion, it can be explained only by the fact that I had beaten him so terribly before that. If I try putting myself in his place, I can imagine that the only thing he cared about was which was worse, which hurt more. I mean, being kissed by somebody I detest is still preferable to having that person kick me in the balls from behind. In that sense it's understandable. But at the time I was pretty amazed. He said, 'More! More! So finally I kept on. That must be it, that the only thing he cared about was which was easier to bear."

It is striking that Bartsch, who describes what he did to his victims so openly and in such detail—even though he knows what revulsion this will arouse in others—is very reluctant to divulge his memories of when *he* was the helpless victim. He has to force himself to tell these things, which he does in a terse and imprecise way. At the age of eight he was seduced by his thirteen-year-old cousin, and later, at thirteen, by his teacher. Here we can observe the pronounced discrepancy between subjective and social reality. Within the framework of a little boy's value system, Bartsch sees himself in the murder scenes as a powerful person with a strong feeling of self-confidence, although he knows everyone will condemn him for these actions and attitudes. In the other scenes, however, the warded-off pain of the humiliated victim comes to the surface and causes him unbearable feelings of shame. This is one of the reasons why so many people either can't remember being beaten as children at all or only remember it without the appropriate feelings, i.e., quite indifferently and "coolly."

I am not telling the story of Jürgen Bartsch's childhood in his own words in order to "exonerate" him, something which the legal profession accuses psychoanalysis of doing, or to place the blame on his parents, but to show that every one of his actions had a meaning that can be discovered only if we free ourselves from the compulsion to overlook the context. I was appalled by the newspaper accounts about Jürgen Bartsch, to be sure, but I was not morally outraged, because I know that acts similar to Bartsch's often appear in patients' fantasies when they are able to bring to consciousness the repressed desire for revenge stemming from their early childhood (cf. page 202). But for the very reason that they are able to talk about and confide these feelings of hatred, rage, and desire for revenge to another person, they do not need to translate their fantasies into deeds. Jürgen had not had the slightest opportunity to articulate his feelings. In his first year of life he did not have a regular care giver, then he was not allowed to play with other children until the time he started school, nor did his parents ever play with him. In school he soon became a scapegoat for the other boys; it is understandable that such an isolated child, who is beaten into obedience at home, could not hold his own in the company of his peers. He had terrible fears, and this caused the other children to persecute him even more. The scene after he ran away from Marienhausen shows the boundless loneliness of this adolescent caught between his "sheltered," middle-class home and the Catholic boarding school. The need to tell his parents everything and the certainty that they would not believe him; his fear of going back home but also his longing to cry his heart out there—isn't this the situation of thousands of adolescents?

In the Catholic school, Jürgen, the well-behaved child of his parents, obeyed all the rules. For this reason he reacted with astonishment and anger when a former schoolmate testified at the trial that Jürgen had "of course" slept with another boy. It *was* possible, then, to get around the rules, but not for children who had been forced from infancy to learn obedience under threat to their life. Such children are grateful to be allowed to serve as altar boys and at least in this way to be closer to the priest, to some other living being.

The combination of violence and sexual arousal that the very small child whose parents treat him as their property is frequently exposed to often finds later expression in perversions and delinquent behavior. Likewise, in the murders committed by Bartsch many features of his childhood are reflected with horrifying exactitude:

1. The underground hiding place where he murdered the children is reminiscent of the cellar, with its barred windows and walls ten feet high, that Bartsch describes as the place where he was locked up.

2. Bartsch selected his victims carefully. He walked through arcades for hours looking for the right boy. His parents had also selected him, before adopting him.

3. Later (not all at once—like his victims—but slowly) he was prevented from living.

4. He sliced the children up with a butcher knife, "with our knife," as he writes. The daily beatings his parents gave him and the sight of the animal carcasses they had butchered combined in Jürgen's imagination to produce an ominous feeling that hung over his life like a sword of Damocles. By finally taking a butcher knife into his hands himself, he tried actively to avert his own destruction.

5. He was aroused when he looked into the children's terrified and helpless eyes. In their eyes he saw himself, along with the feelings he had had to suppress. At the same time he experienced himself in the role of the seductive, aroused adult at whose mercy he once had been.

6. The close connection between kisses and beatings was something Bartsch knew from his mother's way of treating him.

Bartsch's murderous acts demonstrate several mechanisms:

1. The desperate attempt to satisfy his forbidden drives in secret against tremendous odds.

2. The discharge of his bottled-up hatred, unacceptable to society, for his parents and teachers, who forbade him to express his spontaneous feelings and were interested only in his "behavior."

3. The acting out of the situation of being at the mercy of his parents' and teachers' violent behavior, which was now projected onto the little boys in lederhosen (which Jürgen had also worn as a child).

4. The compulsive provocation of society's revulsion and disgust, the same feelings his mother had had when Jürgen went back to wetting and soiling his diapers when he was a year old.

The repetition compulsion is an attempt (the same is true of many perversions) to win the attention of the mother of one's early years. Bartsch's "acts" give the public cause for (*justifiable*) horror, just as, for example, Christiane's provocative behavior, which was actually an attempt to manipulate her unpredictable father (cf. page 112), caused the building superintendents, her teachers, and the police *real* difficulties and unpleasantness.

Those who want to believe that a "pathological sex drive" is the sole motive for murdering children will find many acts of violence in our day incomprehensible and will be unable to deal with them. In this connection, I would like to give a brief description of a case in which sexuality plays no special role but which clearly and tragically reflects the history of the perpetrator's childhood.

The July 27, 1979, issue of *Die Zeit* contains an article by Paul Moor about eleven-year-old Mary Bell, who was put away for life by an English court in 1968 on two counts of murder. She was twenty-two when the article appeared, was still in prison, and had received no psychotherapeutic treatment to date.

I quote from the article:

Two little boys, three and four years old, have been murdered. The clerk of the court in Newcastle asks the accused to rise. The girl replies that she is already standing. Mary Bell, accused of murder on two counts, is all of eleven years old.

On May 26, 1957, seventeen-year-old Betty McC. gave birth to Mary in Dilston Hall Hospital, Corbridge, Gateshead. "Get that thing away from me," Betty is said to have cried, and she recoiled when the baby was put in her arms a few minutes after birth. When Mary was three years old, her mother Betty took her for a walk one day—secretly followed by Betty's curious sister. Betty was taking Mary to an adoption agency. A woman came out of the interview room in tears and said they didn't want to let her have a baby because she was too young and was emigrating to Australia. Betty said to her: "I'm putting this one up for adoption. Take her." Then Betty pushed little Mary toward the stranger and left. . . . In school Mary was a troublemaker: for years she hit, kicked, and scratched other children. She would wring the necks of pigeons, and once she pushed her little cousin from the top of an air-raid shelter onto the concrete eight feet below. The following day she tried to choke three little girls on a playground. At the age of nine she started at a new school; two of her teachers there later stated: "It's better not to delve too deeply into her life and circumstances." Later a policewoman who got to know Mary during her pretrial custody gave the following account: "She was bored. She was standing by the window watching a cat climb up the drainpipe and asked if she might bring it inside. . . . We opened the window, and she lifted the cat in and began playing with it on the floor with a piece of yarn. . . . Then I looked up and at first noticed that she was holding the cat by the scruff of the neck. Then I realized that she was holding the cat so tightly that the animal couldn't breathe and its tongue was hanging out. I ran over and pulled her hands away. I said, 'You mustn't do that, you're hurting it.' She answered, 'Oh, it doesn't feel anything, and anyway I like to hurt little things that can't defend themselves.' "

Mary told another policewoman that she would like to be a nurse—"because then I could stick needles into people. I like to hurt people." Mary's mother Betty eventually married Billy Bell, but on the side she cultivated a rather special clientele. After Mary's trial Betty enlightened a police officer concerning her "specialty"; "I whip them," she said in a tone of voice that indicated to the listener her surprise that he didn't already know this. "But I always kept the whips hidden from the children."

Mary Bell's behavior leaves no room whatsoever for doubt that her mother—who gave birth to her at the age of seventeen and then rejected her, who made whipping people her profession—tormented, threatened, and probably tried to kill her own child in the same way that Mary dealt with the cat and the two little children.* There is no law, however, that would have prohibited her mother's behavior.

Psychotherapeutic treatment is not inexpensive and is often criticized on these grounds. But is it less expensive to lock up an eleven-year-old child for the rest of her life? And what good will that do? A child who has been mistreated at such an early age must be able to tell in some way or other about the wrong that has been done her, about the murder perpetrated on *her*. If she has no one, she will not find the language for it and can tell it only by doing what was done to her. This awakens our horror. But the horror should be directed at the first murder, which was committed in secret and has gone unpunished. Then we might be able to help the child to experience her story on a conscious level so that she will no longer have to tell it by means of disastrous enactments.†

The Walls of Silence

I HAVE presented the story of Jürgen Bartsch in order to show by means of a concrete example how the way a murder is committed can provide clues for understanding the soul murder that occurred in childhood. The earlier this soul murder took place, the more difficult it will be for the affected person to grasp and the less it can be validated by memories and words. If he wants to communicate, his only recourse is acting out. For this reason, if I want to understand the underlying roots of delinquent behavior, I must direct my attention

---

* After this book appeared in German, I learned that Mary's mother, who as a child was schizophrenic, tried not only once but four times to kill her daughter. See Gitta Sereny, *The Case of Mary Bell* (New York: McGraw-Hill, 1972).

† I later learned that Mary Bell, who had become "an attractive woman" in the meantime, was released from prison and had "expressed the wish to live near her mother."

to the child's earliest experiences. Despite my attentiveness, after having written this chapter, when I checked over the passages in the Moor book that I had underlined, I found that I had overlooked the passage that was most important of all for me. It was the passage about Jürgen being beaten as an infant.

The fact that I had passed over this passage, which is of such great importance in corroborating my thesis, showed me how difficult it is for us to imagine an infant being beaten by his or her mother, how difficult not to ward off the image of it but to let the full implication sink in on an emotional level. This explains why psychoanalysts are also so little concerned with these facts and why the consequences of this sort of childhood experience have scarcely been investigated.

It would be a misunderstanding and distortion of my intentions for the reader to think on the basis of this chapter that I am assigning guilt to Frau Bartsch. My very point is to refrain from moralizing and only show cause and effect; namely, that those children who are beaten will in turn give beatings, those who are intimidated will be intimidating, those who are humiliated will impose humiliation, and those whose souls are murdered will murder. As far as morality is concerned, one would have to say that no mother beats her infant without cause. Since we know nothing about Frau Bartsch's childhood, these causes remain obscure. But there can be no doubt that they exist, just as they do in Adolf Hitler's case. Condemning a mother for beating her infant and then pushing the whole matter aside is of course easier than accepting the truth, but it is evidence of a very dubious morality. For our moral indignation isolates even more those parents who mistreat their infants, and adds to the distress that brings them to these acts of violence. Such parents have a compulsion to use their child as an outlet, for the very reason that they are unable to understand this very real distress.

To view all this as tragic is no reason to stand idly by while parents beat their children to shreds, body and soul. It should be a matter of course to take away from such parents the right to raise their children, and to offer these parents psychotherapeutic treatment.

The idea of writing about Jürgen Bartsch did not originate with me. A German reader of my first book wrote me a letter, which I quote here with her permission:

> Books do not help to break open the prisons, it is true, but there are books that give us courage to rattle at the prison gates with new courage. Your book is such a one for me.
>
> At one point in your book you speak of corporal punishment for children and state that you cannot speak for Germany because you are not familiar with the situation there.* I should like to reassure you and confirm your worst suspicions. Do you believe the concentration camps of the Nazi period would have been possible had not the use of physical terrorization in the form of beatings with canes, rug beaters, switches, and cat-o'-nine-tails been the rule in raising German children? I myself am now thirty-seven, the mother of three children, and am still trying with varying success to overcome the devastating emotional consequences of that kind of parental strictness, if for no other reason than that my own children can grow up more freely.
>
> In a "heroic struggle" lasting nearly four years now, I still have not succeeded in getting rid of—or at least humanizing—the aggressive, punitive father within me. If there should be a new edition of your book, then I believe you may safely put Germany in first place as far as child abuse goes. More children are dying on our streets as a result of it than in any other European country, and the legacy of child-rearing methods that is being handed down from one generation to the next lies behind a thick wall of silence and resistance. And those whose inner anguish has forced them, with the help of analysis, to look behind the wall will remain silent, for they know no one will believe them when they report what they have seen there. So that you don't get the wrong idea, let me say that I was not given my whippings in the setting of a lower-class housing development but in the well-off, "harmonious" setting of an upper-middle-class family. My father is a minister.

---

* She misinterpreted my meaning here.

The writer of this letter called my attention to the book by Paul Moor, and thus I owe to her my work involving the life of Jürgen Bartsch, from which I have learned much, including something about my own resistance. I knew of the Bartsch trial at the time but had not familiarized myself with the story. It was the letter from my reader that set me on a path I had no choice but to follow to the end.

On this path I also learned how false the assumption is that children in Germany are more widely abused than in other countries. Sometimes it is very difficult for us to bear an overly painful truth, and therefore we ward it off with the aid of illusions. A frequent form of resistance is that of temporal and spatial displacement. Thus, for example, it is easier for us to imagine that children were mistreated in previous centuries or are so in distant countries than to recognize the truth about our own country, here and now. Then there is another illusion: when a person like the reader just quoted makes the courageous decision not to close her eyes to her history any longer but to face it squarely for the sake of her children, she would like at least to retain the belief that the situation is not so upsetting everywhere, that things are better, more humane in other countries—or were so in other times—than they are in her immediate surroundings. We could scarcely go on living without some hope, and it may be that hope presupposes a certain amount of illusion. Trusting that my readers will be able to hold on to the illusions they need, I should like to present some information pertaining to the child-rearing ideology still tolerated and defended with silence in Switzerland (not only Germany) today. The following examples are taken from the extensive file of the telephone "distress line" in the town of Aefligen, Canton Bern, in Switzerland; they were sent to over two hundred newspapers, only two of which ever devoted an article to the facts described here.*

---

* I later learned that three magazines for parents also decided to publish this documentation.

2/5 *Aargau.* 7-year-old boy is severely mistreated by his father (beaten with fists, whipped, locked up, etc.). According to the mother, she is also beaten. Reason: alcohol and financial straits.

St. Gallen. 12-year-old girl can't stand it at home any longer; her parents whip her with a leather strap every time something goes wrong.

Aargau. 12-year-old girl's father hits her with his fists and gives her a thrashing with his belt. Reason: she is not allowed to have any friends, because the father wants his daughter all to himself.

2/7 *Bern.* 7-year-old girl has run away from home. Reason: her mother always punishes her by beating her with a rug beater. According to the mother, it is all right to beat children until they are of school age, because until then it doesn't hurt them emotionally.

2/8 *Zurich.* 15-year-old girl is very strictly raised by her parents. As punishment, her hair is pulled or both earlobes are twisted at the same time. Her parents are of the opinion that the daughter must be held in close rein because life is harsh, and a child must be made aware of this when still a child, otherwise she will be soft in later life.

2/14 *Lucerne.* Father lays his 14-year-old son on his back over his knee and bends him until his back cracks ("like a banana"). The doctor's certificate indicates a displaced vertebra. Reason for the mistreatment: son stole a pocketknife in a supermarket.

2/15 *Thurgau.* 10-year-old girl is in despair because, as a punishment, her father killed her hamster before her eyes and cut it to pieces.

2/16 *Solothurn.* 14-year-old boy is unconditionally forbidden to masturbate. His mother threatens to cut off his penis if he does it again. According to his mother, everyone who does that ends up in hell. Ever since she discovered her husband doing it, she is leaving no stone unturned to combat this shameful act.

Graubünden. Father strikes his 15-year-old daughter on the head with all his might. The girl loses consciousness. The doctor's certificate indicates a fractured skull. Reason for the mistreatment: daughter came home half an hour late.

2/17 *Aargau.* 14-year-old boy is terribly unhappy because he doesn't have anyone he can talk to. He says it's actually his own fault, because he's afraid of other people, especially girls.

2/18 *Aargau.* 13-year-old boy is forced to perform sexual acts with his uncle. The boy wants to commit suicide, not so much because of the acts themselves as because now he is afraid he is homosexual. He doesn't dare say anything to his parents for fear of being beaten.

Canton of Basel. 13-year-old girl was beaten by her boyfriend (age 18) and forced to have intercourse. Because the girl is very frightened of her parents, she means to keep this all to herself.

Basel. 7-year-old boy is very frightened. He says his anxiety comes over him around noon and lasts until late afternoon. The mother doesn't want to take her son to a psychologist; she says in the first place she doesn't have any money, and anyway, he's not crazy. She does have her doubts, however, because twice he has been about to jump out of the window.

2/20 *Aargau.* Father beats his daughter and threatens to poke her eyes out if she keeps on going with her boyfriend. Reason: the two of them disappeared for two days.

2/21 *Zurich.* Father hangs his 11-year-old son from the wall by his legs for 4 hours. Afterwards, he puts him into a cold bath. Reason: he stole something in a supermarket.

2/27 *Bern.* Teacher repeatedly sets an example by boxing his pupils on the ear, following which the child in question has to turn somersaults without interruption until he or she collapses.

2/29 *Zurich.* 15-year-old girl has been beaten by her mother for 6 years (with a broom, cooking utensils, electric cord). She is desperate and wants to get away from her mother.

In the two years that the distress line has existed, the following methods of physical mistreatment have been reported by the people who take the calls.

Beatings. Box on the ear: Repeated hard blows on the ear with the hand, the fist, the flexed thumb. *Sandwich box on the ear:* Here both hands, fists, or flexed thumbs are used simultaneously. *Hand:* Alternating strong body blows with the hands. *Fist:* Hitting the body alternately with both fists. *Double fist:* Pummeling the body with both hands closed into fists. *Elbows:* Striking the body hard with the elbows. *Arms:* Pummeling the body alternately with the arms and the elbows. *Head blows:*

Hitting or a glancing blow, hitting or scraping with the wedding ring. *Rapping the hands:* Not only teachers but parents as well still use the ruler today. Plastic rulers are especially practical. The hand can be struck on the palm, on the balls of the hand, on the backs of the hand, on the fingers (the fingers must be held up in a closed position). More unusual: rapping with the edge of the ruler.

Electricity. Some children have experienced the "burning whip from the electrical socket": by brief exposure to the current or by having the doorknob on the door to the child's room electrified.

Flesh wounds. Blows that cause wounds: with the bare hand (scratched by fingernails), with fists (cut by a ring), with fork, knife, edge of the knife, spoon, with electrical cord, with a guitar string (used as a whip). Wounds from being pierced: with needles, knitting needles, scissors.

Fractures. Broken bones result from children being hurled across the room, pushed over backwards, thrown out of windows, pushed down the stairs, thrown up the stairs, having car doors slammed on them, being kicked in the chest (broken ribs), trampled on, hit on the head with a fist (skull fracture), and hit with the edge of the hand.

Burns from lighted cigarettes or cigars extinguished on the body, a burning match extinguished on the body, soldering irons used on the body, being doused with hot water, being exposed to electrical currents, being burned with a cigarette lighter.

Choking with the bare hands, electrical cord, car windows (closing the window while the child's head is sticking out).

Contusions. Caused by hitting, slamming of car doors (with injuries to children's fingers, arms, legs, and head), kicking, punching.

Hairpulling. By the handful from head, nape of neck, from the side of the face, the chest, the beard (adolescents).

Hanging. Children have reported that their father punished them by hanging them from the wall by their legs and leaving them there for hours.

Twisting one ear, twisting both ears at the same time, twisting arms behind the back and pushing them up.

"Massaging" with the knuckles: temples, collarbone, shins, breastbone, under the ears, above the neck.

Bending: The child is laid on his back over the father's knee and bent "like a banana."

Bloodletting (rare). A 10-year-old's vein on the inner side of the elbow was punctured and blood drawn until the child could no longer stay awake. After child lost consciousness, its sins were forgiven.

Exposure to cold (rare). Children are exposed to extremely cold temperatures or placed in cold water. Thawing out causes pain.

Immersion. Children who splash in the bathtub are held under water.

Deprivation of sleep (rare). An 11-year-old girl was punished by not being allowed to sleep through the night twice in a row. Every three hours she was awakened or put in cold water while asleep. Sleep deprivation is also used to punish bedwetters. An automatic device placed in the bed awakens the child every time it wets. One boy, for example, was unable to sleep through the night for three years. His nervousness was "taken care of" with medication. His schoolwork suffered. Then his mother gave him the pills only sporadically. As a result, the child became increasingly disturbed in his social behavior: again, grounds for corporal punishment.

Compulsory labor. A method that tends to be used in rural areas. As punishment the child must work all night, clean out the cellar until a state of exhaustion has been reached, or work after school for a week or for a month until eleven o'clock at night and starting at five in the morning (including Sunday).

Eating. The child is forced to eat what it has vomited. After the meal, a finger is stuck down the child's throat to make it vomit. Then the child must eat what it has vomited.

Injections. A salt solution is injected into the child's buttocks, arms, or thighs (rare). A dentist has been known to use this method.

Needles. Children have reported repeatedly that their parents take pins along when they go shopping. When the children want to take something from the shelf, the parents, ostensibly giving them a loving pat on the head, jab them in the neck.

Pills. To solve the problem of children having trouble falling asleep, parents give them large doses of sleeping pills and suppositories. One 13-year-old felt groggy every morning and had difficulty learning.

Alcohol. Beer, liquor, or liqueur is poured into the glasses of toddlers. Then they fall asleep more easily and don't disturb the neighbors with their crying.

Head ramming. One boy reported that his father put his head close to the son's head, then rammed his head with a short, quick blow against the son's. The father boasted about his technique, which had to be practiced so the father wouldn't feel pain himself.

Letting things drop. Letting things drop can be made to look like an accident. The child is asked to help carry something heavy. The adult suddenly lets go and the child's fingers, hand, or foot are injured when the weight falls on it.

Torture chamber. One child and his grandmother reported that the father set up a torture chamber in an unused coal cellar. He bound the child to a "trestle" and whipped him. The whip was selected to match the severity of the punishment. Frequently, the child was left bound overnight.

Why did almost all the journals to whom these devastating reports were sent—journals whose main concern is with "society"—choose to respond with silence? Who is protecting whom and from what? Why shouldn't the Swiss public be informed that in its fair land countless children are being subjected to a lonely martyrdom? What is achieved by silence? Might it not even be helpful for the abusive parents to learn that the anguish of the battered child, who they themselves once were too, is finally being noticed and taken seriously? Like the murders committed by Jürgen Bartsch, numerous crimes against children are an unconscious message to the public about the perpetrators' own past, of which they are often scarcely conscious themselves. Someone who was not allowed to "be aware" of what was being done has no way of telling about it except to repeat it. One would think that the media, who claim to do their best to improve society, could learn to understand this language once they are no longer forbidden to be aware of it.

Concluding Comments

I T may strike the reader as very strange to see three such
dissimilar life histories placed side by side (Christiane F.,
a drug addict; Adolf Hitler; Jürgen Bartsch, a child murderer).
But it was because of this very dissimilarity that I selected
and juxtaposed these figures, for, in spite of their differences,
they share certain features common to many other people as
well.

1. In all three cases we find extreme destructiveness.
Christiane F. directed it against herself, Adolf Hitler against
his real and imagined enemies, and Jürgen Bartsch against
little boys, in whom he was repeatedly murdering himself
while at the same time taking the lives of others.

2. I interpret this destructiveness as the discharge of
long-pent-up childhood hatred and its displacement onto other
objects or onto the self.

3. As children, all three were severely mistreated and
subjected to humiliation, not only in isolated instances but on
a regular basis. From earliest childhood, they grew up in a
climate of cruelty.

4. The healthy, normal reaction to such treatment would
be narcissistic rage of extreme intensity. But because of the
authoritarian form of child-rearing practiced by all three
families, this rage had to be sharply suppressed.

5. In their entire childhood and youth, none of the three
had an adult to whom they could confide their feelings, especially their feelings of hatred. (Christiane is an exception here
insofar as she did meet two people during puberty to whom
she could talk.)

6. All three persons described here felt a strong urge to communicate their suffering to the world, to express themselves in some way. They all showed a special talent for verbal expression.

7. Since the path to safe, verbal communication based on a feeling of trust was blocked for them, the only way they were able to communicate with the world was by means of unconscious enactment.

8. Not until the end of the drama is reached do these enactments awaken in the world feelings of shock and horror. The public at large unfortunately does not experience such intense feelings upon hearing reports of battered children.

9. It lies in the nature of these people's repetition compulsion that they succeeded in winning undivided public attention with their enactments—enactments that ultimately led, however, to their own downfall. Similarly, a child who is beaten regularly also succeeds in winning attention, albeit in the baleful form of physical punishment.

10. All three received affection only as their parents' self-objects and property, but never for their own sakes. The longing for affection, coupled with the eruption of destructive feelings from childhood, brought about their fateful enactments during puberty and adolescence. (In Hitler's case, these enactments filled an entire lifetime.)

The three people described here are not only individuals but also representatives of certain groups. We can better understand these groups (for example, drug addicts, delinquents, suicides, terrorists, or even a certain type of politician) if we trace the fate of an individual back to the concealed tragedy of his or her childhood. The many and varied enactments of such people are essentially a crying out for understanding, but in a way that assures them of anything but society's sympathy. It is part of the tragic nature of the repetition compulsion that someone who hopes eventually to find a better world than the one he or she experienced as a child in fact keeps creating instead the same undesired state of affairs.

When a person cannot talk about the cruelty endured as a child because it was experienced so early that it is beyond the reach of memory, then he or she must *demonstrate* cruelty. Christiane does this by self-destructiveness, the others by seeking out victims. For those who have children, these victims are automatically provided, and the demonstration can take place with impunity and without drawing public attention. But if one is childless, as in Hitler's case, the suppressed hatred may be vented upon millions of human beings, and the victims as well as the judges will confront such bestiality without an inkling as to its origins. Several decades have passed since Hitler conceived the idea of destroying human beings like vermin, and in the meantime the techniques required for such a project have certainly been perfected to the highest degree. Thus, it is all the more crucial for us to keep pace with this development by increasing our understanding of the sources of such intense and insatiable hatred as Hitler's. For, with all due respect for historical, sociological, and economic explanations, the official who turns on the gas to asphyxiate children and the person who conceived this are human beings and were once children themselves. Until the general public becomes aware that countless children are subjected to soul murder every day and that society as a whole must suffer as a result, we are groping in a dark labyrinth—in spite of all our well-meaning efforts to bring about disarmament among nations.

When I was planning the major portion of this book, I had no idea that it would lead me to questions concerning world peace. Originally, my sole concern was to inform parents of what I had learned about pedagogy in my twenty years of psychoanalytic practice. Because I did not want to write about my patients, I chose people who were already known to the public. Writing, however, resembles an adventure-filled journey whose destination is unknown at the outset. Therefore, if I have touched on matters of war and peace, it is only peripherally, for these matters far exceed my competence. But my study of Hitler's life, the psychoanalytic attempt to understand his later actions as an outgrowth of the degradation and humiliation he suffered as a child, was not without its consequences. It inevitably brought me to the topic of the search for peace. What emerged has its pessimistic as well as its optimistic implications.

I designate as pessimistic the thought that we are far more dependent than our pride would like to admit on individual human beings (and not only on institutions!), for a single person can gain control over the masses if he learns to use to his own advantage the system under which they were raised. People who have been "pedagogically" manipulated as children are not aware as adults of all that can be done to them. Like the individual authoritarian father, leader figures, in whom the masses see their own father, actually embody the avenging child who needs the masses for his own purposes (of revenge). And this second form of dependence—the dependence of the "great leader" on his childhood, on the unpredictable nature of the unintegrated, enormous potential for hatred within him—is decidedly a very great danger.

The optimistic aspects of my investigations must not be overlooked, however. In all I have read in recent years about the childhood of criminals, even of mass murderers, I have been unable to find anywhere the beast, the evil child whom pedagogues believe they must educate to be "good." Everywhere I find defenseless children who were mistreated in the name of child-rearing, and often for the sake of the highest ideals. My optimism is based on the hope that public opinion will no longer tolerate the cover-up of child abuse in the name of child-rearing, once it has been recognized that:

1. Child-rearing is basically directed not toward the *child's* welfare but toward satisfying the parents' needs for power and revenge.

2. Not only the individual child is affected; we can all become future victims of this mistreatment.

Steps on the Path to Reconciliation: Anxiety, Anger, and Sorrow— but No Guilt Feelings

Unintentional Cruelty Hurts, Too

W HEN we examine the child-rearing literature of the past two hundred years, we discover the methods that have systematically been used to make it impossible for children to realize and later to remember the way they were actually treated by their parents. Why are the old methods of child raising still so widely employed today? This is a mystery I have tried to understand and explain from the perspective of the compulsive repetition of the exercise of power. Contrary to popular opinion, the injustice, humiliation, mistreatment, and coercion a person has experienced are not without consequences. The tragedy is that the effects of mistreatment are transmitted to new and innocent victims, even though the victims themselves do not remember the mistreatment on a conscious level.

How can this vicious circle be broken? Religion says we must forgive the injustice we suffered, only then will we be free to love and be purged of hatred. This is correct as far as it goes, but how do we find the path to true forgiveness? Can we speak of forgiveness if we hardly know what was actually done to us and why? And that is the situation we all found ourselves in as children. We could not grasp why we were being humiliated, brushed aside, intimidated, laughed at, treated like an object, played with like a doll or brutally beaten (or both). What is more, we were not even allowed to be aware that all this was happening to us, for any mistreatment was held up to us as being necessary for our own good. Even the most clever child cannot see through such a lie if it comes from the mouths of his beloved parents, who after all show him other, loving sides as well. He has to believe that the way he is being treated is truly right and good for him, and he will not hold it against his parents. But then as an adult he will act the same way toward his own children in an attempt to prove to himself that his parents behaved correctly toward him.

Isn't this what most religions mean by "forgiveness": to chastise children "lovingly" in the tradition of the fathers and to raise them to respect their parents? But forgiveness which is based on denial of the truth and which uses a defenseless child as an outlet for resentment is not true forgiveness; that is why hatred is not vanquished by religions in this manner but, on the contrary, is unwittingly exacerbated. The child's intense anger at the parents, being strictly forbidden, is simply deflected onto other people and onto himself, but not done away with. Instead, because it is permissible to discharge this anger onto one's own children, it spreads over the entire world like a plague. For this reason we should not be surprised that there are religious wars, although such a phenomenon should actually be a contradiction in terms.

Genuine forgiveness does not deny anger but faces it head-on. If I can feel outrage at the injustice I have suffered, can recognize my persecution as such, and can acknowledge and hate my persecutor for what he or she has done, only then will the way to forgiveness be open to me. Only if the history of abuse in earliest childhood can be uncovered will the repressed anger, rage, and hatred cease to be perpetuated. Instead, they will be transformed into sorrow and pain at the fact that things had to be that way. As a result of this pain, they will give way to genuine understanding, the understanding of an adult who now has gained insight into his or her parents' childhood and finally, liberated from his own hatred, can experience genuine, mature sympathy. Such forgiveness cannot be coerced by rules and commandments; it is experienced as a form of grace and appears spontaneously when a repressed (because forbidden) hatred no longer poisons the soul. The sun does not need to be told to shine. When the clouds part, it simply shines. But it would be a mistake to say that the clouds are not in the way if they are indeed there.

If an adult has been fortunate enough to get back to the sources of the specific injustice he suffered in his childhood and experience it on a conscious level, then in time he will realize on his own—preferably without the aid of any pedagogical or religious exhortations—that in most cases his parents did not torment or abuse him for their own pleasure or out of sheer strength and vitality but because they could not help it, since they were once victims themselves and thus believed in traditional methods of child-rearing.

It is very difficult for people to believe the simple fact that *every persecutor was once a victim.* Yet it should be very obvious that someone who was allowed to feel free and strong from childhood does not have the need to humiliate another person. In Paul Klee's Diaries we find the following anecdote.

> From time to time, I played tricks on a little girl who was not pretty and who wore braces to correct her crooked legs. I regarded her whole family, and in particular the mother, as very inferior people. I would present myself at the high court, pretending to be a good boy, and beg to be allowed to take the little darling for a walk. For a while we'd walk peaceably hand in hand; then, perhaps in the nearby field where potato plants were blooming and June bugs were all over, or perhaps even sooner, we would start walking single file. At the right moment I'd give my protégée a slight push. The poor thing would fall, and I'd bring her back in tears to her mother, explaining with an innocent air: "She fell down." I played this trick more than once, without Frau Enger's ever suspecting the truth. I must have gauged her correctly. (Age five or six)

No doubt, little Paul was repeating something here that was done to him, probably by his father. There is only one brief passage about his father in the Diaries:

> For a long time I trusted my papa implicitly and regarded his words (Papa can do anything) as gospel. The only thing I couldn't bear was his teasing. On one occasion, thinking I was

alone, I was playing make-believe. I was interrupted by a sudden amused "hmpf!" which hurt my feelings. It was not the only time I was to hear this "hmpf!"

Mockery from a beloved and admired person is always painful, and we can imagine that little Paul was deeply wounded by this treatment.

It would be wrong to say that, because we understand its origins, the harm we compulsively inflict on another person does not cause harm and that little Paul did not hurt the girl. To recognize this makes the tragedy visible but at the same time offers the possibility for change. The realization that even with the best will in the world we are not omnipotent, that we are subject to compulsions, and that we cannot love our child in the way we would like may lead to sorrow but should not awaken guilt feelings, because the latter imply a power and freedom we do not have. Burdened by guilt feelings ourselves, we will also burden our children with guilt feelings and tie them to us for a lifetime. By means of our mourning, we can set our children free.

Distinguishing between mourning and guilt feelings might also help to break the silence between the generations on the subject of the crimes of the Nazi period. Mourning is the opposite of feeling guilt; it is an expression of pain that things happened as they did and that there is no way to change the past. We can share this pain with our children without having to feel ashamed; guilt feelings are something we try to repress or shift to our children or both.

Since sorrow reactivates numbed feelings, it can enable young people to realize what their parents once inflicted on them in the well-meaning attempt to train them to be obedient from an early age. This can lead to an eruption of justifiable anger and to the painful recognition that one's own parents, who are already over fifty, are still defending their old principles, are unable to understand the anger of their grown child, and are hurt and wounded by reproaches. Then the child wishes he or she could take back what has been said and undo all that has happened, because now the old familiar fears that these reproaches will send the parents to their graves return. If children are told early and often enough, "You'll be the death of me yet," these words remain with them all their life.

And yet, even if a person is once again left alone with this awakened anger because his aging parents can bear it just as little as before, the mere admission of this feeling to consciousness can lead out of the dead end of self-alienation. Then at long last the true child, the healthy child, can live, the child who finds it impossible to understand why his parents are hurting him and at the same time forbidding him to cry, weep, or even speak in his pain. The gifted child who adapts to parental demands always tries to understand this absurdity and will accept it as a matter of course. But he has to pay for this pseudo-understanding with his feelings and his sensitivity to his own needs, i.e., with his authentic self. This is why access to the normal, angry, uncomprehending, and rebellious child he once was had previously been blocked off. When this child within the adult is liberated, he will discover his vital roots and strength.

To be free to express resentment dating back to early childhood does not mean that one now becomes a resentful person, but rather the exact opposite. For the very reason that one is permitted to experience these feelings that were directed against the parents, one does not have to use surrogate figures for purposes of abreaction. Only hatred felt for surrogates is endless and insatiable—as we saw in the case of Adolf Hitler—because on a conscious level the feeling is separated from the person against whom it was originally directed.

For these reasons I believe that the free expression of resentment against one's parents represents a great opportunity. It provides access to one's true self, reactivates numbed feelings, opens the way for mourning and—with luck—reconciliation. In any case, it is an essential part of the process of psychic healing. But anyone who thinks that I am reproaching these aging parents would be misunderstanding my meaning completely. I have neither the right nor the grounds to do so. I was not their child, was not compelled by them to be silent, was not raised by them, and—as an adult—know that they, like all parents, could do no differently than behave the way they did.

Because I encourage the child within the adult to acknowledge his feelings, including his resentment, but do not absolve him from these feelings, and because I do not place blame on the parents, I apparently create difficulties for many of my readers. It would be so much simpler to say it is all the child's fault, or the parents', or the blame can be divided. This is exactly what I don't want to do, because as an adult I know it is not a question of blame but of not being able to do any differently. Children cannot understand this, however, and they fall ill in the attempt to do so because of a lack of access to their feelings. Only if the child in the adult suspends his futile attempt to understand can he begin to feel his pain. I believe that the children of those adults who finally dare to face their feelings will benefit as a result.

Perhaps even this explanation cannot clear up the misunderstandings that frequently arise in this connection, for they are not rooted in the intellect. If someone learned from an early age to feel guilty for everything and to regard his parents as beyond reproach, my ideas will of necessity cause him feelings of anxiety and guilt. We can see just how strong his attitude, instilled at an early age, is by observing older people. As soon as they find themselves in a situation of physical helplessness and dependence, they may feel guilty for every little thing and may even regard their grown children as stern judges, providing the children are no longer submissive as they once were. As a result, the grown children feel they have to spare their parents out of considerateness, and the fear of hurting them condemns the children to silence once again.

Since many psychologists never had the opportunity to free themselves from this fear and to find out that parents need not die if they hear the truth about their child, they will be inclined to encourage a "reconciliation" between patients and parents as quickly as possible. If the underlying rage has not been experienced, however, the reconciliation is an illusory one. It will only cover over the rage that has been bottled up unconsciously or has been directed against others and will reinforce the patient's false self, even at the expense of his children, who will certainly sense the parent's true feelings. And yet, in spite of these impediments, there are an increasing number of books in which young people confront their parents more freely and openly and honestly than was previously possible. This fact awakens hope that critical writers will produce critical readers who will refuse to allow themselves to be made to feel guilty (or more guilty) by the "poisonous pedagogy" to be found in the professional literature (in the areas of education, psychology, ethics, or biography).

Sylvia Plath: An Example of Forbidden Suffering

You ask me why I spend my life writing?
Do I find entertainment?
Is it worthwhile?
Above all, does it pay?
If not, then, is there a reason? ...
I write only because
There is a voice within me
That will not be still.

SYLVIA PLATH

E VERY life and every childhood is filled with frustrations; we cannot imagine it otherwise, for even the best mother cannot satisfy all her child's wishes and needs. It is not the suffering caused by frustration, however, that leads to emotional illness but rather the fact that the child is forbidden by the parents to experience and articulate this suffering, the pain felt at being wounded; usually the purpose of this prohibition is to protect the parents' defense mechanisms. Adults are free to hurl reproaches at God, at fate, at the authorities, or at society if they are deceived, ignored, punished unjustly, confronted with excessive demands, or lied to. Children are not allowed to reproach their gods—their parents and teachers. By no means are they allowed to express their frustrations. Instead, they must repress or deny their emotional reactions, which build up inside until adulthood, when they are finally discharged, but not on the object that caused them. The forms this discharge may take range from persecuting their own children by the way they bring them up, to all possible degrees of emotional illness, to addiction, criminality, and even suicide.

The most acceptable and profitable form this discharge can take for society is literature, because this does not burden anyone with guilt feelings. In this medium the author is free to make every possible reproach, since here it can be attributed to a fictitious person. An illustration is the life of Sylvia Plath, for in her case, along with her poetry and the fact of her psychotic breakdown as well as her later suicide, there are also the personal statements she makes in her letters and the comments by her mother. The tremendous pressure she felt to achieve and the constant stress she was under are always emphasized when Sylvia's suicide is discussed. Her mother, too, points this out repeatedly, for parents of suicidal people understandably try to restrict themselves to external causes, since their guilt feelings stand in the way of their seeing the situation for what it actually is and of their experiencing grief.

Sylvia Plath's life was no more difficult than that of millions of others. Presumably as a result of her sensitivity, she suffered much more intensely than most people from the frustrations of childhood, but she experienced joy more intensely also. Yet the reason for her despair was not her suffering but the impossibility of communicating her suffering to another person. In all her letters she assures her mother how well she is doing. The suspicion that her mother did not release negative letters for publication overlooks the deep tragedy of Plath's life. This tragedy (and the explanation for her suicide as well) lies in the very fact that she could not have written any other kind of letters, because her mother needed reassurance, or because Sylvia at any rate believed that her mother would not have been able to live without this reassurance. Had Sylvia been able to write aggressive and unhappy letters to her mother, she would not have had to commit suicide. Had her mother been able to experience grief at her inability to comprehend the abyss that was her daughter's life, she never would have published the letters, because the assurances they contained of how well things were going for her daughter would have been too painful to bear. Aurelia

Plath is unable to mourn over this because she has guilt feelings, and the letters serve her as proof of her innocence. The following passage from *Letters Home* provides an example of her rationalization.

The following poem, written at the age of fourteen, was inspired by the accidental blurring of a pastel still-life Sylvia had just completed and stood up on the porch table to show us. As Warren, Grammy, and I were admiring it, the doorbell rang. Grammy took off her apron, tossed it on the table, and went to answer the call, her apron brushing against the pastel, blurring part of it. Grammy was grieved. Sylvia, however, said lightly, "Don't worry; I can patch it up." That night she wrote her first poem containing tragic undertones.

I THOUGHT THAT I COULD NOT BE HURT

I thought that I could not be hurt;
I thought that I must surely be
impervious to suffering—
immune to mental pain
or agony.

My world was warm with April sun
my thoughts were spangled green and gold;
my soul filled up with joy, yet felt
the sharp, sweet pain that only joy
can hold.

My spirit soared above the gulls
that, swooping breathlessly so high
o'erhead, now seem to brush their whir-
ring wings against the blue roof of
the sky.

(How frail the human heart must be—
a throbbing pulse, a trembling thing—
a fragile, shining instrument
of crystal, which can either weep,
or sing.)

Then, suddenly my world turned gray,
and darkness wiped aside my joy.
A dull and aching void was left
where careless hands had reached out to
destroy

> *my silver web of happiness.*
> *The hands then stopped in wonderment,*
> *for, loving me, they wept to see*
> *the tattered ruins of my firma-*
> *ment.*
>
> *(How frail the human heart must be—*
> *a mirrored pool of thought. So deep*
> *and tremulous an instrument*
> *of glass that it can either sing,*
> *or weep.)*

Her English teacher, Mr. Crockett, showed this to a colleague, who said, "Incredible that one so young could have experienced anything so devastating." When I repeated Mr. Crockett's account of this conversation to me, Sylvia smiled impishly, saying, "Once a poem is made available to the public, the right of interpretation belongs to the reader."

If a sensitive child like Sylvia Plath intuits that it is essential for her mother to interpret the daughter's pain only as the consequence of a picture being damaged and not as a consequence of the destruction of her daughter's self and its expression—symbolized in the fate of the pastel—the child will do her utmost to hide her authentic feelings from the mother. The letters are testimony of the false self she constructed (whereas her true self is speaking in *The Bell Jar*). With the publication of the letters, her mother erects an imposing monument to her daughter's false self.

We can learn from this example what suicide really is: the only possible way to express the true self—at the expense of life itself. Many parents are like Sylvia's mother. They desperately try to *behave correctly* toward their child, and in their child's behavior they seek reassurance that they are good parents. The attempt to be an ideal parent, that is, to behave correctly toward the child, to raise her correctly, not to give too little or too much, is in essence an attempt to be the ideal child—well behaved and dutiful—of one's own parents. But as a result of these efforts the needs of the child go unnoticed.

I cannot listen to my child with empathy if I am inwardly preoccupied with being a good mother; I cannot be open to what
she is telling me. This can be observed in various parental
attitudes.

Frequently, parents will not be aware of their child's narcissistic wounds; they do not notice them because they learned,
from the time they were little, not to take them seriously in
themselves. It may be the case that they *are* aware of them
but believe it is better for the *child* not to become aware. They
will try to talk her out of many of her early perceptions and
make her forget her earliest experiences, all in the belief that
this is for the child's own good, for they think that she could
not bear to know the truth and would fall ill as a result. That
it is just the other way around, that the child suffers precisely
because the truth is concealed, they do not see. This was
strikingly illustrated in the case of a little baby with a severe
birth defect who, from the time she was born, had to be tied
down at feeding time and fed in a manner that resembled
torture. The mother later tried to keep this "secret" from her
grown daughter, in order to "spare" her from something that
had already happened. She was therefore unable to help her
acknowledge to herself this early experience, which was expressing itself through various symptoms.

Whereas the first attitude is based entirely on the repression of one's own childhood experiences, the second one also
includes the absurd hope that the past can be corrected by
remaining silent about it.

In the first case we encounter the principle, "What must
not be cannot be," and in the second, "If we don't talk about
what happened, then it didn't happen."

The malleability of a sensitive child is nearly boundless,
permitting all these parental demands to be absorbed by the
psyche. The child can adapt perfectly to them, and yet something remains, which we might call body knowledge, that
allows the truth to manifest itself in physical illnesses or sen-
sations, and sometimes also in dreams. If a psychosis or

neurosis develops, this is yet another way of letting the soul speak, albeit in a form that no one can understand and that becomes as much of a burden to the affected person—and to society—as his or her childhood reactions to the traumata suffered had been to the parents.

As I have repeatedly stressed, it is not the trauma itself that is the source of illness but the unconscious, repressed, hopeless despair over not being allowed to give expression to what one has suffered and the fact that one is not allowed to show and is unable to experience feelings of rage, anger, humiliation, despair, helplessness, and sadness. This causes many people to commit suicide because life no longer seems worth living if they are totally unable to live out all these strong feelings that are part of their true self. Naturally, we cannot require parents to face something they are unable to face, but we can keep confronting them with the knowledge that it was not suffering per se that made their child ill but its repression, which was essential for the sake of the parents. I have found that this knowledge often provides parents with an "aha!" experience that opens up for them the possibility of mourning, thus helping to reduce their guilt feelings.

Pain over the frustration one has suffered is nothing to be ashamed of, nor is it harmful. It is a natural, human re-action. However, if it is verbally or nonverbally forbidden or even stamped out by force and by beatings, as it is in "poison-ous pedagogy," then natural development is impeded and the conditions for pathological development are created. Hitler proudly reported that one day, without a tear or a cry, he managed to count the blows his father gave him. Hitler imagined that his father never beat him again thereafter. I take this to be a figment of his imagination because it is un-likely that Alois's reasons for beating his son disappeared from one day to the next, for his motives were not related to the child's behavior but to his own unresolved childhood humiliation. The son's imaginings tell us, however, that he could not remember the beatings his father gave him from that time on because having to fight down his psychic pain by identifying with the aggressor also meant that the memory of the later beatings was repressed. This phenomenon can often be observed in patients who, as a result of regaining access to their feelings, now remember events they previously emphatically denied had taken place.

Unlived Anger

IN October 1977 the philosopher Leszek Kolakowski was awarded the Peace Prize of the German Booksellers' Association. In his acceptance speech he spoke about hatred, with special reference to the event that was on many people's minds at that time, the hijacking of a Lufthansa plane to Mogadishu.

Kolakowski said that time after time there have been instances of people who are completely free of hatred and who therefore offer proof that it is possible to live without it. It is not surprising for a philosopher to talk like this if he identifies humanness with *consciousness*. But for someone who has been confronted with manifestations of *unconscious* psychic reality on a daily basis and who sees over and over again how serious the consequences of overlooking this reality are, it will no longer be a simple matter of course to divide people into those who are good or bad, loving or hate-filled. Such a person knows that moralizing concepts are less apt to uncover the truth than to conceal it. Hatred is a normal human *feeling*, and a feeling has never killed anyone. Is there a more appropriate reaction than anger or even hatred in response to the abuse of children, the rape of women, the torture of the innocent—especially if the perpetrator's motives remain hidden? A person who has had the good fortune from the beginning to be allowed to react to frustration with rage will internalize his empathic parents and will later be able to deal with all his feelings, including hatred, without need for analysis. I don't know if such people exist; I have never met one. What I *have* seen are people who did not acknowledge their hatred but delegated it to others without meaning to and

without even knowing they were doing it. Under certain circumstances, they developed a severe obsessional neurosis
accompanied by destructive fantasies, or, if this did not occur,
their children had the neurosis. Often they were treated for
years for physical illness that was really psychic in origin.
Some suffered from severe depressions. But as soon as it became possible for them to experience their early childhood
hatred in analysis, their symptoms disappeared, and with
them the fear that their *feeling* of hatred might cause someone
harm. It is not *experienced* hatred that leads to acts of violence
and destructiveness but hatred that must be warded off and
bottled up with the aid of ideology, a situation that can be
examined in detail in the case of Adolf Hitler. Every experienced feeling gives way in time to another, and even the most
extreme conscious hatred of one's father will not lead a person
to kill—to say nothing of destroying a whole people. But Hitler
warded off his childhood feelings totally and destroyed human
life because "Germany needed more Lebensraum," because
"the Jews were a menace to the world," because he "wanted
young people to be cruel so they could create something new"
—the list of supposed reasons could go on and on.

How are we to explain the fact that, in spite of growing
psychological awareness in the last decades, two-thirds of the
people polled in Germany still believe that corporal punishment is necessary, good, and right for children? And what
about the remaining third? How many of the parents among
them feel compelled to strike their children against their better
judgment and in spite of their good intentions? This situation
is understandable if we take the following points into consideration.

1. For parents to be aware of what they are doing to
their children, they would also have to be aware of what was
done to them in their own childhood. But this is exactly what
was forbidden them as children. If access to this knowledge
is cut off, parents can strike and humiliate their children or
torment and mistreat them in other ways, without realizing

how they are hurting them; they simply are compelled to behave this way.

2. If the tragedy of a well-meaning person's childhood remains hidden behind idealizations, the unconscious knowledge
of the actual state of affairs will have to assert itself by an
indirect route. This occurs with the aid of the *repetition compulsion*. Over and over again, for reasons they do not understand, people will create situations and establish relationships
in which they torment or are tormented by their partner, or
both.

3. Since tormenting one's children is a legitimate part of
child-rearing, this provides the most obvious outlet for bottled-
up aggression.

4. Because an aggressive response to emotional and
physical abuse is forbidden by parents in almost all religions,
this outlet is the only one available.

There would be no incest taboo, say the sociologists, if
sexual attraction among members of a family were not a
natural impulse. That is why this taboo exists in every civilized nation and is an integral part of child-rearing from the
beginning.

I sense a similarity here to the way a child's aggressive
feelings toward the parents are traditionally treated. I do not
know how people in other cultures who have not grown up,
as we have, with the Fourth Commandment have solved this
problem, but wherever I look, I see signs of the commandment
to honor one's parents and nowhere of a commandment that
calls for respect for the child. Could this be analogous to the
incest taboo and indicate that respect is instilled in the child
as early as possible because the child's natural reactions toward the parents can be so violent that parents would have
to fear being beaten by their children or even killed by them?

We constantly hear about the cruelty of the times, and
yet it seems to me there is a ray of hope in the trend to examine
and question inherited taboos. If parents need the Fourth
Commandment to keep their children from expressing natural

and legitimate aggressive feelings from the outset, with the result that the child's only option is to pass this same commandment on to the next generation, then it would be a sign of great progress if this taboo were done away with. If the mechanism becomes conscious, if people are allowed to become aware of what their parents did to them, they would surely try to direct their response to the preceding generation and not the following one. This would mean, for example, that Hitler would not have needed to kill millions of human beings if it had been possible for him as a child to rebel directly against his father's cruelty.

It would be an easy matter to misunderstand my claim that the untold deep humiliation and mistreatment Hitler suffered at his father's hands without being allowed to respond was responsible for his insatiable hatred. Someone may object by saying that an individual human being cannot destroy an entire people on such a scale, that the economic crisis and the humiliation suffered by the Weimar Republic contributed to producing the catastrophe. There can be no doubt that this is true, but it was not "crises" and "systems" that did the killing, it was human beings—human beings whose fathers were able to point with pride to the obedience instilled in their little ones at a very early age.

Many of the facts we have reacted to for decades with moral indignation and uncomprehending aversion can be understood from this perspective. An American professor, for example, has been conducting experiments for years with brain transplants. In an interview with the magazine *Tele*, he reports that he has already succeeded in replacing the brain of one monkey with that of another. He does not doubt that in the foreseeable future it will be possible to do the same thing with human beings. Readers have a choice here: they can be thrilled at so much scientific progress, or they can wonder how such absurdity can be possible and what purpose such pursuits can serve. But a piece of seemingly unimportant information may produce an "aha!" reaction in them, for Professor White speaks of "religious feelings" connected with his endeavor. Questioned by the interviewer, he explains that he had a very strict Catholic upbringing and in the opinion of his ten children had been raised like a dinosaur. I don't know what is meant by this, but I can imagine that this image refers to antediluvian methods of child-rearing. What does that have to do with his scientific work? Perhaps this is the unconscious background for Professor White's experiments: by devoting all his energy and vitality to the goal of one day being able to transplant brains in human beings, he is fulfilling his long-harbored infantile wish to be able to replace his parents' brains. Sadism is not an infectious disease that strikes a person all of a sudden. It has a long prehistory in childhood and *always* originates in the desperate fantasies of a child who is searching for a way out of a hopeless situation.

Every experienced analyst is familiar with ministers' children who were never allowed to have so-called bad thoughts and who managed not to have any, even at the cost of a severe neurosis. If infantile fantasies are finally allowed to come to the surface in analysis, they generally have a cruel and sadistic content. In these fantasies, the early fantasies of revenge of the child who has been tormented by his or her upbringing merge with the introjected cruelty of the parents, who have attempted to stifle or have actually stifled the child's vitality by making impossible moral demands.

Everyone must find his own form of aggressiveness in order to avoid letting himself be made into an obedient puppet manipulated by others. Only if we do not allow ourselves to be reduced to the instrument of another person's will can we fulfill our personal needs and defend our legitimate rights. But this appropriate form of aggression is unattainable for many people who have grown up with the absurd belief that a person can have nothing but kind, good, and meek thoughts and at the same time be honest and authentic. The effort to fulfill this impossible demand can drive sensitive children to the brink of madness. No wonder they try to free themselves from their prison by means of sadistic fantasies. Yet this attempt is also forbidden and must be repressed. Thus, the comprehensible and empathic part of these fantasies remains fully concealed from consciousness, covered over by the gravestone of a dismaying, split-off cruelty. Although this gravestone is not totally invisible, it is carefully avoided and is feared for a lifetime. Nevertheless, there is no other path to one's true self in the entire world than this one leading past the gravestone that has been shunned for such a long time. For before a person can develop an appropriate form of aggressiveness, he or she must discover and experience the old fantasies of revenge, which were repressed because they were forbidden. Only these fantasies can lead one back to genuine childhood indignation and rage, which can then give way to mourning and reconciliation.

The career of the Swiss writer Friedrich Dürrenmatt, who in all probability has never undergone analysis, can serve as an example here. He grew up in a Protestant parsonage, and his first act as a young writer was to confront the reader with the grotesque absurdity, hypocrisy, and cruelty of the world. Even his studied emotional coldness, even the most abrasive cynicism cannot completely erase the traces of his early experiences. Like Hieronymus Bosch, Dürrenmatt depicts an *experienced* hell, even though he probably no longer has any clear memory of it.

The Visit could never have been written by someone who had not learned for himself that hatred finds its strongest and most cruel expression when there are very close ties to the hated object. In spite of all he has sensed so deeply, the young Dürrenmatt consistently displays the coldheartedness acquired by a child who must always conceal his feelings from those around him. In order to free himself from the moral strictures of the parsonage, he must first reject those highly extolled virtues, such as pity, altruism, and mercy, that he has come to distrust, and finally express his forbidden and cruel fantasies in a loud and distorted voice. In his more mature years, Dürrenmatt seems less compelled to conceal his true feelings. In his later works we sense not so much the provocative nature of the earlier ones as the urgent need to do humankind the service of confronting it with uncomfortable truths. For, as a child, Dürrenmatt must have been able to see through the world around him uncommonly well. Because he is able to describe what he has seen in a creative way, he also helps his readers to become more attentive and aware. And having seen things with his own eyes, he has no need to submit to the stultifying influence of ideologies.

This is one form of working through childhood hatred that is of immediate benefit to humankind—it doesn't have to be "socialized" first. Likewise, those who have benefited from analysis will not have the need to inflict harm on others once they have confronted their childhood "sadism." Quite the contrary, they become much less aggressive if they are able to live *with* their aggressions and not *in opposition to* them. This is not a case of sublimation but a normal process of maturation that can begin when certain obstacles have been removed. It does not require any great effort, because the warded-off hatred has been *experienced* and *not abreacted*. These people become more courageous than they were before: they no longer aim their hostility at those "below" them (e.g., their children), but directly at those "above" (who wounded them and thus caused their anger). They are no longer afraid of standing up to their superiors and are no longer compelled to humiliate their partners or their children. They have experienced themselves as victims and now do not have to split off their unconscious victimization and project it onto others. Yet there are still countless numbers of people who utilize this mechanism of projection. As parents they use it on their children; as psychiatrists, on the mentally ill; and as research scientists, on animals. No one is surprised or indignant at this. What Professor White is doing with the brains of monkeys is acclaimed as science, and he himself is quite proud of his activities. Where is the line to be drawn between him and Dr. Mengele, who performed experiments on human beings in Auschwitz? Since Jews were considered nonhuman, his experiments were deemed "morally" legitimate. In order to understand how Mengele was able to remove the eyes and other organs of healthy people, we only have to know what was done to him in childhood. I am convinced that something almost inconceivably horrible to outsiders would be uncovered, which he himself no doubt regarded as the best upbringing in the world, one to which, in his opinion, he "owed a great deal."

The choice of available objects on which a person can take revenge for his or her childhood suffering is practically limitless, but one's own children provide an almost automatic outlet. In nearly all of the old child-rearing manuals, major emphasis is placed on how to combat willfulness and the tyranny of the infant and how to punish infantile "obstinacy" with the severest of measures. Parents who were once tyrannized by these methods are understandably eager to try to free themselves from the burden of the past as quickly as possible by means of an ersatz object; they experience their own tyrannical father in their child's anger, but here they finally have him at their mercy—like Professor White his monkeys.

Analysts are often struck by the fact that their patients regard themselves as very demanding for having the most modest—but vitally important—of needs and by the fact that they hate themselves for this. A man who has bought a house for his wife and children, for example, may find he does not have a room he can retire to, although he ardently wishes for one. That would be too demanding or "bourgeois." But because he feels smothered without this space of his own, he considers abandoning his family and escaping to the desert. A woman who entered analysis after a series of operations considered herself especially demanding because she was not grateful enough for all that she had been granted in life and wanted still more. In analysis it was revealed that for years she had had a compulsion to keep buying new dresses that she really didn't need and seldom wore and that this behavior was in part a substitute for the autonomy she had never been given. From the time she was a little girl, her mother had told her how demanding she was; she was very ashamed and tried all her life to be frugal. For this reason, she did not even consider psychoanalysis. Not until she had had several organs removed in surgery did she reach the point of allowing herself the expense of treatment. And then it slowly became clear that this woman had provided the arena in which her mother tried to assert herself against her own father. No resistance whatsoever had been possible against this tyrannical man. But from the very beginning her daughter accepted a pattern of behavior that made all her wishes and needs look like exaggerated and extravagant demands, which her mother then opposed with moral indignation. As a result, any impulses on the daughter's part in the direction of autonomy were accompanied by guilt feelings, which she tried to hide from her mother. Her most fervent wish was to be undemanding and frugal, while at the same time she suffered from the compulsion to buy and amass unneeded things, thereby proving to herself that she had the demanding nature attributed to her by her mother. She had to undergo many difficult sessions of analysis before it was possible for her to cast aside the role of her tyrannical grandfather. Then it became obvious that basically this woman had very little interest in material things—now that she was able to realize what her true needs were and to be creative. She no longer was compelled to buy what she didn't need in order to make her mother believe she was tyrannically demanding or to secretly seize autonomy for herself, and she was finally able to take seriously her true spiritual and emotional needs without feeling guilty.

This example illustrates several of the ideas advanced in this chapter.

1. Even when the needs a child expresses are quite harmless and normal, she can be perceived by her parents as demanding, tyrannical, and threatening if the parents have suffered under a tyrannical father, for example, without being able to defend themselves against him.

2. A child can respond to these "labels" with demanding behavior that comes from his or her *false self*, thereby embodying the aggressive father the parent is seeking.

3. Reacting to the behavior of the child or later patient

on the level of drives, or even trying to help him or her learn "drive renunciation," would mean ignoring the true history of this tragic substitution and leaving the patient alone with it.

4. There is no need to attempt "drive renunciation" or "sublimation" of the "death wish" if the personal roots of an aggressive or even destructive way of acting are understood, for then psychic energy will of itself be transformed into creativity, provided that no attempts have been made to "educate" the patient.

5. Mourning over what has happened, over the irreversibility of the past, is the prerequisite for this process.

6. This mourning, when experienced in analysis with the aid of transference and countertransference, leads to an intrapsychic, structural transformation and not simply to new forms of interaction with present partners. This distinguishes psychoanalysis from other forms of therapy, especially family therapy.

The Permission to Know

PARENTS are of course *not only* persecutors. But it is important to know that in many cases they play this role *as well*, and very often without even being aware of it. In general, this is a little-known fact; when it is known, it is the subject of much controversy, even among analysts, and it is for this reason that I place so much emphasis on it here.

Loving parents in particular should want to find out what they are unconsciously doing to their children. If they simply avoid the subject and instead point to their parental love, then they are not really concerned about their children's well-being but rather are painstakingly trying to keep a clear conscience. This effort, which they have been making ever since they were little, prevents them from letting their love for their children unfold freely and from learning something from this love. The attitudes of "poisonous pedagogy" are not restricted to outdated child-rearing manuals of the past. There they were expressed consciously and unabashedly, whereas today they are disseminated more quietly and more subtly; nevertheless, they still permeate most major areas of our lives. Their very omnipresence makes it difficult for us to recognize them. They are like a pernicious virus we have learned to live with since we were little.

We are often unaware, therefore, that we can live without this virus and would be better off and happier without it. People of high caliber and with the best intentions, like, for example, A.'s father (cf. page 92), can become infected without even realizing it. If they do not happen to undergo analysis, they have no occasion to discover the virus, no opportunity ever to question later in life emotionally charged convictions they adopted from their parents in early child-hood. In spite of their sincere efforts to bring about a democratic family environment, they simply cannot help dis-criminating against the child and denying his or her rights, for, on the basis of their own early experiences, they can hardly imagine anything else. The early imprinting of these at-titudes in the unconscious guarantees their enduring stability.

There is another factor that also has a stabilizing effect here. Most adults are parents themselves. They have raised their children with the help of an unconscious storehouse filled with their own childhood experiences and have had no other recourse but to do everything the same way their parents did before them. But when they are suddenly confronted with the knowledge that the greatest and most lasting harm can be done to a child at a very tender age, they understandably are filled with often unbearable guilt feelings. People who were raised according to the principles of "poisonous pedagogy" suffer particular anguish at the thought that they may not have been perfect parents, because they owe it to their inter-nalized parents to have made no mistakes. Thus, they will tend to shy away from new ideas and will seek a haven all the more behind the old rules of child raising. They will insist emphatically that duty, obedience, and suppression of feelings are the portals to a good and honorable life and that we become adults only by learning to keep a stiff upper lip; they will find it necessary to ward off all knowledge about the world of their early childhood experiences.

The knowledge we need is often quite close at hand, even "right under our very nose." When we have the chance to observe children of today who are growing up with fewer constraints, we can learn a great deal about the true nature of the emotional life, which remained hidden for the older generation. To give an example:

A mother is at a playground with her three-year-old, who is clinging to her skirt and sobbing as though her heart would break. Marianne refuses to play with the other children. When I ask what the matter is, the mother tells me with great sympathy and understanding for her daughter that they have just come from the train station. The little girl's daddy, whom they had gone to meet, had not been there. Only Ingrid's daddy had gotten off the train. I said to Marianne, "Oh, but that must have been a big disappointment for you!" The child looked at me, large tears rolling down her cheeks. But soon she was stealing glances at the other children, and two minutes later she was romping happily with them. Because her deep pain was experienced and not bottled up, it could give way to other, happier feelings.

If the observer is open enough to learn something from this incident, he or she will be saddened by it and will wonder if the many sacrifices that had to be made were perhaps not necessary after all. Rage and pain can apparently pass quickly if one is free to express them. Can it be possible that there was no need to struggle against envy and hatred all this time, that their hostile power holding sway within was a malignant growth whose magnitude was a consequence of repression? Can it be possible that the repressed feelings, the calm and controlled "balance" one has proudly attained with so much difficulty are in reality a lamentable impoverishment and not an "asset" at all, although one had become accustomed to seeing it as such?

If the observer of the scene described has until now been proud of this self-control, some of the pride may turn to rage, rage at the realization that all this time he or she has been cheated out of free access to feelings. And the rage, if it is really acknowledged and experienced, can make room for a feeling of sorrow over the meaninglessness as well as the inevitability of the sacrifices. The change from rage to sorrow makes it possible for the vicious circle of repetition to be broken. It is easy for those who have never become aware of having been victims, since they grew up believing in the principles of being brave and self-controlled, to succumb to the danger of taking revenge on the next generation because they themselves have been unconsciously victimized. But if their anger is followed by grief over having been a victim, then they can also mourn the fact that their parents were victims too, and they will no longer have to persecute their children. This ability to grieve will bring them closer to their children.

The same thing holds true for the relationship with grown children. I once talked with a young man who had just made his second suicide attempt. He said to me: "I have suffered from depressions since puberty; my life has no meaning. I thought my studies were to blame because they involved so much meaningless material. But now I have finished all my exams, and the emptiness is worse then ever. But these depressions don't have anything to do with my childhood; my mother tells me that I had a very happy and sheltered childhood."

We saw each other again several years later. In the meantime, his mother had undergone analysis. There was an enormous difference between our two meetings. The young man had become creative not only in his profession but in his whole outlook; unquestionably, he was now living *his* life. In the course of our conversation he said: "When my mother loosened up with the help of analysis, it was as though the scales fell from her eyes, and she saw what she and my father had done to me as parents. At first it weighed on me the way she kept talking to me about it—apparently to unburden herself or to win my forgiveness—about how they had both in effect squelched me as a young child with their well-meaning methods of raising me. In the beginning I didn't want to hear about it, I avoided her and became angry with her. But gradually I noticed that what she was telling me was unfortunately entirely true. Something inside me had known it all along, but I was not allowed to know it. Now that my mother was showing the strength to face what had happened head-on, not to make excuses, not to deny or distort anything, because she felt that she, too, had once been a victim—now I was able to admit my knowledge of the past. It was a tremendous relief not to have to pretend any longer. And the amazing thing is that now, in spite of all her failings, which we both know about, I feel much closer to my mother and find her much more likable, animated, approachable, and warm than I did before. And I am much more genuine and spontaneous with her. The insincere effort I had to make is over. She no longer has to prove to me that she loves me in order to hide her guilt feelings; I sense that she likes me and loves me. She also doesn't have to prescribe rules of behavior for me anymore but lets me be as I am because she can be that way herself and because she is herself less under the pressure of rules and regulations. A great burden has fallen from me. I enjoy life, and it all happened without my having to go through a lengthy analysis. But now I would no longer say that my suicide attempts were unrelated to my childhood. It's just that I wasn't permitted to see the connection, and that must have intensified my feeling of desperation."

This young man was describing a situation that plays a role in the development of many mental illnesses: the repression of awareness dating back to early childhood that can become manifest only in physical symptoms, in the repetition compulsion, or in psychotic breakdown. John Bowlby has written an article entitled "On Knowing What You Are Not Supposed to Know and Feeling What You Are Not Supposed to Feel," in which he reports on similar experiences.

In conjunction with this story of a potential suicide, it was instructive for me to see that even in severe cases analysis may not be necessary for a young person as long as his parents are able to break the ban of silence and denial and assure their grown child that his symptoms are not pure fabrication or the result of overexertion, of "being crazy," of effeminacy, of reading the wrong books or having the wrong friends, of inner "drive conflicts," etc. If the parents are able to stop desperately fighting their own guilt feelings and as a result need not discharge them onto the child but are willing to accept their fate instead, they will give their children the freedom to live not *against* but *with* their past. The grown child's emotional and physical wisdom can then be in harmony with his intellectual knowledge. If mourning of this nature is possible, parents will feel close to their children rather than distant from them—a fact that is not well known because the attempt is seldom made. But when mourning is successful, the false demands of child-rearing are silenced and true understanding of life takes their place. This understanding is accessible to anyone who is ready to rely on what his own experience tells him.

Afterword

AFTER I finished the manuscript of this book and sent it to the publisher, I was talking about problems of child-rearing with a younger, very empathic colleague whose work I regard highly and who is himself the father of two children. He said it was a shame that psychoanalysis still has not worked out any guidelines for humane pedagogy. I expressed doubt that there could be such a thing as humane pedagogy, having learned in my analytic work to recognize even the more refined and subtle forms of manipulation that pass for pedagogy. Then I explained my firm conviction that all pedagogy is superfluous as long as children are provided with a dependable person in early childhood, can use this person (in D. W. Winnicott's terms), and need not fear losing him or her or being abandoned if they express their feelings. Children who are taken seriously, respected, and supported in this way can experience themselves and the world on their own terms and do not need adult coercion. My colleague was in complete agreement, but he thought it important for parents to be given more concrete advice. Then I quoted my sentence that appears on page 132: "If parents are also able to give their child the same respect and tolerance they had for their own parents, they will surely be providing him with the best possible foundation for his entire later life."

After giving a short, spontaneous laugh, my colleague looked at me very gravely and after a moment's silence said, "But that isn't possible . . ." "Why not?" I asked. "Because . . . because . . . our children do not use coercive measures against us, they don't threaten to leave us when we are bad. And even if they say it, we know they wouldn't do it . . ." He became increasingly reflective and then said very slowly, "You know, now I wonder if what is called pedagogy may not be simply a question of power, and if we shouldn't be speaking and writing much more about hidden power struggles instead of racking our brains about finding better methods of child-rearing." "That's exactly what I have tried to do in the book I have just finished," I said.

It is the tragedy of well-raised people that they are un-aware as adults of what was done to them and what they do themselves if they were not allowed to be aware as children. Countless institutions in our society profit from this fact, and not least among them are totalitarian regimes. In this age when almost anything is possible, psychology can provide dev-astating support for the conditioning of the individual, the family, and whole nations. Conditioning and manipulation of others are always weapons and instruments in the hands of those in power even if these weapons are disguised with the terms *education* and *therapeutic treatment*. Since one's use and abuse of power over others usually have the function of holding one's own feelings of helplessness in check—which means the exercise of power is often unconsciously motivated —rational arguments can do nothing to impede this process.

In the same way that technology was used to help carry out mass murders in the Third Reich in a very short space of time, so too the more precise kind of knowledge of human behavior based on computer data and cybernetics can con-tribute to the more rapid, comprehensive, and effective soul murder of the human being than could the earlier intuitive psychology. There are no measures available to halt these de-velopments. Psychoanalysis cannot do it; indeed, it is itself in danger of being used as an instrument of power in the train-ing institutes. All that we can do, as I see it, is to affirm and lend our support to the human objects of manipulation in their attempts to become aware and help them become conscious of their malleability and articulate their feelings so that they will be able to use their own resources to defend themselves against the soul murder that threatens them.

It is not the psychologists but the literary writers who are ahead of their time. In the last ten years there has been an increase in the number of autobiographical works being written, and it is apparent that this younger generation of writers is less and less inclined to idealize their parents. There has been a marked increase in the willingness of the postwar generation to seek the truth of their childhood and in their ability to bear the truth once they have discovered it. The descriptions of parents found in the books of such writers as Christoph Meckel, Erika Burkart, Karin Struck, and Ruth Rehmann and in the reports of Barbara Frank and Margot Lang would scarcely have been conceivable thirty or even twenty years ago. The same holds true for America, where more and more books about childhood (by Louise Armstrong, Charlotte Vale Allen, Michelle Morris, Florence Rush, and many others) have been appearing recently that display an authenticity and honesty unknown heretofore. I see great hope in this as a step along the road to truth and at the same time as confirmation that even a minimal loosening up of child-rearing principles can bear fruit by enabling at least our writers to become aware. That the academic disciplines must lag behind is an unfortunate but well-known fact.

In the same decade in which writers are discovering the emotional importance of childhood and are unmasking the devastating consequences of the way power is secretly exercised under the disguise of child-rearing, students of psychology are spending four years at the universities learning to regard human beings as machines in order to gain a better understanding of how they function. When we consider how much time and energy is devoted during these best years to wasting the last opportunities of adolescence and to suppressing, by means of the intellectual disciplines, the feelings that emerge with particular force at this age, then it is no wonder that the people who have made this sacrifice victimize their patients and clients in turn, treating them as mere objects of knowledge instead of as autonomous, creative beings. There are some authors of so-called objective, scientific publications in the field of psychology who remind me of the officer in Kafka's *Penal Colony* in their zeal and their consistent self-destructiveness. In the unsuspecting, trusting attitude of Kafka's convicted prisoner, on the other hand, we can see the students of today who are so eager to believe that the only thing that counts in their four years of study is their academic performance and that human commitment is not required.

The expressionistic painters and poets active at the beginning of this century demonstrated more understanding of the neuroses of their day (or at any rate unconsciously imparted more information about them) than did the contemporary professors of psychiatry. During the same period, Freud's female patients with their hysterical symptoms were unconsciously reenacting their childhood traumata. He succeeded in deciphering their language, which their conventional doctors had failed to understand. In return, he reaped not only gratitude but also hostility, because he had dared to touch upon the taboos of his time.

Children who become too aware of things are punished for it and internalize the coercion to such an extent that as adults they give up the search for awareness. But because some people cannot renounce this search in spite of coercion, there is justifiable hope that regardless of the ever-increasing application of technology to the field of psychological knowledge, Kafka's vision of the penal colony with its efficient, scientifically minded persecutors and their passive victims is valid only for certain areas of our life and perhaps not forever. For the human soul is virtually indestructible, and its ability to rise from the ashes remains as long as the body draws breath.

Bibliography

Allen, Charlotte Vale. *Daddy's Girl*. New York, 1980.

Ariès, Philippe. *Centuries of Childhood: A Social History of Family Life*. Translated by Robert Baldick. New York, 1962.

Armstrong, Louise. *Kiss Daddy Good-night*. New York, 1978.

Bowlby, John. "On Knowing What You Are Not Supposed to Know and Feeling What You Are Not Supposed to Feel," *Journal of the Canadian Psychiatric Association*. 1979.

Braunmühl, Ekkehard von. *Antipädagogik* [*Antipedagogy*]. Weinheim and Basel, 1976.

——. *Zeit für Kinder* [*Time for Children*]. Frankfurt, 1978.

Bruch, Hilde. *The Golden Cage: The Enigma of Anorexia*. New York, 1978.

Burkart, Erika. *Der Weg zu den Schafen* [*The Way to the Sheep*]. Zurich, 1979.

Epstein, Helen. *Children of the Holocaust: Conversations with Sons and Daughters of Survivors*. New York, 1979.

F., Christiane. *Christiane F.: Autobiography of a Girl of the Streets and Heroin Addict*. Translated by Susanne Flatauer. New York, 1982.

Fest, Joachim C. *The Face of the Third Reich: Portraits of Nazi Leadership*. Translated by Michael Bullock. New York, 1970.

——. *Hitler*. Translated by Richard and Clara Winston. New York, 1974.

Fromm, Erich. *The Anatomy of Human Destructiveness*. New York, 1973.

Handke, Peter. *A Sorrow Beyond Dreams: A Life Story*. Translated by Ralph Manheim. New York, 1974.

281

Heiden, Konrad. *Der Führer: Hitler's Rise to Power.* Translated by Ralph Manheim. Boston, 1944.

Helfer, Ray E., and C. Henry Kempe, eds. *The Battered Child,* 3rd ed. Chicago, 1980.

Hitler, Adolf. *Mein Kampf.* Translated by Ralph Manheim. Boston, 1943.

Höss, Rudolf. *The Autobiography of Rudolf Höss: Commandant of Auschwitz.* Translated by Constantine Fitz-Gibbon. New York, 1959.

Jetzinger, Franz. *Hitler's Youth.* Translated by Lawrence Wilson. London, 1958.

Kestenberg, Judith. "Kinder von Überlebenden der Naziverfolgung" [Children of Survivors of Nazi Persecution], *Psyche* 28, 249–65.

Klee, Paul. *The Diaries of Paul Klee: 1898–1918.* Edited, with an Introduction, by Felix Klee. Berkeley and Los Angeles, 1964.

Kohut, Heinz. *The Analysis of Self.* New York, 1971.

———. "Überlegungen zum Narzissmus und zur narzisstischen Wut" [Reflections on Narcissism and Narcissistic Rage], *Psyche* 27, 513–54.

Krüll, Marianne. *Freud und sein Vater* [*Freud and His Father*]. Munich, 1979.

Mause, Lloyd de, ed. *The History of Childhood.* New York, 1974.

———. "Psychohistory: Über die Unabhängigkeit eines neuen Forschungsgebietes" [Psychohistory: On the Independence of a New Area of Research], *Kindheit* 1, 51–71.

Meckel, Christoph. *Suchbild: Über meinen Vater* [*Wanted: My Father's Portrait*]. Düsseldorf, 1979.

Miller, Alice. *Prisoners of Childhood* (published in paperback as *The Drama of the Gifted Child* [1983]). New York, 1981.

———. *Du Sollst Nicht Merken* (to be published in English as *Thou Shalt Not Be Aware*). Frankfurt, 1981.

Moor, Paul. *Das Selbstporträt des Jürgen Bartsch* [*The Self-Portrait of Jürgen Bartsch*]. Frankfurt, 1972.

Morris, Michelle. *If I Should Die Before I Wake*. Los Angeles, 1982.

Niederland, William G. *Folgen der Verfolgung [The Results of Persecution]*. Frankfurt, 1980.

Olden, Rudolf. *Hitler*. Translated by Walter Ettinghausen. New York, 1936.

Plath, Sylvia. *Letters Home: Correspondence 1950–1963*. Selected and edited with commentary by Aurelia Schober Plath. New York, 1975.

——. *The Bell Jar*. New York, 1971.

Rauschning, Hermann. *The Voice of Destruction*. New York, 1940.

Rehmann, Ruth. *Der Mann auf der Kanzel: Fragen an einen Vater [The Man in the Pulpit: Questions for a Father]*. Munich and Vienna, 1979.

Rush, Florence. *The Best Kept Secret: Sexual Abuse of Children*. New York, 1980.

Rutschky, Katharina. *Schwarze Pädagogik [Black Pedagogy]*. Berlin, 1977.

Schatzman, Morton. *Soul Murder: Persecution in the Family*. New York, 1973.

Schwing, Gertrud. *The Way to the Soul of the Mentally Ill*. New York, 1954.

Sereny, Gitta. *The Case of Mary Bell*. New York, 1972.

Sheleff, Leon. *Generations Apart: Adult Hostility to Youth*. New York, 1981.

Smith, B. F. *Adolf Hitler: His Family, Childhood, and Youth*. Stanford, 1967.

Stierlin, Helm. *Adolf Hitler: A Family Perspective*. New York, 1976.

Struck, Karin. Klassenliebe *[Class Love]*. Frankfurt, 1973.

——. *Die Mutter [The Mother]*. Frankfurt, 1975.

Syberberg. Hans-Jürgen. *Hitler, a Film from Germany*. New York, 1982.

Theweleit, Klaus. *Männerphantasien [Male Fantasies]*. Frankfurt, 1977.

Toland, John. *Adolf Hitler*. New York, 1976.

Winnicott, D. W. *Playing and Reality.* New York, 1971.

Zenz, Gisela. *Kindermisshandlung und Kindesrechte [Mis-treatment of Children and Children's Rights].* Frankfurt, 1979.

Zimmer, Katharina. *Das einsame Kind [The Lonely Child].* Munich, 1979.